CRITICAL JUNCTIONS

CRITICAL JUNCTIONS

Anthropology and History beyond the Cultural Turn

Edited by

Don Kalb

and

Herman Tak

Berghahn Books

NEW YORK • OXFORD

Published in 2005 by
Berghahn Books

www.berghahnbooks.com

© 2005, 2006 Don Kalb and Herman Tak
First paperback edition published in 2006

Library of Congress Cataloging-in-Publication Data

Critical junctions : anthropology and history beyond the cultural turn /
edited by Don Kalb and Herman Tak.
    p. cm.
Includes bibliographical references and index.
ISBN 1-84545-008-6 (alk. paper)--ISBN 1-84545-029-9 (pbk. : alk. paper)
    1. Ethnohistory. 2. Anthropology—Methodology. 3. Historiography.
I. Kalb, Don, 1959–. II. Tak, Herman.

GN345.2.C75 2004
303.4—dc22

                                                      2004055427

British Library Cataloguing in Publication Data

A catalogue record for this book is available from
the British Library.

Printed in the United States on acid-free paper

CONTENTS

PREFACE

This is a book about theory and method in the humanities and social sciences. It reacts to what has become known as the "cultural turn," a shift toward semiotics, discourse, and representations and away from other sorts of determinations that started in the early 1980s and that has dominated social thinking for a long string of years. The book is based in a reconsideration of the meeting of two disciplines that helped to launch the cultural turn: anthropology and history. Specifically, it criticizes the ideas of hermeneutics and "thick description" (Clifford Geertz) that have come to play a key role in the encounter of anthropology and history and then in the cultural turn. It led to the renewed cherishing of what Gupta and Ferguson have called paradigms of "peoples and places," saturated pictures of universes, both small and large, of meaning in a more or less frozen standstill—an intellectual precursor to the cultural xenophobia of our times. Against this, the present book embraces praxis and "critical junctions": the connections in space (in and out of a place/in and out of a group), the relations through time, the internal and external relations of power and dependency, and what Eric Wolf has called the "interstitial relations" between apparently separate institutional domains. In this way the book adds to the current revival of institutionally based "global ethnography," which studies "up and outward" (the journal *Ethnography* is a good example).

An important aspect of this is a rethinking of what class means and does, and how to study it. The big issue is how to integrate in one vision class-structured, situated, embodied social interaction and the rarely immediately visible "movers and doers" in time and space. By revisiting the early debate on anthropology and history, the book looks at the work of non–cultural turn authors such as Norbert Elias, Max Gluckman, David Harvey, E. P. Thompson, Raymond Williams, and Eric Wolf in an attempt to make new openings for an ethnography of agency and experience that is fully grounded in the relational vehicles of power in space and time.

This collection emerged from a special issue of *Focaal—European Journal of Anthropology* titled "Historical Anthropology: The Unwaged Debate" (no. 26/27, 1996), edited by Don Kalb, Hans Marks, and Herman Tak. The issue celebrated the first ten years of the journal (then only published in the Netherlands). Several papers from this collection were subsequently discussed at a session at the American Anthropological Association meetings in San Francisco, November 1996, organized by August Carbonella, Kalb, and Tak. They were rewritten in the next years, waiting for the editors to finally bring them together in the present book.

We are grateful for the patience of the authors and the publisher, which has been really extraordinary. Recurrent removals to other places and to new employers have slowed the publication of this book almost beyond credibility. Don Kalb thanks Gus Carbonella, Gerald Sider, and Herman Tak for comments on the introduction. Participants to a lively discussion in the Staff Colloquium of the new Sociology and Social Anthropology Department at Central European University, Budapest, October 2003, made helpful comments leading to further revision. Special thanks are due to professor Chris Hann, director of the Max Planck Institute for Social Anthropology, Halle, Germany, who facilitated Don's month-long stay at the institute in October 2002 in which the draft of the introduction was written. Herman Tak also thanks Ewa and Max for allowing him several days off during their summer holidays in 2004. Hans Marks did crucial work in helping to conceptualize and bring about the initial debate. He was subsequently swamped by other work, but we remain grateful for his input. Marion Berghahn of Berghahn Books kept her interest, for which we thank her, as well as for her ability to find outstanding reviewers: several important shortcomings in the draft introduction were pointed out, leading to another rewrite.

The book is dedicated to all those (including Ellen) who have helped with loyalty, labor, genius, and friendship to realize over a full two decades the undertaking that has been the inspiration for this book—*Focaal*.

INTRODUCTION
Critical Junctions—Recapturing Anthropology and History

Don Kalb and Herman Tak

But it *was* but a myth, useful in the way that myths are—it provided an easily grasp-able, suggestive, powerful image. It highlighted the principles by which we think, though not the devious paths by which we reached our condition.

— Ernest Gellner, *Language and Solitude: Wittgenstein, Malinowski and the Habsburg Dilemma* (1998)

People cannot be reduced to texts any more than they can be reduced to objects.

— Michael Jackson, *Paths toward a Clearing: Radical Empiricism and Ethnographic Enquiry* (1989)

This collection of studies and essays seeks to address the pitfalls of, and the alternatives to, what has become known as the "cultural turn" (or the "historic turn") in the social and human sciences. The cultural turn has been a multi-farious and pretty pervasive phenomenon in Western universities and modes of social knowledge since the early 1980s, when, in Bill Sewell's phrasing, a "kind of academic culture mania has set in" (Sewell 1999: 36). It embraced parts of anthropology, sociology, social theory, gender studies, literary stud-ies, various branches of history, and science studies and laid the philosophical groundwork for the expansion of the field of cultural studies. Our precise target here is much more limited than this broad movement, though directly of relevance to it. It concerns first of all the relatively narrow terrain where exercises in anthropology and history have been blurred and combined. We have a particular rationale for focusing on this conjunction. This happened to be the site where both the analytic promises as well as the difficulties involved in the meeting of humanist and social science approaches soon became obvious.[1] Anthropologists were looking to history for fresh analytic approaches that could help them move beyond the static and bounded pictures of communities produced by participant observation and cultural description. Many historians, however, in retrospect appeared rather interested in precisely the enclosed cultural interpretation that the historical anthropologists were reacting against. Historical anthropology and anthropological history were often like ships passing each other in the night.

The contributions in this collection are concerned with recapturing some of the openings onto cultural analysis that have been worked out before as well as alongside the mainstream of recent poststructuralist and postmaterialist writing (another ID for the cultural turn), mainly in anthropology but not limited to it. The authors share in the conviction that the turning away from "the social" and the political, the relative neglect of praxis, and the resultant obsession with "meaning," symbols, and signs, at least in the particular forms that have been developed over the two preceding decades, has been a form of analytic "deforestation" (Eric Wolf) that we can not be content with. Above all, they feel deeply uneasy about the privileging of statics over dynamics, of supposed local expressive universes over translocal social connections, of the complacencies of place and identity over the deeply contentious issues of place making, struggle, and personal becoming in a wider and hugely uneven global space of modern projects. In a sense, the authors presented here are all concerned about the generalization from anthropology to the other human sciences of "a lack of systematic sociology," which, according to Sherry Ortner (1994: 377), had always already been characteristic of the symbolic anthropologies that had prepared the way for the cultural turn.

Bonnell and Hunt are right that we need to "revitalize the social" (1999: 11). But how should we do that? If positivism and structural functionalism are not the answer, what are the basic starting points? Sure, a reconstructed Marxism, Foucault, Elias, Bourdieu, perhaps even Lacan, offer necessary openings. But what needs strong emphasis now beyond their particular conceptual and visionary encouragements is what we call "critical junctions." "The social" as seen in modernist social thought has precisely suffered from a neglect of the systematic appraisal of critical junctions. That is our claim for reinventing the social.

What do we mean by it? The notion of critical junctions intends to summarize the core analytical value of four closely interconnected sets of social relations for understanding any human collectivity, sets that have been relatively neglected in a social science that took its modernist subdivisions and differentiations of time, space, and institutions—markets, states, civil societies, etc.—as truths rather than just claims and programs.[2] These are relations through time, relations in space, relations of power and dependency (internal as well as external), and the interstitial relations between nominally distinct domains such as economics, politics, law, the family, etc. These include remembered, desired, repressed, and imaginary relations as well, which may be less empirical in the narrow sense of the term but not less real or discoverable. Such relations may be of a floating, transitory network character, or they may be of more institutionalized solidity; they can be largely horizontal or hierarchical, but they are always and necessarily dynamic and dialectical. Together, these four sets of critical junctions, in their mutual interweaving, largely shape the place-making projects, capacities, aspirations, and frustrations of modern subjects.

One important subtheme of the book is a rethinking along these lines of that once core critical junction of modernity, class, and class formation (in particular the essays by Carbonella, Kalb, and Sider). Class has never attained much attention in anthropology, but it was one of the main culprits of the culturalist critique against reductionism within history and sociology in the 1980s and 1990s (see below and Carbonella, Kalb, this book; see Eley and Nield 2000a, 2000b, and Kalb 1997, for a full account of the debate). All the sins of a mechanical and reductionist approach to human actors, which the cultural turn was reacting against, came together, it was more or less claimed, in the concept of class. Class reduced meaning-seeking persons and human subjects to economic dopes, short-term rational actors, and instrumentalist advantage seekers, preventing social analysts from seeing what people were "really after" and discovering "otherness."

Revisiting that debate about class now and shifting the terms, perspectives, and methodological alliances as inspired by our relational vision of critical junctions allows us to recapture some of the basic issues that were at stake in anthropology's self-critique and its turn toward history in the 1970s, and to do so in ways that suggest strong alternatives to the culturalist escape from the alleged reductionism of class in its positivist disguise while retaining crucial moments of an expanded vision of class that were part and parcel of, for example, Eric Wolf's interest in history. Critical junctions approaches help to open up new ways of envisioning and tracing class anthropologically, while preventing reductionism, essentialism, and teleology (Kalb 1997; Tilly 2001). This seems all the more important today, now that the only two classes that feel they can legitimately speak of themselves as *a class* are the capitalist class and "the middle classes." The first does so in order to act offensively and collectively on its interests (as a class for itself in the Marxian sense), the second to defend itself desperately against the onslaught of the first by claiming moral superiority over anyone else and therefore the right to state support, just as the *Mittelstand* of old. In the end, we indeed propose our critical junctions to fight—even though modestly—some cruel ironies of history.

Critical junctions are also proposed as a counterpoint to the global open space of the liberals and the postmodernists, believing local outcomes to be largely contingent as local communities choose from an abundant menu of global offerings in finance, economics, ideologies, and cultural images. Arjun

Appadurai's (1996) well-known argument about "scapes" emphasized precisely the mutual disjunctions among such domains of global activity in order to get rid of the overly rigid and comprehensive core-periphery schemas of World Systems Theory that believed that finance, economics, political ideologies, and cultural images all traveled in fixed packages and there was little localities could choose. Against his disjunctions, we come up with critical junctions—junctions among such domains but also with the other three fields of inter-junction that we have identified. This is because we claim that places and place making projects are still embedded in very determinate and identifiable sets of critical junctions, and because we think that their identification means a step forward in social science. This is not to deny contingency, emergent proper-ties, or human action. It is, rather, to situate it. Ours is an effort to retain some of the more systematic and comprehensive character of global relationships of inequality, even though our vision is more differentiated and contingent than the stories of old (see also Friedman 2003).

In the original problem statement that we sent to our contributors there was no mention of our notion of critical junctions. Instead, we focused in a more straightforward way on the two different visions of the rapprochement of anthropology and history—the ships passing in the night—that emerged in the 1980s. For example, we asked whether they agreed with a divide within the confluence of anthropology and history between what we called historical anthropology on the one side and anthropological history on the other. All of them agreed with that claim, and they supported our view that anthropo-logical history tended to study historical epochs as static temporal blocks of meaning, just like anthropologists used to see the village as a concretization of a wider semiotic universe. Historical anthropology, on the other hand, seemed rather in search of evolving practice—including discursive practice—within competing networks of power and counterpower, either in the past, the pres-ent, or the future. There was little disagreement about this.

We also inquired about the function of scale reduction as a research tool in both paradigms. We proposed that historical anthropologists should use the local site of research often prescribed by the initiation rituals of their discipline as a window onto wider and evolving landscapes of power—as a discovery procedure to get at critical junctions, we would now say. This claim was appre-ciated in spirit but sometimes criticized in form because of the different tradi-tions our authors were working from. Handelman, for example, with his roots in the Manchester School, rejects the idea of scale reduction entirely. In his reading, it leads to "freezing" the flow of practice and cutting snapshots out of a wider and dynamic field of social praxis in time and space. This makes sense for him who emphasizes studying up and outwards and following up through time. Scale reduction in the anthropological history mode indeed does pre-cisely what Handelman criticizes, as he stresses in pointing to the examples of Geertz and Darnton. Others, such as Carbonella or Silverman and Gulliver, consider the issue of scale reduction from the political economy tradition in

U.S. anthropology and recognize both the opportunities as well as the dangers. Giordano, with his emphasis on the elite manipulation of symbols, is somewhat agnostic about the merits and shortcomings of the smaller scale as a window onto wider vistas.

Throughout the book, authors keep coming back to these initial guiding questions of our project (except Kalb and Musante, whose contributions were written at a later stage). As we see them now, these are core methodological issues for a social or human science that is increasingly turning to the study of place making in the context of what in the course of this project we have increasingly begun to define as our set of critical junctions.

This introduction then represents a standpoint arrived at well after the project. It frames its discoveries and advances well beyond the starting points that we shared with our authors. It was the dialogue with them that showed us this way. It was also the social science context at large during the rather long incubation of this book that pushed us to go further than we originally aspired to do. The cultural turn became much more seriously debated around the millennium than in the years before. This invited us to respond in more general ways to more overarching issues. Our starting point in the anthropology and history debate, precisely because it had been an early crossroads in what happened to become the cultural turn, allowed us to make new inroads, often by rediscovering old ones.

This book, then, is not quite unique in its critical rethinking of programs, forms, and fashions of sociocultural analysis that have emerged under the banner of this cultural turn.[3] On the contrary, the critique, although always present, has by now become an articulate and broadly shared stance, above all perhaps in anthropology. This is ironic, since anthropology initially played such a significant role in offering building blocks for the "turnists." For some time, certainly in the United States, anthropology exercised a strong culturalist attraction for researchers in other academic fields, first of all through Clifford Geertz's example of hermeneutic "thick description." The subsequent radicalization of the "thick description" program in the postmodernist movement in anthropology associated with George Marcus, Michael Fisher, and James Clifford, for whom Geertz willy-nilly functioned as an imaginary father figure (see Kuper 1999), gave the culturalists a further impetus. But as the Geertzian perspective on cultural difference and meaning was appropriated by the highbrow disciplines associated with the Western canon, such as literary studies and history, and as its homegrown postmodernism collapsed, unease among critical anthropologists slowly turned into explicit critique. Even more paradoxical: as "talking culture" (Stolcke 1995) became the daily bread of public opinion, circulating between mass media and policy makers in ever more ethnically and socially divided Western countries on a neoliberal course in the 1990s, anthropologists across the board wallowed in their own superficial success. "Cultural fundamentalist" (ibid.) imaginaries subsequently went into higher gear as the inherent conflicts of U.S.-led globalization became lethally linked with local and older fights, and the world scene turned into a virtual bonfire of xenophobia, cultural superiority, humiliation, and "othering." Anthropologists all over the board sensed their errors, refused to serve as Huntington's handmaiden in picturing the clash of civilizations, and changed into vociferous skeptics.

It should thus be conceded from the outset that a critical take on culture as propounded here is far from original in anthropology these days. According to Gupta and Ferguson (1997: 2) it represents "the leading position" within anthropology. Therefore, we should not try to rehearse at length the older debates on Geertz and others in this introduction; but they do figure in one way or another in all the contributions to this book. Instead, we will point out that we entirely support the contemporary critical conviction that culture is not simply shared and that it cannot be treated as a coherent system of orderly meanings with a logic of its own, to be abstracted from human action, utterance, and belief as embodied in public symbols associated with specific "peoples and places." In the words of Adam Kuper, we strongly refute such "extreme idealism" (1999: 120). Instead, we emphatically agree that it makes sense to "write against culture" (Abu Lughod 1991). We are also aware that culture is often just a "politically correct euphemism for race" (Kuper 1999: 240). Culture, we claim, must rather be seen as the evolving, shifting, fragmented and contested knowledge implicated in human praxis and relationships, generally forged as such "in response to identifiable determinants" (Wolf 1982: 387). We agree that instead of any organic wholeness, its parts are actually dependent on specific institutional, juridical and administrative arrangements and therefore are an inevitable aspect of projects of domination, control, and resistance. Moreover, the sources and users of such "cultural materials" are much of the time spatially (and temporally) separated, as well as deeply socially divided. This nexus is captured in the terms of deterritorialization and reterritorialization, a flow that inescapably culminates in cycles of dominance, dependence, and resistance. Culture, therefore, is never just "signification" or meaningful order, but also, and at the same time, imposed disorder, social amnesia, "silencing," and "misrecognition" on behalf of some and at the expense of others, even though nobody may be in perfect control. All in all, in the words of the late Ernest Gellner, culture theory easily "ignores the importance of physical and economic coercion in society, and the manner in which these can decide internal cultural options, it tends to be far too egalitarian as between cultures, and to obscure the … technical superiority of some over others" (1998: 186).

This is the by now little disputed ground upon which we stand. The authors in this collection contribute their own specific arguments to aspects of this debate-out-off-the-"culture mania" of the 1980s and 1990s. They do so by rereading, elaborating, and criticizing pre- and noncultural turn modes of describing and explaining structures of experience, feeling, subjectivity, and action in human societies, as well as criticizing the works that have pointed the way for the "turnists." The purpose is to articulate perspectives that are more dynamic, relational, material, and explanatory; perspectives that help to envision what we have called critical junctions. We highlight the still unexhausted possibilities developed among others in the work of scholars such as Norbert Elias (Rebel), Max Gluckman (Handelman), Eric Wolf (Carbonella, Kalb, Musante, Rebel), E. P. Thompson and Raymond Williams (Carbonella, Kalb, Sider), David Harvey (Carbonella, Kalb), and elite-theorists such as Mosca and Pareto (Giordano). Such openings are discussed as such, but they are also developed in the analysis of concrete and original case studies.

Having made these large introductory moves, we can now slow down and ask more precise questions. In particular we should ask what are the theoretical and methodological implications of critical junctions, which spring from the confluence of anthropology and history as explored in the contributions below. Secondly, we will discuss what the cultural skepticism implies for an ethnographic research practice which seems so methodologically tied up with the thick description model and the consequent prioritizing of local knowledge, implying bottom-up cultural order rather than top-down imposition. We will discuss these issues by way of a discussion of the more confirmative, but, as we shall see, to some extent self-defeating, positions on culture and the cultural turn proposed by recent interdisciplinary theorists such as Bill Sewell, Marshall Sahlins, and Richard Biernacki, and compare their visions with those of the present authors.

Template, Time, and Struggle

While in the course of the 1990s the mood regarding culture in anthropology circles was gradually turning gloomy, in history a more positive appraisal clearly prevailed. Even while Lynn Hunt and Vicky Bonnell in a recent collection admitted that it was time to go "beyond the cultural turn," emphasizing that their book demonstrated a continued belief in the relevance of "the social" and of "social explanation," the tone was rather that culture-as-meaning remained a liberating discovery for practitioners of social history (Bonnell and Hunt 1999: 1–35). Most of them had been trained on the basis of largely positivistic, reductionistic, reified, and quantifiable notions of what the social actually was. In a note Bonnell and Hunt thank William Sewell for bringing the apparent staying power of the social to their attention. In his own contribution, however, Sewell writes about his early exercises in the "new social history," American style, associated with the journal with the telling name *Social Science History*, culminating in his dissertation on the social stratification of Marseille, a quantitative study. Down in the Marseille archives Sewell must have felt frustrated, prohibited from engaging in any humanistic sense with the historical subjects of his study, not even with the historical urban landscape that they had left behind. Anthropology helped him, and it remains illuminating to hear why: "I experienced the encounter with cultural anthropology as a turn from a hardheaded, utilitarian, and empiricist materialism—which had both liberal and *marxisant* faces—to a wider appreciation of the range of possibilities, both in the past and in the present. Convinced that there was more to life than the relentless pursuit of wealth, status, and power, I felt that cultural anthropology could show us how to get at that 'more'" (Sewell 1999: 35–36). Sewell developed that 'more' in his important book on *Work and Revolution in France: The Language of Labor from the Old Regime to 1848* (1980). Anthropology, above all in the figure of Clifford Geertz, conveyed meaning, life-worlds, contingency to him: discovery, instead of prefabricated, anachronistic, and reductionistic categories.

Note that this was exactly what had driven Clifford Geertz in developing his interpretivism in the 1960s and 1970s: the opposition against positivism, objectification, reductionism, and variables-based universalism.[4] While such positivism was hardly to be found among anthropologists, in other social disciplines it was a majority position, and an intolerant one at that, claiming to represent the scientific itself. Geertz's eloquent itinerary from Parsonian social science toward the humanities helped dissenters such as Sewell to envision alternatives. In a sense, Geertz demonstrated by concrete example what Habermas in the European social theoretical context of the same struggle against positivism was arguing for in the abstract: the inescapable reality and legitimacy of intersubjective, communicative values and truths. Alas, culture gave few tools for rethinking the problematic positivist vision of the social itself. It offered a way out, yes, but was not in itself a weapon to successfully reengage and reappropriate the lost object of the social through theoretical struggle. It was more exit than voice, even though, ironically, voice was precisely seen as the lost moment to be recovered. Interpretivism moved the conceptual terrain out of the orbit of the relational—or in any case potentially relational, since the problem for social science was precisely the methodologically individualist and economically reductionist reading of the social—and into the circle of the semiotic. We want to show the consequences for the analysis of human practice and temporal change by taking Sewell's work as an example of the methodological split that necessarily occurs if culture takes precedence over practice and relationality.

In his recent essays Sewell remains loyal to his initial liberating moment of culture, the culture of Geertz, Sahlins, Benedict, and Boas, and ultimately of Herder and the German neo-Kantians. He is not convinced by recent anthropological culture-doubts and argues that anthropology, or any other social science, can "yet do without," echoing James Clifford's effective apology (Clifford 1988: 10). Throughout he is fair about the impact of practice, action, institutions, power, and the actual permeability of boundaries on the culture concept. But in the end he remains ambivalent. While backing away from the "thick coherence" that Geertz and Sahlins induce, he concedes to culture a "thin coherence" and contends that it does have "autonomy" and a "logic of its own." "Culture," he writes, "may be thought of as a network of semiotic relations cast across society, a network with a different shape and different spatiality than institutional, or economic, or political networks" (Sewell 1999: 49). Culture in this sense becomes close to a compact of signifiers abstracted from written language, codified law, institutional charters, and formal practices, precisely the sources that Sewell had used for his *Language of Labor*. Culture for Sewell is thus a "great tradition," "a model of and for" the world in Geertz's sense, a template. He attributes to it a "distinct semiotic logic … in a roughly Saussurean sense," operating via distinctions and oppositions (ibid.: 49).

But beware, the culture of the social historian and political scientist Sewell is "thin," not "thick," and the difference illustrates the ambiguities of culturalism in historiography. For Sewell it means that while culture may have an autonomous logic, that logic must in the end remain "open-ended, not closed" (ibid.: 50). This is so because it is "interlocked in practice with other structures—economic, political, social, spatial, and so on" (ibid.: 51). As a consequence, times change, Sewell concludes, and adaptations of cultural patterns to developments in other institutional fields will therefore always be necessary.

This is the point at which Sewell's formulations become confusing. Either culture is autonomous and operates according to a logic of its own, roughly Saussurean if need be; or it is not autonomous and is operated within an interlocking set of institutional practices, including specialized institutions for culture production, set in motion by identifiable and interested actors, who may or may not face resistance. It is the one or the other, and it makes a difference for how we think and talk about social existence. Somewhat later in this text, Sewell concedes that if cultural significations happen to become "thickly" coherent and therefore strongly determinant of human action, it can only be so precisely because of the enclosing practices of these institutional mechanisms and not because of its internal grammars (ibid.: 53–55). Culture's logic, then, is merely formal and its substance and direction are first of all produced by interested actors in history and in situ who apparently have a space of experience, practice, and connectivity not fully absorbed by culture's predated signifying grids. Ergo culture is not autonomous. Hence change.

Later in the same text, having set out to save culture, Sewell retreats again from this practice-based conception. "Cultural coherence," he writes, "to the extent that it exists, is *as much* [my emphasis] the product of power as it is of semiotic logic" (ibid.: 57). He then finishes with a conciliatory and slightly contradictory note: while he recognizes that at this stage in human history we should not longer assume strongly bounded and cohesive cultures linked to places and peoples, we nevertheless must retain the sense of "particular shapes and consistencies of worlds of meaning in different places and times and a sense that in spite of conflicts and resistance, these worlds of meaning somehow hang together" (ibid.: 57–58). So we are left with "thin" difference of a "somehow" sort. This is good as an ethical code for living, but for social theory and methodology it throws up more dilemmas than it solves.

Ambivalences thus abound, and they are not irrelevant. It is power, most critical anthropologists will nowadays say, that produces the "somehow," that is how boundaries and coherence can be explained, not by meaning itself. Explanations of culture by culture are tautologic. What Sewell seems attached to, then, and entirely rightly so, is contingency, history, and discovery, wrapped together in the postmodern feel-good notion of difference. But is culture, even if just "thinly coherent," really necessary to get there? If indeed totalities exist, must they then be expressive totalities? Or can they also be, to use Michael Burawoy's (1985) distinction, socially structured totalities? Or, if the connotation of a totality is a bit overstretched for our postmodern sensibilities, can it just be a social formation? One does not need to be a rigid scientific Marxist or Foucauldian believer to have an idea that such social formations do exist and crystallize around core institutions of power that coordinate dominant modes of production, technology, and social relations. And at the least since Lenin, Luxemburg, and Trotski we know that such identifiable social formations interact and interpenetrate through global space in hierarchical ways, forming world systems, if you like, and that consequently their boundaries are variable and contested, that they have always been like that and that they must increasingly be so under the intensifying onslaught of new financial, political, and military imperialisms and the associated corporate marketing drives. Difference between such formations is therefore not necessarily authentic, pristine, or prior; it also always forms the outcome of precisely these global asymmetrical interactions, as Sider emphasizes in his contribution. Culture as template is a poor way to get at these historical dynamics, relationalities, and connectivities. Culture, even if thin, remains a vision of horizontal and synchronic difference. We need ways to get at thick history and dense space instead of thin culture. Hence critical junctions—in space, time, and institutional domains.

William Roseberry, in his early critical piece on Geertz's cockfight, was right that, *pace* Sewell's dismissal (Sewell 1997: 36), it is the material production of culture that must be explained, 'material' in this context just being another word for the institutionalized, power-laden process of consequential social praxis (Roseberry 1989: 17–29). Or as Sider says in his contribution to this volume, it is not difference but differentiation that must be explained. Practice and power are by now the established conceptual ways to prevent "the extreme idealism" (Kuper 1999: 120) of culture. But by themselves these notions may still be too momentary and place-bound. The idea of critical junctions serves to wed them analytically to networks of space and time. Indeed, the concern with diachrony and the rejection of idealism are not two different things: they spring from the very same commitment, as does the issue of space and place. Halfway formulations such as Sewell's leave us in an awkward split.

Why is this split theoretically unproductive? The ambiguities about culture surfaced already in an older and interesting article by Sewell on class protest in France. It is useful to have a look at that text because it graphically illustrates the theoretical problems that emerge when the problem of culture is linked to that of historical change and struggle. It was a critique of Charles Tilly's vision in *The Contentious French* and other publications of a transition in popular protest repertoires from reactive (corporate and backward looking) to proactive (class based and forward looking) as facilitated by central state formation and capitalist accumulation and concentration (Tilly, Tilly, and Tilly 1975; Tilly 1986). The brunt of the criticism was that Tilly was "blind" to "the cultural dimension" (Sewell 1990: 546) of protesting sodalities. The consequence of this theoretical neglect was that Tilly, according to Sewell, overestimated the importance of 1848 in helping to bring about the proactive repertoire and overlooked the "foundational" importance (ibid.: 534) of the French Revolution. It was also a neglect, Sewell argued, of the contingencies of political struggle and the critical imagination in favor of anonymous and large-scale social forces that mechanically work out their apparently inevitable *telos*. The French Revolution of 1789, Sewell claimed, created a "cultural foundation" for proactive civic protest, because it helped to invent and institutionalize the modern notion (fantasy we would nowadays perhaps say) of the nation as a free association of citizens and of the popular insurrection as a democratic act expressing the will of "the people." Here was a template, a foundational moment for modern political repertoires, claims Sewell: a model of and for the world, in the Geertzian sense.

But, as Giordano emphasizes in his contribution to this book, foundational moments are always manipulated by elites and contenders through time, responding as they do to new pressures and opportunities. While Sewell the theorist of culture-as-an-autonomous-semiotic-field should have little patience for such skirmishes on the ground, Sewell the social historian readily concedes the point. The empirical part of his essay thus shows what he cannot articulate in theory: that the allegedly civic template of the revolution was first used to rule out all public and corporate associations in a paranoid celebration of "the nation" as the single legitimate and organic form of the public, repressing all forms of democratic deliberation and protest. It was then selectively implemented from above by the centralizing police-state policies of subsequent emperors and kings. But it was also gradually appropriated and reframed by organizations of young rebellious workers in a handful of dynamic cities, who, assisted by local republican intellectuals, bent it toward their interests and lent it a more radical and proactive twist. Their rereading of the revolutionary heritage highlighted the legitimacy of social rights and class-based civic action, a reading that increasingly helped them, in 1830, 1848, and 1870, to overcome their mutual divisions and forge a common front against exploitative employers and the authoritarian state. What is essential is that this outcome should not be assumed to have been encrypted already in the proceedings of the revolutionary parliament in 1789, as Sewell the cultural theorist must imply. Rather, it was produced in a historical dialectic of power and counterpower projects, in mobilization, bargaining, and compromise, in institutional expansion responding to large-scale social change along Tilly's lines, and most tangibly through waves of strong urban popular resistance. Instead of the unfolding of an autonomous cultural logic toward its own natural end, the outcome, then, was contingent on power balances, struggles, and events, on working-class action and republican organization in a series of identifiable neighborhoods in several politically significant locales. These concrete rebellious groups and these particular locales remain of immense significance in having created in praxis the civic reading of the rather plastic template of the revolution, even if hindsight does indeed suggest that the processes of accelerated capital concentration, intensified proletarianization and modern state-formation, as propelled by deadly rivalries among European states and cutthroat competition among producers and entrepreneurs—Tilly's large-scale processes—were indeed shifting European power balances to such an extent that the general strengthening of civic and social rights on a national level became a likely outcome. And yes, this aggregate result may rarely have been envisioned by any single contentious actor in any particular site.

We should thus see the revolution of 1789 not as a finished cultural template for modern citizenship, but as one dramatic moment in a long syncopated sequence of violent social and cultural confrontations in the transformation of a whole historical regime toward its own form of modernity. Each punctuation produced its own newly invented, revised, or restored additions to the cultural archive, which could function as a new resource for the next episode (see also Rebel, this book). What happened at any one point in time always preselected what could possibly happen in the next, and the next act always led to reinterpretations of prior events, a temporal dialectic that altogether produced the social and institutional heritage that we call modern French (and European) society. And indeed a spatial dialectic, too, as it unfolded in between a set of localized actors within various evolving French urban landscapes in dialogue with the political center, and was subsequently exported and responded to all over Europe. Similarly, "the cultural foundation" (ibid.: 534) of the Ancien Régime by itself could never have explained "the experimentation in the forms of social relations" (ibid.: 538) among Parisian intellectuals that preceded the revolution of 1789 and prefigured its idiom, except perhaps in the sense of suggesting some core themes of protest such as the critique on privilege. The relational and historical experiments of the Parisian professional bourgeoisie in its rebellion against the injustices of the empire run from Versailles taught them about the meaningful alternatives. Likewise, workers in 1848 and later, in Lyon, Toulouse, or Paris, learned from their own evolving social relations and the struggles they fought, and in so doing they developed their language, their knowledge, their politics, and their utopias. And of course they did so in reference, though not necessarily in reverence, to what was there before ("framing" in the words of social movement researchers such as Doug MacAdam, Sid Tarrow, and Charles Tilly 2001; "cultural materials" according to Eric Wolf; "tradition" in Raymond Williams 1988).

Gerald Sider in his contribution encourages us to see how cultural forms are both derived from and feed back into the social relations that people enter into in the course of their everyday struggles for making their "own" history. For him, culture is a hopelessly static term that cannot capture the ongoing cognitive, emotional, and relational fights that people must wage in order to comprehend in meaningful and materially consequential ways the relations and institutional environments by which various forms of disorder are imposed on them. Struggle (and perhaps experience) is the overarching term for him, not culture, even though he remains dissatisfied with the utilitarian and largely purposive connotation of the term in both the liberal and Marxist imaginaries.

Sider's vision, it is important to note, is not necessarily at odds with Sewell the social historian who finds it hard to integrate the culture-as-template notion of Sewell the culture theorist in his research on temporal change, as we have seen. True, Sider's examples come from ethnography among concrete localized people rather than from historical research on states, epochs, and great traditions that are stretched out in time and space. His language accordingly is aimed more to capture action and flow and social connectivity than macro historical events, long-term historical sequences, and aggregate societal outcomes. As Handelman remarks in his contribution, praxis and flow necessarily fade when temporal distance and geographic scale increase. Kalb's essay tries to bring these foci together in an alternation of perspectives on experience, memory, praxis, struggle, structural power, and path-dependent and externally linked social process. His contribution shows how the study of evolving social structures in wider temporal and geographic frames can be linked with the microanalysis of practice, experience, and imagination, and vice versa, allowing more dynamic insights in power and social possibilities than either the small-scale/compressed time frame of classical ethnography or the macro historical study can offer on their own.

But culture-as-template theories, on the other hand, find little confirmation with Sider, Kalb, Handelman, or any of the other culture-critics represented in this book. Anthropologists, it is true, should admit that their object and methods lend themselves more readily to a critical stance toward culture-as-template visions than those of historians. Ethnography conventionally deals with local action and praxis. It may be increasingly aware of global connectedness and deterritorialized flows in cultural software, but it often remains weak in perceiving the sheer weight of great traditions as embodied in grand institutional, juridical, and lexical architectures, and associated fantasies of order, justice, and redemption, such as those of states or even civilizations, as they impinge on local life.[5] Sewell is not unduly impressed by the fixity and solidity of an edifice so grand, and at the same time so capillary, as the modern French state, even while on closer inspection such edifices are under continuous revision and repair. Is the magnitude of the object itself perhaps the reason for his embrace of the template of culture? One of the original reasons for anthropologists to conjoin their locally based perspectives with historical ones was precisely the effort to envision the great tradition of the nation and the global hierarchies of the world system in their manifold links with the locality and vice versa, as Silverman and Gulliver remind us in their chapter.

Rebel's contribution to this book meets Sewell on his own ground. He carefully develops a critique on culture-as-template perspectives in historical studies of holocaust-forms in Central Europe. His great concern, of course, is to prevent the unsavvy cultural determinism that "provincial judges" such as Goldhagen have been propounding in the course of the academic culture wave of the 1980s and 1990s. Two methodological moments are basic to Rebel's construction. First, he takes pains to discern between culture as template on the one hand, and what Eric Wolf has called "the engram" on the other, a series of articulate and variably institutionalized memories within a cultural heritage that can at any moment be mobilized and updated and serve as visions for action. They can also be left in the archive. The point is that they are available, and that their actual use and outcome are open and contingent upon the pressures, potentialities, and actors of the moment. The engram in Rebel's case concerns the illegal but customary temporary reintegration into established German villages and "home towns" of marginalized, stigmatized, and segregated groups of dispossessed siblings through the institution of internal policing actions or external paramilitary activities, which seems to have been operative since at least the late Roman Empire. Secondly, he is in search of a "configuration" in the sense of Norbert Elias, a specific set of social relationships with a dynamic and developmental rhythm of its own, such as Elias had analyzed between the French court and its nobles. He concentrates on the Austrian Empire and identifies such figuration in the *Grundherrschaft* and inheritance laws of the Empire, explicitly introduced for enhanced central accumulation and liquidity in imperial Vienna. This figuration, according to Rebel, eventually produced a "misrecognized" and therefore traumatized category of brutalized outsiders in a *Heimat* whose rhetorics were saturated with ideas of belonging, honor, and caring. Its victims, Rebel argues, were preselected for "known but hidden" forms of gradual annihilation or were allowed to informally and temporarily regain their honor through martial and policing functions. Wolf's concept of the engram allows Rebel to prevent the teleology of cultural templates while at the same time retaining the human possibilities, including the destructive ones, that are stored in great traditions and that can be reappropriated and updated at different times under new pressures. Their actualization and meaning, however, remain fully dependent on praxis, institutional process, creativity, and the core social relationships involved in power projects—Elias's figuration, as also Giordano emphasizes. Process, thus, remains open, multilineal, and guided by praxis; explanation is social and contingent rather than based in any firm cultural logic.

Place, Space, and Linkage

Compare the entirely contrastive evaluations by Don Handelman and William Sewell of Geertz's well-known parable of Cohen the Jew in his introduction to *The Interpretation of Cultures* (1973). Cohen is a Moroccan Jew whose sheep are stolen by unfriendly Berbers. He is compensated by "his" friendly Berbers, and then fined again by the French authorities who have made pacts with Berbers illegal. Handelman wonders why Geertz at this supposedly most programmatic moment of his oeuvre tells just "a framed snapshot" that can at best be "read and reread in search of embedded meanings" but never serves to interrogate the actual sequences and linkages backward into French colonialism, outward into Berber politics, or forward into Cohen's goal-oriented practices. "Practice," Handelman therefore concludes, "goes nowhere, except to be swallowed and regurgitated recursively by culture." Sewell, on the other hand, finds it "a good metaphor of the sort of dynamic, relational, differentiated cultural analysis" that he finds himself advocating (1997: 51). It is a characteristic "confusion of tongues," he proclaims, that can lead to the transformation of cultural systems. But Handelman does not believe in cultural systems transforming themselves, not even so much in confusion. He is interested in the actual use that actors make of symbols, in human practice and human becoming. The snapshot of confusion, which can only be produced by halting time, experience, and action, is in Handelman's opinion inhabited by all but flat characters: in reality the French, the Berbers, and Cohen knew very well what they were doing and why, but the picture tells us very little about this, nor about their relational unfolding.

Rereading Robert Darnton's famous essay (1985) on the Cat Massacre in eighteenth-century Paris, Handelman demonstrates that the same "snapshot" principles operate in the forms of micro history that have found inspiration in Geertz's thick description. Such micro histories always work by assuming a macro cultural universe, a template in Wolfs' words. Epochs thus become "blocks of meaning" for the historian just as cultures become enclosed signifying universes for the interpretivist anthropologist. But micro-history and ethnography could be inspired by another tradition, too, Handelman reminds us. Interpretivism, as well as Malinowskian or Boasian ideas of ethnography, take the local as an unproblematic instance of a larger cultural universe, but the Mancunian tradition of situational analysis and the extended case study, derived first of all from Max Gluckman, calls for "studying up and outwards" (Burawoy 2000) and invites us to follow the flow and interactions of practice through time and throughout space. Here is an ethnographic tool for seeing Wolf's engram at work. Handelman calls for a spatialized and dynamized ethnography of practice instead of the localized interpretivism of synchronic meanings derived from a hypothesized encompassing semiotic cosmos. His is a plea for thick micro-history through time in contrast to the conventional ethnographic collapse of a flat cultural universe in place.

In his own examples here Handelman is more concerned with temporal flow than spatial linkage, while Musante, Carbonella, Kalb, Sider, Silverman and Gulliver, and Rebel take the perspective more explicitly into space and write on the deeply contested politics of place making within wider landscapes of organized power. Not surprisingly, several of them work in a tradition linking the anthropology of Eric Wolf to macro historical sociologists such as Elias and Tilly or British Marxists such as Harvey, Williams, Hobsbawm, or Thompson.

The political economy tradition in U.S. anthropology, as well as French anthropological Marxism, was already interested in spatial articulation and linkage perspectives, even though the inclination persisted to assume that non-Western places had somehow been pristine, authentic, and uncorrupted by "others" prior to European encroachments, while the complexities of the encroaching itself, too, were not always fully understood. Such assumptions of authenticity are absent in the work presented here, which is also mostly on Northern contexts. Carbonella, for example, shows how memory and place making among paper mill workers in the northeastern United States are closely tied to both local as well as national efforts at reshaping the spatial grids of industrial relations under which the reproduction of these communities proceeds. The local in itself is an insufficient site for grasping these wider landscapes of power that structure local capacities for action and critical memory. Similarly, Kalb's electrical workers in one of the core sites of electronics production in the modern world, the Netherlands, are tied to, and intensely cope with, the particular social and cultural regimes that have emerged in order to link the locality as well as the small nation profitably to world markets for labor-intensive manufactured goods. These regimes thrived on coalitions between employers and parents. Such alliances facilitated exploitation within the family and between generations and sexes, and generated deeply complex struggles about gender, youth, discipline, and profitability, as expressed among others in social policy. Carbonella and Kalb are rare examples of anthropologists who find their ethnographic subjects in the historical heartlands of Western industry, a step still hard to take for the discipline itself. A perspective on critical junctions is a methodological sine qua non for such openings.

Musante turns the perspective around. While Carbonella and Kalb must "study up and outwards" to map the critical junctions shaping their local scenes, Musante shows how prior struggles with the state continue to inform local protest against state-imposed globalization policies in a Mexican municipality. Globalization does not arrive spontaneously, *pace* neoliberalism and postmodernism alike; it arrives as a state-imposed project that continues a long sequence of class-structured fights about land and indigenous rights and at best adds a new twist to them.

Giordano is also concerned with place making in encompassing landscapes of power. His landscapes are more exclusively geopolitical and military than socio-economic. In his discussion of saints he makes the interesting observation that sanctification in the Russian Orthodox church has mostly been aimed at "warrior-saints," while the Balkans have increasingly seen the creation of "victim-saints"—Serbia is no special case. He relates such differences in myth making to a crucial contrast in national experience: the difference between the continuously precarious integrity of Russian statehood thanks to martial cunning, versus the regularly interrupted, subjected, and as yet still contested state traditions of Balkan civilizations, with all the profound insecurity, humiliation, and repression that this may entail.

These essays present new perspectives and fresh questioning of the space-place nexus. For all its investment in local fieldwork and ethnography, classical anthropology can hardly be said to have contributed much to an analytical understanding of place making, although Appadurai (1996) and Gupta and Ferguson (1997a, 1997b) have recently suggested important conceptual steps.[6] Indeed, place was paradigmatically treated as a cultural microcosm derived from a larger one. It was not a problem to begin with and was often selected on the basis of mere chance and luck rather than its expected analytical properties or its potential for theoretically relevant discovery. The ethnographic ambition was often simply also to fill in another blank on the map. Apart from several inexcusable mystifications, there were also various good reasons for this light touch. But both internal developments within social science and external processes within the world are pressing for a critical junctions agenda that requires more explicit analytical acumen in relating the local to macro-scale structures and developments, and vice versa. "There is nothing mere to the local," Appadurai aptly notes (1996), since place making in modern environments of powerfully engulfing global flows, institutions, and networks, must increasingly become an intense domain of research and analysis, as well as popular concern, action and imagination. It is the historically established interactions of any territory within global space, their timing, and the emergent linkage practices of the local throughout space that count first of all; and histories of both, the local itself as well as any locale's linkage pattern at large, are important vehicles in bringing prevailing as well as subaltern and possible landscapes about. The local, from this perspective, always hosts some crucial global properties, which cannot always be uncovered from a more aggregate perspective, as Silverman and Gulliver emphasize and various contributions demonstrate. The local opening onto critical junctions thus can deepen the scope of general theories by suggesting limits, conditions, and interacting or intervening mechanisms and relationships that come inevitably into play as global forces become enmeshed in specific contexts of time and space, and then as a rule produce slightly unexpected outcomes. Concrete abstractions, to use Marx's vocabulary, are always much more complicated than universal abstractions, and, in point of fact, the latter only realistically exist in the shape of the former. This is the agenda of discovery that the emphasis on critical junctions promises.

From the perspective of the politics of place-making, the indulgence with culture as template has produced some very unsavvy results in some classical anthropologies of the local. They have first done so, as Sider discusses, by envisioning a static, authentic culture "of a people" with inherent rules that supposedly reigned prior to the incorporation in the Western system. Such anthropological constructions of culture were often projections of bourgeois fantasies about well-ordered, internally coherent worlds. Sider cites the example of the "dreamtime" of Aboriginal populations in Australia, which is "largely a Euro-Australian fantasy about Aboriginal culture, that the native peoples must now participate in sustaining" in order to protect their territorial claims in court. They are forced to use our fantasies to resist our brutalities, Sider remarks.

Secondly, such blunders continue to happen in classical structuralist anthropologies when they suggest that marginalized populations, in spite of colonization and the destruction of erstwhile relationships, actually heroically sustain their traditional worlds. Marshall Sahlins is a case in point. In a 1999 paper he exclaims that modernity is indigenized by Eskimo peoples in the Arctic North. Against twentieth-century modernist predictions that their hunting and gathering culture would disappear as a consequence of capitalism and modernity, he contends that money and city life on the contrary have been boldly appropriated by indigenous peoples as subsidies in order to sustain traditional kin-based livelihoods in circumpolar territories. As in Captain Cook (1995), events are fully swallowed by cultural structure, and Western imposition is retrospectively reversed and apparently totally manipulated by a resistant culture. Instead of the complex and contradictory politics of place making against the odds, Sahlins sees just cultural heroism. Not surprisingly, action, practice, relationships, linkages, flow, let alone exploitation and power, are minimized to the point of irrelevance, while the simple fact of the location of some in the wilderness, the continuation by them of hunting and gathering, and above all the adherence by a few to the mythologies presumably of old, are magnified beyond all proportions to make this spurious claim. As we have claimed above, anthropologies of place making cannot but demonstrate that modernity was always more complex than classical social theories anticipated. But to argue its entire irrelevance, except as a boon to continuity, is grotesque, certainly in respect to people among whom alcoholism and suicide after the fact have produced among the lowest life expectancies in the modern world while their territories now sustain a mere fraction of the children born there.

What such classical failures minimally demonstrate is that place making is never just a local event. It happens while wider landscapes of power impinge on local terrain. Not in the abstract, but in the concrete: by inserting it forcibly in a specific slot and incorporating it in a particular mix of institutional hierarchies, networks, market flows, and chains of familial and friendship connections. It is the historically established linking mix of any locale that generates in its turn the opportunities for newly emergent junctions, as people move out of the locality in search of resources and come back with new information, assets, and widened networks. Place making is as much based in the movements in and out, as it is in what moves those who do not move. It is about connectivity and about how particular sets of critical junctions help to shape the visions and resources of locally consequential actors.

Classical field research has therefore rightly been encouraged to change its single-site inclinations to more multi-sited ambitions. As translocal connecting networks become ever more salient in the reproduction of local life, field research cannot afford to stay put. It can expand its analytical horizon by incorporating archive and library research, as was recommended in the initial move toward history, as Silverman and Gulliver recount. But it can also follow networks "upwards and outwards" via participant observation, secondary sources, and interviews, as illustrated by Gluckman's classic example of situational analysis (see Handelman, this book). It can even "study through" (Randeria 2003): connecting contexts of decision making at high levels of authority, such as the World Bank or government departments, to local concerns, mobilizations, and outcomes. There are scores of critical junctions that must be brought into view if the fallacies of classical anthropology are to be prevented. Meanwhile, the actual scale of the local may well be changing, too: from the proverbial village to the wider agricultural landscape, to the industrial district, to urban or even global regions; or following the spatial and social linkages made by transmigrants (for instance, Grillo 2002); or explore the connections in networks of transnational protest (for example, Edelman 2002).

Discovery, Dilthey, and Realism

In a recent series of texts, historical sociologist Richard Biernacki (1995, 1999) has made some provocative proposals concerning the study of culture. Cultural turnists, he claimed, have treated culture as an ontological and foundational reality that practically suffused cases and remained stable over time (Biernacki 1999), much like classical anthropology, he could have added. Therefore, he says, the case study was their preferred tool to show how culture remained itself amid change in other factors. Thus, history and anthropology could both stay what they were: idiographic exercises. So far his critique is not principally different from ours. But in the next maneuver he diverges strongly from what we have been implying. He recommends a comparative procedure that asks, and tests, whether culture is actually a relevant differentiating factor among other variables in various cases. But in so doing, culture turns into a nominalistic, ideal type-like construct designed by the researcher to identify horizontal difference between cases. He presents his own work as an example. In *The Fabrication of Labor* (1995) he sets out to demonstrate that cultural knowledge about the social relationships of production, the wage, profitability and accounting in English and German woolen factories in the late eighteenth and nineteenth centuries differed in significant ways. In fact, he not only discovers synchronic differences in how the wage and profitability are conceived in these countries, but also infers dynamic consequences for the emergence of counterknowledges and resistance. Marx could only have discovered the hidden dynamics of the workday in industrial capitalism from a location in Germany, he claims, since it was there that time had actually become a measure of accounting and factory discipline, not in England. This is, he suggests, what determined the nature of place in these two different national industrial landscapes, other factors, such as technology and size of ventures, being equal.

His case is a bold one and anthropologists and historians would be well advised to take up the challenge. By interrogating the explanatory status of culture among other empirical factors, he is injecting a healthy dose of skepticism concerning the old German neo-Kantian project of a separate charter for the cultural sciences (*Geisteswissenschaften*) and the accompanying bipolarization between nomothetic-universalist and idiographic-particularist approaches. It also works against the overtly idealist idea of culture as holistic meaning and foundational template. Indeed, Wilhelm Dilthey, who has been credited with drafting the separate constitution of the cultural sciences in Wilhelmine Germany, seems never to have believed that hermeneutics could have been sufficient in its own right. For him, empirical knowledge, comparison, and identification of causal regularities had to complement the procedures of hermeneutic interpretation to arrive at valid historical understandings (Morris 1997: 330–337). It is time that anthropologists and historians revisit their one-sided readings of Dilthey and Weber. Dilthey, like Geertz, argued against the hegemony of the natural science model in order to secure some space for human freedom, action, and understanding. Like Geertz, he sought the way out by focusing too exclusively on meaning versus mechanical determination rather than the other possible route of critique: relationality versus individualism, even though that was always also implied. Thus, Biernacki's provocations do occasion a rethinking. But while he sends idealism out through the front door, he immediately brings it in again through the back door. He remains entirely within the orbit of classical positivism in his epistemology and methodology and therefore forecloses a re-elaboration of the relational critique.

It is here that a useful anthropological alternative finds its opening. Biernacki's quasi-experimental design necessitates a nominalist attitude to concepts. Culture becomes just a nominal construct created by the researcher to discover variance among cases. But what is he measuring, then? Whatever its precise definition, is culture really a separate variable that can actually occur in isolation in social life and be measured as such? Are we to believe that it is not also operating in something called the economy, or society, or politics, and vice versa?[7] Is it not a place-bound interaction effect produced by other variables given particular contexts of space and time—critical junctions? In Biernacki's concrete case of the comparison of woolen production in England and Germany the respective trajectories of proletarianization, market liberalization, and industrialization differ between the two countries in terms of sequence and timing, as does, of course, the class character of the regime. Moreover, the units are interlinked by a forwardness-backwardness connection. Why take out one aspect (ideas, knowledge, etc.), privilege it, and repress the weight of the whole structured totality of context, timing, and sequence? All the usual reservations about external validity of positivist and nominalist designs obtain here. They can be summarized in the proverbial metaphor of the French fry cutter. The potato is now cut in chunks that can be nicely handled separately, but the potato itself is gone. Biernacki readily admits so, but seems little concerned about what he has lost in the act. What he has lost is precisely the raison d'être of anthropological method: the integrity of context and the ontological assumption of a relational totality, our critical junctions. Biernacki's method therefore necessarily leads to ideal types and away from realism. Anthropology, Eric Wolf would say, is about interstitial relations, about the real-life interconnections between nominally distinct spheres of social life (for example, Wolf 2001: 49–63). It is the anthropological mission among the social and human sciences to move beyond the ideal types.

While his positivism would not suggest so, Biernacki is in fact too good a researcher to be unaware of all these anthropological intricacies. In his monograph he shows how the slow rollback of feudal relations and the limitations on market exchanges in the pre-1873 German-speaking lands had important consequences for labor law and the ordering of emergent industrial relations. This continental context produced a significantly different social environment for waged work and thinking about capitalist productivity compared to England, which was thoroughly commercialized at an early stage, before the expansion of manufacturing as an industry. Thus, his own material demonstrates that knowledge and culture, far from being independent factors, were part and parcel of wider and different national contexts/trajectories. He even extends his case by additionally drawing Italy and France into the comparison, identifying their peculiarities on the basis of his discoveries of contrasts in Germany and England, and the causal regularities in social relations and trajectories that they suggest.

Thus, Biernacki's provocation for anthropology is real, but it does not lay in the methodological considerations he has offered to us. In fact, I would contend that in his methodological articles he entirely seems to misrepresent his own research process. He pretends that it has been his positivist, experimental research design, testing whether culture (knowledge, law) made a difference, which allowed him to make his conclusions. But one can hardly imagine it did. Testing needs rigorous prior categories, hypotheses, and operationalizations. It is simply not suited for making new discoveries. It is meant for establishing correlations and distributions between known variables, not for finding out new ones. It necessarily reproduces the nominalist distinctions and cannot discover the dynamic complexities of situated and embodied social becoming. Instead of his misconceived overture with idealism, positivism, and nominalism, Biernacki should have thought more systematically about his method of discovery.

A critical junctions agenda in anthropology and history can add to our scholarly discoveries provided we become more self-conscious about methodological choices. In his discussion of Gluckman's method for "studying up," Handelman emphasizes that its potential for discovery is optimally exploited if it is used outside the old methodological bipolarity of induction versus deduction, the common terms associated with fieldwork and testing. Rather, it should proceed according to what Charles Peirce has called "abduction." Abduction refers to a dialectical process of hypothesis formulation on the basis of prior and comparative knowledge, then looking for new, surprising, or unanticipated phenomena in a fresh case that cannot be explained by the prior hypotheses, and subsequently specifying, modifying, and reformulating these hypotheses, or introducing entirely new ones, to account for the anomaly.[8] In my eyes, this is what has probably happened to Biernacki. Having started the study of historical vocabularies of labor law and management in one case, he apparently discovered anomaly and counterintuitive findings in the second case. He then was forced to explain the contrast. In trying to do so he discovered causal regularities that can account for the divergence between the two cases. He subsequently even extends his explanation to two new and intermediate cases (Italy and France), all along the way introducing new distinctions and inserting novel conditions. Abduction as a method of discovery in fieldwork fits well into Imre Lakatos's notion of scientific programs. Programs must remain in place, according to Lakatos, until their capacity for generating new insights by way of accounting for anomalies through the rephrasing of previous questions and hypotheses, is fading (Lakatos 1976, 2000).

From a critical junctions perspective on space, time, and interstitial relations in anthropology, discovery and context are inseparable. Why? Anthropology, against the preferences of many anthropologists, is legitimately expected to contribute to universal and comparative knowledge about human civilizations and human history. But it is inclined to do so with a programmatic digression into local outcomes.[9] As stated earlier, local outcomes generally exhibit properties with important implications for our understanding of global process. Few authors would doubt that the twentieth century has added tremendously to the modes of connectivity between people and places, even in some respects having reached planar scale after 1989. Whether we like to call that process globalization, cosmopolitanism, imperialism, stepped-up financial capitalism, or what not, it is clear that such processes fragment as they unite and localize while they globalize. The one-world notion is a great, and perhaps inhuman, fantasy, and the classless society is as far away as ever. This is not only because global process is uneven or power-/profit-driven, however central that in itself may be. It is also because global processes, such as market expansions, the spread of capitalist relationships, state and empire formation, incorporation in national and subsequently transnational juridical spaces, participation in primary, secondary, and tertiary education, all such universalizing forces, simply cannot foreclose locally differentiating outcomes. Global process must necessarily interact with prior local histories, political experiences, divisions of assets, and divisive relations of gender, race and class, which make starting points diverge. And such divergence becomes magnified in its spiraling consequences for local sites in an environment of stepped-up rivalry and competition, which is scripted in the very rules of the global game. Local outcomes are therefore never merely locally produced, as Appadurai (1996) rightly implies. They are willy-nilly composites of global-local interactions, critical junctions if you like. Such patterned and emergent critical junctions ultimately serve to select between what Michael Mann has called "zones of peace and zones of turmoil" (Mann 2001), between spirals downward into the zones of catastrophe, such as Central Africa, and spirals upward into the gated communities of the happy few, with infinite layers for the majority of humankind in between. Context, therefore, by itself is crucially about discovery. It is about discovering the timing, trajectories, and patterning of social practice as it extends from the local outward into space, and from the global downward onto territorialized life, producing anomalies all along. Context as discovery is just another word for, as well as the programmatic denial of, the lazy *ceteris paribus* formulae of the proverbial global consultant or the Chicago economist. As we know, in reality the other things are never just equal or indifferent. On the contrary, they *make* the whole difference; for the local, for the global, as well as for the progress of our knowledge. Context is about how space and place, global and local histories interconnect to produce a multiplicity of interlinked modernities. It is the critical junctions that must be discovered and explained.

Notes

1. Some of the relevant items are Bonnell and Hunt 1999; Christiansen 1984; Comaroff and Comaroff 1992; Dirks, Eley, Ortner 1994; Ginzburg, 1992, 1997; Gulliver and Silverman 1992; Hunt 1989; Le Roy Ladurie 1975; Levi 1991; Lüdtke 1989; Mintz 1985; Sahlins 1985, 1995; Scheider and Rapp 1995, Sharpe 1991; Stone 1979; Sider 1982, 1990; Sider and Smith 1997; Tilly 1984; Wolf 1964, 1982; 1999, 2001.
2. In this respect our work is entirely sympathetic to Gupta and Ferguson 1997a, 1997b; Tilly 2001; Trouillot 1991, 2002; and Wallerstein et al. 1996.
3. For other critiques, see, for example, Bonnell and Hunt 1999; Brightman 1995; Brumann 1999; Fox 1991; Fox and King 2002; Gellner 1987, 1998; Gingrich and Fox 2002; Gupta and Ferguson 1997a, 1997b; Kuper 1999; Ortner 1997; Stolcke 1995; Thomas 1991.
4. The characteristic positivist counterreaction was formulated by Paul Shankman 1984. May we note that the first issue of *Focaal—European Journal of Anthropology* (as yet without the postfix), started in Nijmegen in 1985 by Don Kalb, was dedicated to a discussion of Geertz's work. In his article with co-student and co-editor Roland Bonsen, Kalb thought that it was a non-debate, among others because both largely left out the "social dimension."
5. In this sense one should make the ironic remark that Huntington (1996) is regrettably still "better" in history than Hannerz (1992) or Appadurai (1996).
6. See also Kalb 2000, 2002, and 2004 for suggestions on place, space, and linkage in the anthropology of globalization, post-socialism, and development, respectively. Low and Lawrence Zuniga's recent anthology of the anthropology of space and place (2002) shows the slow learning process among anthropologists and the influence of critical geography on the more innovative recent departures in the discipline.

7. For an extended discussion of this issue from the perspective of class versus culture approaches, see Kalb 1997: 1–24. The new economic sociology and institutional economics, as well as economic anthropology, has of course bridged these antinomies too. See Gudeman 2001; Narotzky 1998; Ortiz and Lees 1992.

8. Similar formulations can be found at various places in Wolf's work, for example, 2001: 49–63; also in Elkana 2000.

9. If the strong agreement between the younger Wolf (1964) and the older Geertz (1999) on this organizing vision for the anthropological discipline would be an index of actual unanimity among its current practitioners, the *Methodenstreit* of which this book is a product would have been unnecessary.

References

Abu-Lughod, Lila. 1991. "Writing Against Culture." In *Recapturing Anthropology: Working in the Present*, ed. Richard G. Fox, 137–162. Santa Fe: School of American Research Press.

Appadurai, Arjun. 1996. *Modernity at Large*. Minneapolis: University of Minnesota Press.

Biernacki, Richard. 1995. *The Fabrication of Labor, Germany and Britain, 1640–1914*. Berkeley: University of California Press.

———. 1999. "Method and Metaphor after the New Cultural History." In *Beyond the Cultural Turn*, ed. Victoria Bonnell and Lynn Hunt, 62–94. Berkeley: University of California Press.

Bonnell, Victoria, and Lynn Hunt, eds. 1999. *Beyond the Cultural Turn*. Berkeley: University of California Press.

Brightman, Robert. 1995. "Forget Culture: Replacement, Transcendence, Relexification." *Cultural Anthropology* 10, no. 4: 509–546.

Brumann, Christoph. 1999. "Writing for Culture: Why a Successful Concept Should Not Be Discarded." *Current Anthropology* 40 (supplement): 1–27.

Burawoy, Michael. 1985. *The Politics of Production*. London: Verso.

Burawoy, Michael, et al. 2000. *Global Ethnography*. Berkeley: University of California Press.

Christiansen, Palle Ove. 1984. "Interdisciplinary Studies and Conceptual Eclecticism: On Historical Anthropology, the History of Everyday Life and the Study of Life Modes." *Etnologia Europaea* 14, no. 1: 32–43.

Clifford, James. 1988. *The Predicament of Culture*. Cambridge, MA: Harvard University Press.

Comaroff, John, and Jean Comaroff. 1992. *Ethnography and the Historical Imagination*. Boulder: Westview Press.

Darnton, Robert. 1985. *The Great Cat Massacre and Other Essays*. New York: Vintage Books.

Dirks, Nicholas, Geoff Eley, and Sherry B. Ortner, eds. 1994. *Culture/Power/History: A Reader in Contemporary Social Theory*. Princeton, NJ: Princeton University Press.

Edelman, Marc. 2002. "Toward an Anthropology of Some New Internationalisms: Small Farmers in Global Resistance Movements." *Focaal—European Journal of Anthropology* 40: 103–123.

Eley, Geoff, and Keith Nield. 2000a. "Farewell to the Working Class?" *International Labor and Working-Class History* 57: 1–30.

———. 2000b. "Reply: Class and the Politics of History." *International Labor and Working-Class History* 57: 76–87.

Elkana, Yehuda, ed. 2000. *The Paradoxes of Unintended Consequences*. Budapest: CEU Press.

Fox, Richard, ed. 1991. *Recapturing Anthropology: Working in the Present*. Santa Fe: School of American Research Press.

Fox, Richard, and Barbara King, eds. 2002. *Anthropology beyond Culture*. Oxford: Berg.

Friedman, Jonathan, ed. 2003. *Globalization, the State, and Violence*. Walnut Creek, CA: Altamira Press.

Geertz, Clifford. 1973. *The Interpretation of Cultures*. New York: Basic Books.

———. 1998. "The World in Pieces." *Focaal—Tijdschrift voor Antropologie* 32: 91–117.

Gellner, Ernest. 1987. *Relativism and the Social Sciences*. Cambridge: Cambridge University Press.

———. 1998. *Language and Solitude: Wittgenstein, Malinowski and the Habsburg Dilemma*. Cambridge: Cambridge University Press.

Gingrich, Andre, and Richard Fox, eds. 2002. *Anthropology, by Comparison*. London: Routledge.

Ginzburg, Carlo. 1992. *Clues, Myths, and the Historical Method*. Baltimore: Johns Hopkins University Press.

———. 1997. *The Cheese and the Worms*. Baltimore: Johns Hopkins University Press.

Grillo, Ralph. 2002. "Transnational Migration, Multiculturalism, and Development." *Focaal—European Journal of Anthropology* 40: 135–149.

Gudeman, Stephen. 2001. *The Anthropology of Economy*. Oxford: Basil Blackwell.

Gulliver, Philip, and Marilyn Silverman, eds. 1992. *Approaching the Past: Historical Anthropology through Irish Case Studies*. New York: Columbia University Press.

Gupta, Akhil, and James Ferguson, eds. 1997. *Culture, Power, Place: Explorations in Critical Anthropology*. Durham, NC: Duke University Press.

———, eds. 1997. *Anthropological Locations: Boundaries and Grounds of a Field Science*. Berkeley: University of California Press.

Hannerz, Ulf. 1991. *Cultural Complexity*. New York: Columbia University Press.

———. 1996. *Transnational Connections*. London: Routledge.

Hunt, Lynn, ed. 1989. *The New Cultural History*. Berkeley: University of California Press.

Huntington, Samuel. 1997. *The Clash of Civilizations*. New York: Simon and Schuster.

Jackson, Michael. 1989. *Paths toward a Clearing: Radical Empiricism and Ethnographic Enquiry*. Bloomington: Indiana University Press.

Kalb, Don. 1997. *Expanding Class: Power and Everyday Politics in Industrial Communities, The Netherlands 1850–1950*. Durham, NC: Duke University Press.

———. 2000. "Localizing Flows: Power, Paths, Institutions, and Networks." In *The Ends of Globalization: Bringing Society Back*, ed. Don Kalb et al., 1–33. Lanham, MD: Rowman and Littlefield.

———. 2002. "Afterword: Globalism and Postsocialist Prospects." In *Postsocialism: Ideals, Ideologies and Practices in Eurasia*, ed. Chris Hann, 317–334. London: Routledge.

Kalb, Don, Wil Pansters, and Hans Siebers, eds. 2004. *Globalization and Development: Themes and Concepts in Current Research*. Dordrecht: Kluwer Academic Publishers.

Kuper, Adam. 1999. *Culture: The Anthropologists' Account*. Cambridge, MA: Harvard University Press.

Lakatos, Imre, E. Zahar, and J. Worral, eds. 1976. *Proofs and Refutations*. Cambridge: Cambridge University Press.

Le Roy Ladurie, Emanuel. 1975. *Montaillou, village Occitan de 1294 à 1324*. Paris: Gallimard.

Levi, Giovanni. 1991. "On Microhistory." In *New Perspectives on Historical Writing*, ed. Peter Burke, 93–114. University Park: Penn State Press.

Low, Setha, and Denise Lawrence-Zuniga, eds. 2002. *The Anthropology of Space and Place: Locating Culture*. Oxford: Blackwell.

Lüdtke, Alf, ed. 1989. *Alltagsgeschichte*. Frankfurt am Main: Campus Verlag.

MacAdam, Doug, Sid Tarrow, and Charles Tilly. 2001. *Dynamics of Contention*. Cambridge: Cambridge University Press.

Mann, Michael. 2001. "Globalization after September 11." *New Left Review, Second Series* 12: 51–72.

Mintz, Sidney. 1985. *Sweetness and Power: The Place of Sugar in Modern History*. Harmondsworth, UK: Penguin.

Morris, Brian. 1997. "In Defence of Realism and Truth: Critical Reflections on the Anthropological Followers of Heidegger." *Critique of Anthropology* 17, no. 3: 313–340.

Narotzky, Susana. 1998. *New Directions in Economic Anthropology*. London: Pluto Press.

Ortner, Sherry B. 1994. "Theory in Anthropology since the Sixties." In *Culture/Power/History: A Reader in Contemporary Social Theory*, ed. Nicholas Dirks, Geoff Eley, and Sherry B. Ortner, 372–411. Princeton, NJ: Princeton University Press.

Randeria, Shalini. 2003, "Domesticating Neo-liberal Discipline: Transnationalisation of Law, Fractured States and Legal Pluralism in the South." In *Shared Histories and Entangled Modernities*, ed. Wolf Lepenies, 146–182. Frankfurt: Campus Verlag.

Roseberry, William. 1989. *Anthropologies and Histories: Essays in Culture, History, and Political Economy*. New Brunswick, NJ: Rutgers University Press.

Sahlins, Marshall. 1985. *Islands of History*. Chicago: Chicago University Press.

———. 1995. *How Natives Think: About Captain Cook for Example*. Chicago: University of Chicago Press.

———. 1999. "What is Anthropological Enlightenment? Some Lessons of the Twentieth Century." *Annual Review of Anthropology* 28: i–xxiii

Schneider, Jane, and Rayna Rapp, eds. 1999. *Articulating Hidden Histories: Exploring the Influence of Eric R. Wolf*. Berkeley: University of California Press.

Sewell, William H., Jr. 1980. *Work and Revolution in France: The Language of Labor from the Old Regime to 1848*. Cambridge: Cambridge University Press.

———. 1990. "Collective Violence and Collective Loyalties in France: Why the French Revolution Made a Difference." *Politics and Society* 18, no. 4: 527–552.

———. 1997. "Geertz and History: From Synchrony to Transformation." *Representations* 59: 35–56.

———. 1999. "The Concept(s) of Culture." In *Beyond the Cultural Turn*, ed. Victoria E. Bonnell and Lynn Hunt, 35–62. Berkeley: University of California Press.

Shankman, Paul. 1984. "The Thick and the Thin: On the Interpretive Theoretical Paradigm of Clifford Geertz." *Current Anthropology* 25, no. 3: 261–279.

Sharpe, Jim. 1991. "History from Below." In *New Perspectives on Historical Writing*, ed. Peter Burke, 24–41. University Park: Penn State Press.

Sider, Gerald. 1982. *Culture and Class in Anthropology and History: A Newfoundland Illustration*. Cambridge: Cambridge University Press.

———. 1993. *Lumbee Indian Histories: Race, Ethnicity, and Indian Identity in the Southern United States*. Cambridge: Cambridge University Press.

Sider, Gerald, and Gavin Smith, eds. 1997. *Between History and Histories: The Making of Silences and Commemorations*. Toronto: University of Toronto Press.

Stolcke, Verena. 1995. "Talking Culture: New Boundaries, New Rhetorics of Exclusion in Europe." *Current Anthropology* 36, no. 1: 1–24.

Stone, Lawrence. 1979. "The Revival of Narrative: Reflections on a New Old History." *Past and Present* 85: 3–24.

Thomas, Nicholas. 1991. "Against Ethnography." *Cultural Anthropology* 6, no. 3: 306–322.

Tilly, Charles. 1984. "The Old New Social History and the New Old Social History." *Review* 7, no. 3: 363–406.

———. 1986. *The Contentious French*. Cambridge, MA: Harvard University Press.

———. 2001. "Relational Origins of Inequality." *Anthropological Theory* 1, no. 3: 355–372.

Tilly, Charles, Louise Tilly, and Richard Tilly. 1975. *The Rebellious Century, 1830–1930*. Cambridge, MA: Harvard University Press.

Trouillot, Michel-Rolph. 1991. "Anthropology and the Savage Slot: The Poetics and Politics of Otherness." In *Recapturing Anthropology*, ed. Richard Fox, 17–44. Santa Fe: School of American Research Press.

———. 2002. "Adieu, Culture: A New Duty Arises." In *Anthropology Beyond Culture*, ed. Richard Fox and Barbara King, 37–60. Oxford: Berg Publishers.

Wallerstein, Immanuel, et al. 1996. *Open the Social Sciences.* Stanford: Stanford University Press.

Williams, Raymond. 1988. *Keywords.* London: Fontana Press.

Wolf, Eric. 1964. *Anthropology.* Princeton, NJ: Princeton University Press.

———. 1982. *Europe and the People without History.* Berkeley: University of California Press.

———. 1999. *Envisioning Power.* Berkeley: University of California Press.

———. 2001. *Pathways of Power: Building an Anthropology of the Modern World.* Berkeley: University of California Press.

Chapter One

Microhistorical Anthropology
Toward a Prospective Perspective

Don Handelman

Nothing made sense and neither did everything else.

— Joseph Heller, *Catch-22*

The relationship between anthropology and history is one of inequality. This is no less so for the relationship between anthropology and microhistory. History, one of the noble disciplines in the "history" of Western thought, has as an emblem the muse, Clio. Anthropology has anyone who at times is everyone, at times someone, so often nameless and unvoiced. In their relationship, anthropology is the junior partner, a Johnny-come-lately to the professional telling of pastness within intellectual worlds whose denizens believe in the existence and importance of the time-depths of history, probably since these also are perceived as the sources of knowledge.

This asymmetric relationship continues to dominate the relationship between these disciplines. Consider an advertising leaflet from a decade or so ago for the trendy interdisciplinary journal, *History and Anthropology* (the lineal sequencing of this journal's title tells, of course, the whole story of the hierarchy between these disciplines). The leaflet blurb states that the journal will stress the "mutually destabilising relationship" between history and anthropology, and then continues as follows: "History *demonstrates* the contingency of anthropology, and the multivocality of anthropology *can question* the authoritative claims and narrative forms of conventional history" (my emphases). This discourse spells out the metamessage of hierarchy and subordination through

Notes for this chapter begin on page 47.

which the reader is intended to frame the relationship between the disciplines. History's capacity to deconstruct anthropology is unconditional, its rhetoric imperiously declarative; anthropology's capacity to deconstruct history is qualified, more possible than actual, and in any case, partial. One can add that since anthropology is formed through historically constituted moments, its epistemological status is in the historian's grip.[1] Anthropology is encompassed, in the Dumontian sense, by history.

In contrast to the above depiction of anthropology in relation to history, I propose here that there is no epistemological distinction in principle between an anthropology grounded in the study of social practice and an anthropology that does microhistory. Social practice necessarily glides, slips, or trips retrospectively into microhistory; microhistory emerges prospectively from the temporal practices of social life. Practice—the doing, and therefore the creation of social life—produces microhistories of living, just as these microhistories shape the living of lives. This most intimate of relationships between social practice and microhistory seems to hold for history constructed by the professional, the outsider; for indigenous history, created by those who live through their own temporal sequences and trajectories; and for history done by the insider who is a professional historian. The hierarchy between these disciplines is erased.

Scale reduction is a central methodological problematic in the doing of history by professional historians and by anthropologists who do history. Nonetheless, scale reduction is less of a problem in the relationship between social practice and microhistory. Rather, this relationship enables our understanding of social life as put together through an ongoing clash and synthesis of mundane and extraordinary events.

The editors of this volume distinguish between two paradigms that relate anthropology and history. Both paradigms use scale reduction in order to ask very different questions. One paradigm, anthropological history, refers to the decoding of collective representations within historical periods. The other, historical anthropology, addresses theoretical issues that are not limited to period, place, or group. Yet these paradigms omit a significant development in the history of British social anthropology, one that I am calling a microhistorical anthropology of social practice. Under other rubrics, this perspective flourished through the work of the Manchester School founded by Max Gluckman.[2] The Manchester approach continues to resonate in varieties of social anthropology that emphasize the strong connection between field research and social practice, without becoming engorged by the nihilistic recursiveness of much reflexive anthropology (Handelman 1994). The Mancunians did not perceive their work as microhistory. Yet, understood in this way, their perspective is highly suggestive for the study of social practice in real time, since, for example, this approach necessarily engages with the problematic of "emergence" in social life (Handelman 1977), especially in the domain of the micro.[3] Emergence is strongly related to that which, further on, I call "prospective" microhistory.

As I suggested above, this approach to microhistory is less dependent on methods of scale reduction than are the paradigms of anthropological history and historical anthropology. The praxis, indeed the fusing, of social practice and microhistory modifies the conditions under which extensive scale reduction seems inevitable for all sorts of historical anthropology. In order to sharpen the focus of microhistorical anthropology, I will distinguish between this and that which I will name (using an ironic oxymoron) atemporal microhistory. This is the interpretive, hermeneutic microhistory done both by anthropologists and historians, in which social practice is minimal while scale reduction is major. For the purpose of this discussion, atemporal microhistory may be thought of as part of anthropological history.[4]

A major proponent of scale reduction in anthropology is Clifford Geertz. His strategy of ethnography is "to draw large conclusions from small, but very densely textured facts" (Geertz 1973a: 28). He is present here as an anthropologist who does "microscopic" ethnography (ibid.: 21), and whose cultural relativism and very brief mentions of "thick description" have had serious impact on anthropological history, in particular on the "new cultural history" (Hunt 1989; see also Walters 1980), but also on the "new historicism" (Veeser 1989; see also Ermarth 1992). In his introduction to thick description, Geertz (1973a) illustrates "thickness" through an example of ethnography that is historical but that approximates atemporal microhistory. Given Geertz's influence, this example will be discussed further on. In keeping with Geertz's dictum of large and small in ethnography, the editors of this volume characterize anthropological history in terms of a scale reduction in which large questions are applied to small-scale settings. Therefore, expansion of scope and scale reduction go hand in hand.[5]

My discussion proceeds as follows. I address atemporal microhistory through Geertz and through the cultural historian Robert Darnton (influenced by Geertz). Here social practice is nearly absent. Consequently the linkage between small-scale settings and temporal movement is limited. I then address microhistorical anthropology through the Manchester School ideas of situational analysis and the extended case-study method. Here social practice and temporal trajectories come to be linked—indeed, social practice is shown to be a temporal trajectory. Thus, the glide into microhistory is continuous (even though, as I noted, this relationship to temporality was rarely understood as history by protagonists of the Manchester School).

Following the above, I will mention briefly two of my own older studies on welfare bureaucracy that at the time I did not think of as microhistory. At this juncture I will make the additional distinction between retrospective and prospective microhistory. Retrospective microhistory reconstructs pastness, as this moves toward or into the present. Prospective microhistory begins with presentness and moves into the future, as present becomes past (thereby creating future). The first of my own studies exemplifies retrospective microhistory, and the second, prospective microhistory. Overall, the significance of scale reduction varies with the emphasis on social practice. Scale reduction is greater in atemporal microhistory than it is in microhistorical anthropology. Within microhistorical anthropology, scale reduction is more relevant to retrospective microhistory than it is to prospective microhistory. The *prospective attitude* to microhistory is most involved with social practice that itself creates futures, and so this attitude is the least influenced by scale reduction. In conclusion, I briefly note resonances between the approach of the Manchester School and some postmodernist thinking on history.

Atemporal Microhistory

How can history of any sort be called atemporal? I suggest that atemporal history comes into being when it ignores or holds in abeyance movement through time.[6] But only through giving signal importance to temporal movement can practice be made a central issue of analysis. Microhistory moves toward the atemporal when its practitioners begin to ignore the conditions of its formation and movement through time. Certainly, this is a relative matter. Nonetheless, it is then that the historical phenomenon or setting is held constant, more "frozen in time," as it were, and treated as if it contained the cultural information on social practice needed to decode its meanings. The setting is formulated (despite disclaimers to the contrary) something like a microcosm of more comprehensive cultural orders that are brought to bear to explicate its significance. The interpretive moment moves from the culture within which the setting is embedded into the setting itself, in order to unpack or decode its densely packed meanings. These in turn are understood to be significant for the embedding culture. This is how large conclusions about culture can be drawn directly from small facts embedded within it.[7] Time is spatialized (a close kin of textualized), and therefore is (at least partially) disabled (see, for example, Sharron 1982). Social practice (with its crucial potential to generate new, emergent properties through time) is subordinated to cultural themes and symbols, becoming wholly their product. History as temporal process is crippled and made quite irrelevant to interpretation. The historical is turned into just another ethnographic place, another Aristotelian container of various happenings and things brought into conjunction with one another. The temporality of history is backgrounded more than foregrounded in atemporal microhistory; and temporal process (regardless of its scale) is made into yet another artifice of interpretation.[8] Commenting on Le Roy Ladurie's *Montaillou: The Promised Land of Error*, Gertrude Himmelfarb (1989: 662) argues that this work "is nothing like narrative history in the traditional sense, which is not confined to a single event but rather connects in a narrative sequence a series of events over a significant span of time."

Geertz (1973a: 6) takes "thick description" from the philosopher Gilbert Ryle.[9] To illustrate thick description, Ryle contrasts three boys who contract the eyelids of their right eyes. One has an involuntary twitch, and so closes his eyelid without deliberation. The second closes his eyelid deliberately, producing what we recognize as a wink. The third parodies the wink by producing it in a way (overemphasized, accompanied by a grimace) that ridicules the second and perhaps also the first. This may lead to complicated plays on meaning (rehearsing the wink or its parody, faking a wink in order to deceive another, and so forth). Ryle contrasts the adequate "thin description" of the behavior done in common by all three boys (the rapid contraction of the right eyelid) with the interwoven, complex messages that winking (as a cultural category, adds Geertz) communicates. The latter is "thick," layered, polysemic, recursive description.[10]

This discussion of Ryle is followed immediately in Geertz's text by an example of thick description, a narrative set in Morocco in 1912, soon after the arrival of the French. The narrative revolves around Cohen the Jew who is robbed by unfriendly Berbers, but who invokes his trading pact (the institution had been outlawed by the French) with his own Berber allies and thereby succeeds in extracting extensive damages in sheep from the robbers' tribe. Nonetheless, the sheep are confiscated by the French, who jail Cohen as a spy for the Berbers. Eventually Cohen returns home without his sheep. The story is recounted by Geertz as historical, but this seems of little interest to him. He is fascinated by the story's "thickness" of scope—Jews, Berbers, French, institutionalizing power, institutionalized economic relationships, conflict and thwarted interests—the mesh, tear, and clash of cultural categories, the interwoven messages of convergence and contradiction. And all this within the microscopic size of the tale. The story is given little significance as, say, a moment of temporal process. It has quite the same epistemological status as the description it follows in Geertz's text—Ryle's discussion of winking. So one may well ask, why highlight so prominently as thick ethnographic description a story told to Geertz five decades and more after its (supposed) occurrence? Why did Geertz not use as his illustration of thick description something with the presentness of practice, something he himself had observed (for example, the telling of the tale itself, if one wished to stick to narrative)? The "thickness" is semantic rather than one of practice (see also Biersack 1989: 74).

I suspect that Geertz pretends to the significance of thick description in microhistory, while strategically using the distancing provided by time past to implicitly buttress his argument for the textualization of culture, for the metaphor of culture as an ensemble of texts—indeed, for an argument that undermines historical process (e.g., Roseberry 1982: 1022). More distant in time, more cleanly "textualized," more easily divorced from practice. The textualization of culture is the single worst move of Geertz's creative and at times brilliant scholarship (Handelman 1994: 346). With each reading, each interpretation, the literal text is "thickened," involuted, groping within itself to reach beyond. Nonetheless, the frame of the text does not change, nor do the characters, nor the mise-en-scène. Regardless of the variety and multiplicity of readings, the parameters of the text are closed, unless it is literally rewritten. Radical change cannot be generated from within the text itself, but only from without by someone akin to a deus ex machina. Lurking within Geertz's textualization of culture are the premises of an antiquated model of culture in which radical change occurs only through contact between cultures. Applied to culture, in effect to context, the text metaphor makes these highly rigid and inflexible in their boundaries, substance, and process. Culture is essentialized by the text metaphor.

Geertz (1989–1990: 329) once commented that the relationships between anthropology and history are a matter of "textual tactics." In tactical, or more accurately, strategic terms, the text metaphor fights temporal process to a near standstill, fragmenting and freezing temporal dynamics into framed snapshots like that of Cohen and his sheep, into still photographs that (like rituals and other symbolic forms) can be pored over, "read" and reread in search of embedded meanings. It is hardly surprising that the most celebrated of Geertz's thickened descriptions, the Balinese cockfight (Geertz 1973b), is a nonhistorical study of a bounded ritual form as "text"; and that of his major historical works, the one that attends most closely to history (Geertz 1965) often meanders without point, while another (Geertz 1980) dramatizes royal rituals within which indigenous history is embedded and made synchronic. One could conclude that, generally speaking, temporality is too processual for Geertz to deal with through hermeneutics (see Biersack 1989: 80). In one of his most recent works, he takes a different tack, throwing himself headlong into the crosscurrents and undertows of time, history, and change—into metaphors of squalls and twisting streams, swirls and confusions—and comes close to drowning in the process (Geertz 1995). Perhaps atemporal microhistory is more controllable, safer, and not all that oxymoronic.

What happens, then, when a distinguished cultural historian of eighteenth-century France adopts a Geertzian attitude to ethnography and microhistory, to entering culture through ritual, and to reading culture like a text? For one thing, Robert Darnton (1985) produces another exemplar of thickened description (Chartier 1985: 683). Yet, for another, his historical work verges at times on atemporal microhistory. Darnton's study has received a good deal of attention in print (Chartier 1985; Fernandez 1988; LaCapra 1988; Mah 1991), and here I will not go into what he and his critics have to say, and to one another. But I will point out how easily (in the manner of Geertz) Darnton the microhistorian slides into an atemporal landscape.

"Workers Revolt: The Great Cat Massacre of the Rue Saint-Severin" tells of how in the fourth decade of the eighteenth century, on the orders of their master, the apprentices in a Parisian printing shop killed all of the local cats they could get their hands on, including their mistress's favorite, La Grise, whom they had been told expressly to leave alone. Some of the cats were put through a mock trial, swiftly judged guilty, and hung from a miniature gibbet. The workers did all this in a spirit of great fun, enthusiasm, and frivolity. Even though the master and mistress came upon the workers in the midst of their cat massacre, and even though she recognized her favorite on the gibbet, the workers were left to continue their carnivalesque antics. According to Darnton's rendition of the brief text written by one of the revellers some twenty years after the event, the apprentices were not made to suffer for executing La Grise. This text of six pages forms the basis of Darnton's interpretation of the multiple meanings of the event, including the question with which he begins—why the workers found what they did so funny. For Darnton the event is replete with symbolic significance for France of the period, way beyond the tiny confines of a nondescript printing shop.

To explain this little, local, and, more likely than not, privately invented ritual of killing cats, Darnton brings to bear a Gargantuan array of signifiers that he claims were integral to the culture of the period. However, Darnton freezes the "period" in very broad scope. According to Chartier (1985: 689), these signifiers are taken by Darnton from multiple sites and times between the sixteenth and nineteenth centuries, in a (indiscriminate, is the implication) reification of Frenchness, of French culture. These signifiers include the symbolism of cats, sexuality, witchcraft, cuckolding, the torture of animals, initiation rites in printing shops, legal trial, charivari, fête, bawdy street theatre, Mardi Gras, and so on. Unless one accepts (as Geertz says he refuses to admit) that the microscopic is also a microcosm of the macro level of cultural order, this linkage between micro and macro feels quite forced—indeed, it seems like the artifice of the interpreter. But, too, this is an artifice that denies to persons the capacities to invent "culture" through their practices: in other words, to create micro-forms of action and practice that may well not come to have a broader cachet. This artifice denies that form and meaning often are emergent processes, emerging from practice itself, whose significance is first and foremost in the micro domain of everyday living.

Darnton argues that full of resentment against the debasing conditions of their work, livelihood, and living conditions, and using their extensive cultural repertoire of symbols and meanings, the workers staged a rebellion in play, a dramatic joke, against their master and mistress and got away with it because their uprising was (merely, is the implication) symbolic and playful.[11] In this kind of scale reduction, however, the metamessage is not left in the micro domain of meaning. So, continues Darnton: "A half-century later the artisans of Paris would run riot in a similar manner [hardly, given the playfulness of the printing apprentices], combining indiscriminate slaughter with improvised popular tribunals. It would be absurd to view the cat massacre as a dress rehearsal for the September Massacres of the French Revolution, but the earlier outburst of violence did suggest a popular rebellion, though it remained restricted to the level of symbolism."[12] With all due disclaimer, the tiny, obscure cat massacre is torqued into revolutionary upheaval.[13]

The cat massacre (like Cohen, his sheep, and the Balinese cockfight) seems on the surface to be preoccupied with practice, with how people do what they do in fashioning their lives in particular settings. Yet their practice does not produce further practice through sequences of living and doing—there are no emergent properties, no agents or agencies of creativity in these microethnographies of Geertz and Darnton. Agents (like Geertz in his own work) operate as *bricoleurs*. Yet in these works practice goes nowhere, except to be swallowed and regurgitated by culture. Geertz in the cockfight and Darnton in the cat massacre are obsessed with the reductionism of explaining the cultural provenance of every symbolic element that may be remotely relevant. For all the clever talk of textured, interwoven levels of meaning, there is especially in the cat massacre a much cruder arithmetic quality of symbols added to symbols, ritual forms to ritual forms, as if this could explain the social dynamism of the event, its relationship to culture, and culture to history.

Yet what is *temporal* about the cat massacre, apart from Darnton's concern to illuminate something of an epoch? Bluntly put, the only temporal shape to the cat massacre is that its *mentalité* is reputed to have taken place in some particular past. In this regard, period and place function much as people and place do for the anthropological ethnographer. Geertz (1989–1990: 323) comments in this regard: "Dealing with a world elsewhere comes to much the same thing when elsewhere is long ago as when it is far away." In atemporal microhistory, time is sliced into periods, each slice itself an atemporal reservoir of culture and social organization, amenable to much the same interpretations as are done on the latter by anthropologists. This kind of history is most vulnerable to losing the grounds of its own formation—the construction and shaping of movement through time, the emergence of structured process. This loss produces the slip into atemporal history.

The ease with which Darnton does slide (or stumble?) into atemporal microhistory is highlighted in his response to Chartier's (1985) critique. Darnton (1986: 232–234) offers a reanalysis of the cat massacre by shoving history further into the background in pursuit of "structure" in the printing shop. He sets up a matrix of two sets of binary opposition, between culture (work) and nature (sex) on the one hand, and between the domestic (the household) and the wild (street life) on the other. Using this matrix, he argues that the apprentices and pet cats occupied the same disputed space, competing for food and for a position closer to master and mistress. The pet animals inverted structure, displacing the human apprentices in the more privileged position (the cats received table food; the boys, cat food, and so forth). By hanging the cats, the boys reversed this inversion and once more restored a properly ordered hierarchy to the conflation of categories. Darnton, the interpreter of textualized cultural thickening, comes out of the structuralist closet, distant indeed from the embrace of native history.

Microhistorical Anthropology

To reiterate, there is no principled discontinuity between an anthropology grounded in social practice and microhistory. This is a partial solution to the problem of scale in microhistory. Yet this solution is not available to atemporal microhistory, so long as practitioners of the latter insist that the sole alternatives to extreme scale reduction are to play fast and loose with the complexities of cultural life, or to use crude typologies to pigeonhole complicated phenomena (Geertz 1983: 13). No doubt there must be scale reduction in all description (given the necessity of selecting the details to include, to emphasize, to forget, and so forth). Nevertheless, the ongoing grounding of analysis in practice lessens the discontinuity between description and analysis without sacrificing conceptualization, while opening the way to the emergence of microhistory.

Max Gluckman's insight was to treat the very description of social life as a means to the *expansion* (rather than the reduction) of scale. He advocated beginning analysis with observations of the practices of others, but staying with their practices through loops of increasing scope and complexity. He argued for a more dialectical attitude through which social practice and analysis were played *through* one another. By contrast, Geertz assumes discontinuity in cultural integration, and thereby uses the microscopic (e.g., Cohen and his sheep) and the ritualistic (e.g., the Balinese cockfight) to protect himself against being overwhelmed by the very discontinuity he has built into hermeneutic interpretation. Gluckman let the practices of others lead to and reveal conflicts in the disordering and ordering of their social life, without bounding off the discontinuities that were revealed. Here I discuss briefly Gluckman's idea of "situational analysis," its expansion by others into the "extended case-study" and the relationship between the microhistory implicated by these conceptions and scale reduction.

Gluckman first outlined his understanding of "social situation" in *Analysis of a Social Situation in Modern Zululand*, first published in two parts in 1940 and 1942.[14] In this work (Gluckman 1958: 2) he wrote as follows:

> As a starting point for my analysis I describe a series of events as I recorded them on a single day. Social situations are a large part of the raw material of the anthropologist. They are the events he observes and from them and their inter-relationships he abstracts the social structure, relationships, institutions, etc., of that society. By them, and by new situations, he must check the validity of his generalisations ... I have deliberately chosen these particular events from my note-books because they illustrate admirably the points I am at present trying to make, but I might equally well have selected many other events or cited day-to-day occurrences ... *I describe the events as I recorded them, instead of importing the form of the situation as I knew it from the whole structure of modern Zululand* into my description. [my emphasis]

Gluckman points to the relative closeness of scale between the interactions he observed and the inscriptions in his field notes. Despite the inevitable ruptures and alienations between what is happening and what is written down, there is significant continuity between them.

The social situation he discusses was the opening of a bridge in Northern Zululand by the Chief Native Commissioner, an event attended by the Regent of Zululand and by European and Zulu government officials, missionaries, chiefs, and various tribesmen. Gluckman's description is sequential. Thus, in schematic outline, as the European cars approached the bridge, they were directed by Zulu in full war dress. The Europeans gathered on one side of the bridge, the Zulu on the other. The Regent joined the Zulu, and the European Commissioner, the Whites. The clan songs of the Zulu warriors were halted by the Regent, a Christian, and hymn singing led by a missionary (during which the warriors removed their head gear) opened the proceedings. The Europeans and the Regent made speeches thanking one another. The Commissioner gave the Zulu a head of cattle to slaughter, so that they could pour its gall at the foot of the bridge to ensure safety and good fortune, and then cook and eat its meat. The Zulu warriors led the cars of the Europeans across the bridge to break the opening ribbon, after which the cars returned to the European side. The Europeans retired to their shelter for tea and cakes, some of which the Commissioner sent across to the Regent. In turn, from among the Zulu drinking beer and waiting for their meat to cook, the Regent sent over four pots of brew. Although the Europeans left soon after, the Zulu continued the gathering for the rest of the day.

So far, in this description of practice, scale reduction is minimal. The bridge opening is represented not as a story (for example, one told to Geertz) about a story (Cohen and his sheep) retold to the reader by the anthropologist (Geertz). Nor is it an authored text that tells a story (the cat massacre) about an event (the cat massacre), such that text, story, and the event that the story is purported to index are treated as one and the same in the historian's (Darnton's) interpretation. The bridge opening (*pace* postmodernists) is a quite straightforward piece of ethnographic description from the viewpoint of the anthropologist. With Gluckman's emphasis on practice, extreme scale reduction would defeat his purpose.

Gluckman does not use this social situation as a microcosm of colonial South Africa (Sider and Smith 1997: 7). Had he done so, scale reduction would immediately become a highly prominent and problematic issue. Instead, close to the scale of that which occurred at the bridge, the situation offers certain social categories for analysis. Gluckman takes the categories of people who gather together at the bridge, and the juxtapositions of their behaviors, as threads to follow into the wider society (rather than the opposite, as Geertz and Darnton do, of speedily using the macro to interpret the micro). He thereby exposes how these threads ravel and unravel in weaving a social fabric.

Above all, Gluckman stressed the apartheid between the Europeans and the Zulus, such that the cleavage that separated them was so much more powerful and far-reaching than the exchanges that linked them. He underlined that this cleavage depended on the control of the Whites over the Zulu, a domination ultimately based on force and repression. Gluckman's rendering of the structure of colonial Zululand is grounded in the practices of the people who compose this ordering and who reproduced this through numerous social situations, of which the bridge opening was one. Gluckman (1958: 9) then expands the scope of his method, by arguing for comparisons between the social situations in order to reveal more of the underlying structure. Bruce Kapferer (1987: 10) has commented that through his antireductionist stance, Gluckman "dramatically showed that the whole was inscribed in the process of its parts." In my formulation, the key term here for microhistory is process, not structure. Nonetheless, Gluckman's stance still was distant from microhistory, process, and issues of emergence.

To explain how the bridge opening was composed as it was, Gluckman turned to macrohistory, particularly that of the Zulu peoples. As Chandra Jayawardena (1987: 33) pointed out, Gluckman's concept of the social situation is "a historical precipitate. It is the point of convergence of a series of processes, operating through time, which could have possibly taken other paths, but did not, and which brought a miscellany of customs and people to the opening of the bridge." Nevertheless, the early vision of comparing situations with one another that Gluckman offered still was intended in a more static sense to expose the complexities of social structure. As Gluckman (1967: xiv) wrote, "it was still the social morphology that we were aiming to present."

Two developments shifted situational analysis toward microhistory. One was the elaboration of the social situation into the extended case study (Gluckman 1961; van Velsen 1967), while the other was the *prospective* vision of emergence and change that the first offered. In his later understanding of the social situation, Gluckman argued vigorously and vehemently that it was not to be understood simply as ethnographic description nor as what he termed an "apt illustration," an example that illustrated some generalization. The apt illustration merely buttresses and embellishes a generalization reached deductively or inductively. In either instance the researcher knows where he wants to go, and the apt illustration is chosen to support the researcher's suppositions. However, the ethnographer who follows closely the social practices (in my terms) through which situations are constituted learns that they lead more in certain directions and less in others. Gluckman's commonsense field research dictum—follow your nose wherever it leads you—meant that whatever people were practicing would emerge from the ethnographic data.[15]

In terms of the logic of this method it made excellent sense to follow some of the same people from one situation into others. These social situations were treated as a series that emerged through time, invoked different contexts of action, created variance in continuities and discontinuities, evoked inconsistencies in self-presentation, and, for that matter, generated values and norms, all the while staying close to "lived realities" (Kapferer 1987: 10), that is, close to the scale at which people in interaction shaped their lives. Looked at in this way, the relationships among persons were neither categorical nor static through time, but instead were changing, sometimes in patterned ways, sometimes in new ones. Moreover, and of no less importance, the actions, relationships, and phenomena that emerged were only sometimes anticipated by or predictable from initial conditions. Often they were not.

This of course is microhistory, if not in the direction usually posited by the historian or the anthropologist. As Jayawardena (1987: 41) states: "Those social situations (or historical events) are significant that re-arrange social structures in such a way as to alter the possibilities of action. To use Gluckman's terms, the significance of events arises not from their repetitiveness [i.e., from their reproduction] ... but from their consequences in changing structures."[16] Further elaborations of situational analysis made it more actor and choice oriented (Kapferer 1972), connecting people and events through ego-centered social networks (e.g., Garbett 1970). The agency of individuals was given greater scope through time, just as this flexibility was constrained in emergent ways by the very kinds of interaction (Handelman 1977) and social relationships that these individuals developed.

The serial approach of the extended case study opened time/space (descriptively and analytically) to the practice of process, in other words, to the recognition that new social and cultural phenomena are continuously practiced (and interpreted) into being. These include both the random and the near predictable (Shermer 1995: 70). The problematic of emergence should be on the agenda of all scholars of social life (including the historical). So long as the anthropologist does not perceive social life as the reductionist instantiation of norms and values, or as the dialectical outcome of interplay between the ideal and the real, then social life needs to be understood as processual in its prospective accomplishments of making something of the random and the predictable, and of all in between. The problematic of emergence is that of the creation of social life through practice, and of how this is done in the micro domains in which we live most of our lives most intensely.[17]

Emergence, one can argue, is *intrinsic* to interaction through time, as is how the emergent effects its own emergence and so, too, the conditions that enabled it to come into existence (Mihata 1997: 32, following G. H. Mead). For example, Max Weber (1964: 119) was adamant about the probabilistic, prospective nature of the social relationship: "Let it be repeated, and continuously kept in mind, that it is only the existence of the probability that, corresponding to a given subjective meaning complex, a certain type of action *will* take place, which constitutes the 'existence' of the social relationship" (my emphasis).[18] The extended case-study method followed particular, living human beings through their uncertain daily lives, as these lives came into being, prospectively. I think it fair to say that the anthropologists who followed such paths of research were often surprised by the emergent character of microsocial living, even when they organized emergent phenomena into vehicles for discussing cyclical processes (as, for example, Turner [1957] did with the idea of "social drama"). In my view, no other perspective developed through anthropology has been as sensitive in charting the processual, indeterminate character of social life as has that of social situation and extended case study. This has significant implications for microhistorical anthropology.

In studying emergence the anthropologist continues to stay fairly close to the scale on which social practices are done. To study process through a series of emerging, observable events or social situations is to do a form of microhistory, but one that usually is not recognized as such. Instead of going back in time (regardless of the length of the duration), one goes forward, following the emergence and development—unfolding, reproductive, haphazard, chaotic—of social practices in the present as these become futurities. The microhistory of reproduction and emergence is *prospective* history, rather than retrospective. Nevertheless, prospective history is no less history than is the retrospective. Evens (1995: 15) points out: "The consideration that no social situation can be perfectly delineated beforehand, but always remains open and uncontrollable to some degree, bespeaks a certain hierarchical relationship between the situation and its participants—the participant ever relates to the situation as part to whole. The resulting 'structure of encompassment' is ... an open or dynamic structure." Evens argues that this coming into being of that which I am calling the prospective, which depends on choice, is a moral structure of becoming. In this sense, prospective microhistory is the creation and re-creation of moral existence in relation to the grounds of everyday existence.

The most likely, quite prosaic reason that prospective history is not recognized as such is that history has been defined first and foremost by historians. Collingwood, following Dilthey, argued that the historian could not represent historical events as if they had presentness, given their remoteness in time and the historian's inability to observe, yet his need to depend on inference. Thus, Collingwood (1957: 54) stated: "The historian's business is to know the past, not to know the future." Yet as Jayawardena (1987: 43) points out, the study of social situations "can also reveal potentialities that, though now submerged, could become dominant." Indeed, many anthropologists do prospective history, especially prospective microhistory, without recognizing it as such. This was so for myself, as well.

Retrospective Microhistory, Prospective Microhistory

To exemplify retrospective and prospective microhistory, respectively, I will contrast in brief two of my older studies on welfare bureaucracy. As I understood them then, these analyses concerned reproduction and emergence. Now I understand them also as forays in microhistory. The first instance (Handelman 1976) takes up the emergence of relationships between a household and a welfare department in Israel during close to two decades (1950–1969). It is retrospective microhistory—a historical reconstruction of events—based on files and other archival records, and on interviews. Though I knew the major protagonists of the household in 1969, the analysis depended to a high degree on my premises and on my particular choice of rational exchange theory to discuss the data.

The second instance (Handelman 1978) lasted some two weeks, was based to a high degree on the practices of some of the protagonists, and was almost entirely prospective. This instance took up a question that a social services department in Newfoundland was required to answer—whether an under-age teenager had been physically abused by her father. Here I was able to use observations, as well as interviews and records, to follow the case as it happened. For that matter, as the case developed into the future (into that of the protagonists, as well as mine), I was able continuously to shift back and forth between the events as they occurred, the interpretations given by officials, and my own. My own interpretation became more phenomenological. My inferences were highly conditioned by events as they emerged—despite my ethnographic selection I had much less control of that which was occurring or would occur next. These two instances illuminate some significant differences between retrospective and prospective microhistory.

Unlike historians, anthropologists need analytical reasons for doing history. That is, anthropologists address their historical data theoretically. Historians, on the other hand, may relate to their materials on people in place through time very much like ethnographers desiring to amass as much information as possible on the peoples they study. In the first instance—the case of the Israeli household and the welfare department—I initially made three assumptions. One, based retrospectively on archival records, proposed that there are persons who come to desire a long-term affiliation with the department for the sake of benefits entailed in such a relationship. Another, based on exchange theory, proposed that faced with a situation of choice, persons attempt to expand and to elaborate their sources of benefits within the limitations of incomplete information. The third, based on welfare department ideology, proposed that the department attempts to terminate client affiliation as soon as possible.

Putting together retrospection, theory, and native ideology enabled me to address my miscellaneous materials with a research question: "given a bureaucratic agency which is oriented toward terminating the affiliations of clients as speedily as possible, and given clients who are more or less interested in terminating their welfare affiliation, how is it that their affiliation becomes more complex and endures for a lengthy period of time?" (Handelman 1976: 224). Put like this, the question turned me toward the negotiated properties of social order, toward the significance of choices made by individuals and by coalitions, and toward the resources, means, and forums that persons attempted to mobilize in order to further their interests of the moment.

Working retrospectively, I divided the contacts between the household and the welfare department into seven consecutive phases that followed the changing fortunes (and the structural reasons for these) of the former in relation to the latter. I called these phases by the following titles, which were intended to evoke a sense of how the relationship developed: "First contacts with bureaucracy," "The affiliation of a welfare client," "The legitimation of a social case," "Closure of economic alternatives," "The consequences of structural dependence—diminished responsibility and bureaucratic disengagement," and "From welfare career to sheltered career." Without going into detail it is clear that I organized my data into a narrative for the case, as it emerged historically from its past toward my present. The analytical story line tells how the sequence of negotiated transactions between household and department over the conditions of the termination of affiliation unexpectedly produced a career-line of clientship oriented wholly toward extracting welfare benefits. This career-line of clientship emerged slowly and delicately through numerous transactions between the household and many official agencies, despite the desire of both household and department to cease their relationship. Had I not attended to the many details in chronological sequence, the qualities of uncertainty, indeed of the emergence of the unexpected, of the ironic appearance through time of the opposite of what was intended by both parties, would have been lost, had I related to the case only as a flattened, synchronic present. My analysis had unearthed the unexpected; and my narrative for this analysis was intended to provide a logic to explain the unexpected, in senses somewhat similar to those advocated by Peirce and Ginzburg.

In this instance, influenced by the form of the extended case study, I turned it into retrospective history. I think I was meticulous in attending to the available details of the case, yet undoubtedly the construction of the story was mine. So too was the stress on the emergence of contradiction between initial conditions and intentions and further developments. I doubt whether any of the protagonists would have understood the story line quite as I did, had I explained it to them as such (something that I did do in the following instance). Extensive scale reduction is inherent in any kind of retrospective history, even when the tenets applied are intended to minimize this. The issue is not just of small ethnographic foci being made to yield magnified inferences, in the manner of Geertz, Darnton, and so many others. If scale is a proportion, then the ratio here is between the kind of data available and the scholar's input to make this into something comprehensible and of theoretical interest. In retrospective history of any kind, micro or macro, the scholar's shaping of meaning and significance is enormous in proportion to the data available.

This proportion of scale reduction shifts to no small degree in prospective microhistory. Instead of reduction, one may argue that there is "scale magnification" in the prominence of detail. In the instance of suspected abuse from Newfoundland (Handelman 1978; see also Handelman 1983, 1987), I did not make my premises explicit to myself. Instead I followed the sequential occurrence of events as the protagonists (especially the social workers) practiced and fashioned these. To a substantial degree the narrative was theirs. My theoretical questions emerged first and foremost from their practices: from their actions, reactions, interpretations, and their striving to give meanings to that which was occurring, the emergence of an occupational, cultural form—the case. This is reflected in how I wrote this work. Each event is described and then is followed by my own interpretive commentary. My theoretical approach became strongly phenomenological as I struggled to make sense of my data in response to the social workers' struggle to make sense of their own.

Here I give only the barest outline of this extended case. The social services department received a telephone call from a parish priest, reporting on an instance of possible child abuse, the maltreatment of an underage teenage niece by her uncle. The very next day one of this man's underage teenage daughters was brought to the hospital where the hospital social worker took the daughter's story describing how her father beat her, and a medical examination was done. The daughter was removed from the family household and placed under the temporary protection of the social services department. The issue for the social workers was whether the girl's father had indeed beaten her, and if so, whether she should be removed from the household for a protracted period. The following day a social worker collected information from various sources, including official ones, about the family. A few days later she visited the family home where the teenage niece, for her part, said she preferred to remain within the household.

From here on, in various settings and contexts, the numerous family members, adults and children, changed their own accounts, contradicted one another's stories, and continued to do so for various reasons. From the perspective of the social workers there were numerous shifting story lines, and the surprising and the unexpected dominated their attempts to synthesize a unifying and unified narrative. Unable to ascertain the validity of different claims to truth, to what had "really happened," they left the matter to the family court to decide. The judge himself could not decide who had done what to whom, but he ruled that the daughter be removed from the family home for a period of one year. As the instance of suspected abuse had begun to emerge as a case, the social workers were convinced that the father had cruelly beaten his daughter. Two weeks later, by the time of the court hearing, serious contradictions dominated the case; and the social workers, unexpectedly, were uncertain as to what had occurred. Nonetheless, they asserted that since family relationships were so poor, it was better for all concerned if the daughter were removed from the household. Though they accepted the official disposition of the case, the social workers continued to be anxious personally about their inability to establish the truth value of reality.

Their practices and mine interacted dialectically within me, for my understanding of what was emerging in phenomenal terms. But their course of practice required closure—consequently, the practices of the welfare bureaucracy demanded that there be a formal conclusion to the suspicions raised by the case. (I, however, did not demand such closure within myself. Writing the text, exposing the problematics and processes of a logic of interpretation, was sufficient "closure" for my purposes.) Moreover, as the events accrued through time, as the shaping of the case emerged, the significance of the conclusions grew. But the events were not strung together as a sequence of additions to a known story line. Instead, the events were given different momentum and direction as they shifted one way and another. Once and again contradiction emerged out of consensus, ambiguity out of certainty. Prospective microhistory made the story more theirs than mine, while my theoretical choices were more in keeping with the spirit of what was happening to them. Working fairly closely to the scale of events (in the mode of the extended case study) and discussing them as I did was possible only through prospective microhistory.

The field anthropologist who interacts face to face with the same people through time necessarily does a prospective microhistory of social practice. Here scale reduction may be fairly limited. In comparison with the historian, the "time of experience" of the ethnographer, the time when the ethnographer experienced events, is highly resonant with the "time of knowledge," the period during which he analyzes these field materials (Motzkin 1992 on the historian). But when the ethnographer does retrospective microhistory, social practice recedes from view, scale reduction increases, experience becomes more minimal, and knowledge increases proportionately (Kracauer 1969: 104–138). If the scholar fixes on a setting in the past and treats this ethnographically, then he is more likely to do atemporal microhistory, which increases the trends given above.

Prospective, Postmodern?

Life is what happens to you while you are making other plans.

— William Gaddis

The Mancunian commitment to the study of social practice foreshadowed developments in aspects of postmodernist thinking. In particular, the prospective microhistory of the extended case study resonates with some postmodernist views of temporality and history. This deserves a few words. The use of the extended case study tries not to prejudge temporal sequences (and their rhythms) nor spatial dimensions that the prospective emergence of a study acquires in interaction with the anthropologist's understanding (and instincts). This is due less to a concern for "objectivity" and more to a concern with that which is occurring in the prospective sense. This following of interaction among a (relatively?) unfixed, "fuzzy" set or agglomeration of persons, this lack of fixity of boundaries in time, space, and place, resonates to a degree with some postmodernist perceptions of dimensionality (e.g., Ermarth 1992; Friedland and Boden 1994).

The prospective perspective makes it crystal clear that temporal rhythms and shapes are created rather than enacted (Ermarth 1992: 56), or perhaps are created anew while enacted.[19] The prospective perspective on practice actively represents the present becoming past as it is becoming future and demands that we acknowledge that the experience and knowledge of pastness are necessarily representational and therefore symbolic. Pastness exists through, is grasped through, symbolic forms, mentally, materially, and is therefore a matter of convention, not of nature (Ermarth 1992: 31). Within the extended case study, the prospective perspective emphasizes the *local* in the emergence of history (Ermarth 1992: 66). Local conditions, local considerations, and local knowledge shape prospective microhistory in the first instance. In this regard, there is always a plurality of prospective microhistories, a multiplicity of microhistorical trajectories.

The prospective perspective is open to a sense of struggle against narrative necessarily being lineal (Lee 1959), given the twists, turns, and surprises of living. Different rhythms of living exist in tandem and intersect. Time may be less seamless and more episodic, opening the study of social situations to different senses of causality. Temporality, as this emerges from a series of events, may turn on itself, changing effects into causes, creating feedback loops that turn into the adumbrated (perhaps reflexive) connectivities among the emergent segments of an extended case study. The twisting, surprising, and looping qualities of emerging social life may index the phenomenal hybridity of social existence as this comes into existence (one could reread Mitchell's [1956] classic study of the Rhodesian copper belt in terms something like these).

These points suggest that, *contra* Geertz, Ginzburg, and the rest, it is of no less significance to draw *small conclusions from small, deeply and densely woven facts* than it is to draw large conclusions from small facts.[20] The relative lack of reduction in scale of the former tells us never to forget that the living of lives in ordinary circumstances is informed by meanings that derive from and are practiced (and interpreted) through the small-scale character of everyday living. That this changes in extraordinary circumstances that implode or explode the everyday does not detract from just how important it is for anthropologists to learn of everyday social worlds in their own emergent circumstances. First and foremost, everyday worlds are constituted by small facts that have immediacy for particular, named human beings. In this respect, prospective microhistorical anthropology can become that which microhistory—atemporal or retrospective—never can. Evans-Pritchard (1961: 20) once commented that "history must choose between being social anthropology or being nothing." I would amend this to state that microhistory can never become anthropological unless its practitioners are prepared to erase the boundaries between history and anthropology, while recognizing that the substantial scale reduction they must practice likely distorts the phenomena they address and shape. For that matter, whether microhistorians recognize this or not, they are engaging in some form of symbolic anthropology—it is not so much that "the past is a foreign country" (Lowenthal 1985) as that pastness exists only through representations and their interpretation.

Though I have not discussed any sort of macrohistorical anthropology, the contrasts with microhistory seem significant. But this may be so mainly because we distinguish between macro and micro in history and anthropology as if there were a difference in principle—a difference of level. Since we seem to believe in (or at least accept heuristically) disciplinary premises about the coherence of culture, structure, social order, and so forth, the macro order is understood as a higher-order level that encompasses the micro. Therefore, it is simpler theoretically to derive the social practices of the micro-level from macro-level assumptions about practice than it is to move in the converse direction, constructing macro-level order from micro-level practices—as Kracauer (1969: 126) comments, the latter arrive at the former in a "damaged state." (Indeed, the positing of levels as encompassing and encompassed makes the possibility of constructing macro from micro virtually impossible.) But this may say more about the realities of our disciplines than those of the people we study. Nevertheless, the practice of prospective microhistory should push us to apprehend not only how native theory emerges from and is reconstituted by native practice, but also the implications of this for the contingent status of our own macro-level concepts.

Notes

My thanks go to Terry Evens for his incisive comments on this essay.

1. The journal editors and members of the editorial board are split evenly between anthropologists and historians. More recently the rhetoric of the journal's blurb became less contentious. It now states that: "*History and Anthropology* continues to address the intersection of history and social sciences and focuses closely on the interchange between anthropologically-informed history, historically-informed anthropology and the history of ethnographic and anthropological representation. It is now widely perceived that *the formerly dominant ahistorical perspective within anthropology* [my emphasis] severely restricted interpretation and analysis." In this formulation the problematic (phrased as "ahistory") still lies within anthropology. There is no mention that history has suffered (which it has) by not being anthropologically informed.

2. Gluckman and his colleagues took what we call "practice" as integral to the generation of social living, rather than theorizing its existence in the manner of Bourdieu (1977) or, to a lesser extent, de Certeau (1984). Indeed, the Manchester School did not use the language of practice. Nonetheless, there are strong affinities between Gluckman's work and that of Bourdieu, as Kapferer (1987) points out.

3. I am using the term "micro" to index a *domain* of social life, in which human beings and their practices have an immediacy of existence, such that each is a function of the other in the "nowness" of their togetherness. The domain is not a level. The latter exists in hierarchical relationship with other levels, perhaps encompassing and being encompassed by them. In this regard, the domain theoretically can have more autonomy from other domains than has the level in relation to other levels. The usual usage in social science of the terms "macro" and "micro" is that of indexing levels, such that the former level is understood to encompass and

to include all elements and forms of organization of the latter level. This is a questionable assumption. I prefer to think of each as a domain, in terms of which each has a considerable degree of autonomous organizational existence from the other. Though highly vulnerable to the power of the macro, the micro generates its own emergent patterns of living and existence, which are not easily derived from, and therefore subsumed by, the kinds of macro classifiers to which anthropologists have become accustomed—culture, society, social organization, and the like. In these terms, the micro is *never* a simple reflection of the macro. Postmodern influences in anthropology do not seem to address this kind of problematic.

4. However, my intention is not to posit a dualism in which atemporal microhistory eschews social practice in favor of interpretation, while prospective microhistory exists through social practice but eschews interpretation. Practice does not exist without choice (possible and actual); choice requires decisions; and decision depends upon interpretation. In this regard the praxis of interpretation and practice was crucial to the Mancunian extended case study (Evens 1995: 5–19). Nonetheless, as I noted, there is a difference in emphasis, such that interpretive anthropology foregrounds interpretation and backgrounds practice, while the extended case study foregrounds the praxis of practice and interpretation.

5. Geertz's notion of scale is more complicated than those of some anthropologists (e.g., Barth 1978a) and cultural historians (e.g., Ginzburg 1993; Chartier 1982: 32) who tend to equate scale with size. Geertz argues that scale is a ratio. The reduction of scale (down to some unspecified point) magnifies the accessibility to configurations of meaning, to native cultural logic and knowledge. In terms posed by Barth (1978b: 254), Geertz explicitly links scale to a "discovery procedure." This invokes scale as a system of correspondence between different magnitudes. Ginzburg (1989), too, through his conjectural or evidential paradigm (which Muir [1991: xviii–xix] compares to Peirce's logic of abduction), emphasizes the semiotic discovery of large patterns of meaning through discovering connections among small, even tiny, signs.

6. In terms of temporality, a minimalist conception of indigenous history from an insider's perspective should evaluate the following conditions of temporal formation and practice: the existence of time as a scheme of classification (Gell 1992) that enables temporal synchronization among persons; time as movement (with whichever cultural rhythms such movement is understood or felt to have) so that temporality is capable of distinguishing among times (Wilcox 1987); the engendering of memory by time, and the significance attributed to remembering. In more etic terms, the ethnographer may distinguish periodicity in terms of contrasts like "hot" and "cold" (Lévi-Strauss 1966), while recognizing that the activation of such categorical temporal rhythms is an analytical device (Motzkin 1992).

7. I ignore critiques of the essentialism of assumptions about highly unified or integrated "cultures." In terms of my argument, the setting may be loosely bounded or it may be embedded in shifting multiplicities of "culture." The logic of inference of connections between setting and embedment will stay the same.

8. This sort of microhistory is most vulnerable to critiques of synchrony (e.g., Clifford 1988).

9. Elsewhere (Handelman 1994: 345) I have suggested that "thick description" is one of the many memorable phrases that Geertz has authored or advertised. These are catchy—something like scholarly jingles, erudite slogans, scholastic pop tunes—and have entered the folk life of anthropology and cognate disciplines. But the project of these turns of phrase is not that of concept or theory formation.

10. At times, thick description bears a close resemblance to Gregory Bateson's use of metacommunication—communication about communication—in relation to tangled hierarchies. Witness his discussion of the playful nip (Bateson 1972: 180; Handelman 1998: 69). Thick description also resonates with Goffman's (1970) conception of framing, itself beholden to Bateson's thinking.

11. No one to my knowledge has suggested in print that this interpretation is out-and-out simplistically functionalist (which of course it is), probably because it is so stylishly clad in fashionable discourses of hermeneutic interpretation, "thickness," and the textualization of culture.

12. See Darnton 1985: 98. Especially in view of Darnton's qualified claim that the cat massacre was an index of the revolution to come, one must read Mah's (1991) critique. Mah shows just how artificial and fragile is Darnton's claim, and that even this respected historian is not averse to suppressing ethnographic facts from his brief source text in the interest of reaching large conclusions from small-scale facts. Apart from Mah, none of the commentators on Darnton's cat massacre (who include a historian, an anthropologist, and a literary theorist) seem to have read the brief source text, though it is easily available.

13. There is a body of work in anthropology that insists emphatically on the significance of small-scale social creations or inventions for small-scale social orders. These creative thrusts enable small-scale social orders to reconstitute themselves through changing practice (see Roberts 1951, 1964; McFeat 1974; Handelman 1977; and chapters 4 and 5 in Handelman 1998). Small conclusions from small, densely textured facts have little or no place in a discipline so given over to the aggrandizement of meaning. Tom McFeat's (1974) *Small-Group Cultures* is an instructive case in point. McFeat's pathbreaking book theorizes the micro-domain of human action, practice, and meaning in order to illuminate how small-scale social units reproduce themselves through time. So much anthropological research was and is done on small-scale groups or categories (regardless of how permeable these are) that constitute the living of lives in the everyday. McFeat, following Roberts and others, argues that the micro is not merely a derivation of, nor a reflection of, macro structures and processes, but is the domain that enables us to live as we do much of the time, often in contradiction to or rupture from the macro. However, anthropologists like Geertz and historians like Darnton insist on large conclusions from small facts, thereby excising much of the significance of the micro from the living of lives. Needless to say, McFeat's book was utterly ignored by anthropologists.

14. I note wryly that Sider and Smith (1997: 3) refer to this work both in their text and bibliography as "Analysis of *the* Social Situation in Modern Zululand" (my emphasis). One of Gluckman's responses might have been that there was no one unified social situation of modern Zululand, but rather a great multitude of social situations that were generated by contradictory and complementary forces through the interactions of people. *The* social situation would turn this into a macro- rather than a micro-scale formulation. *Contra* Sider and Smith, Gluckman's monograph on a social situation predated his exchange with Hobsbawm in Manchester by many years. The thrust of Manchester School anthropology was to treat small-scale interactions not as direct representations, in and of themselves, of great cultural coherences but rather as uncovering whatever it was that people in interactions and relationships created and destroyed. The studies of the Rhodesian copper belt stressed heterogeneity and multiplicity in the generation of emergent micro-forms of social organization (e.g., Mitchell 1956) that themselves were influential in ordering urban social life, often in conflicting and discordant ways, through that which Abbott (1992: 439) has referred to as "processes that involve multiple contingent sequences of events that are moving at different speeds."

15. Edward Muir (1991: xviii–xix) draws attention to the parallels between the "evidential" or "conjectural" paradigm of Carlo Ginzburg and the Bologna School of microhistory and the logic of abduction put forward by Peirce. Abduction indexes creative and rigorous guesswork as the logic that introduces new ideas. I think the case can be made that in social anthropology the study of the social situation and especially the extended case study are related in their logic of inquiry to this idea. In this regard, see also Egmond and Mason's (1997: 33–36) argument on discovery procedure in morphology and microhistory.

16. Manchester social anthropology had its impact on social historians (e.g., Davis 1975, 1984), but this lessened with the turn to cultural history (Hunt 1989).

17. Generally, I prefer the terms "creation" and "emergence," because both retain qualities of uncertainty and open-ended indeterminacy that are lacking in terms like construction and constructivism. The latter overly stress the conscious, rational, planned organization of social life.

18. A further implication of the emergence of relationship is that this connectivity cannot be reduced to the individual participants in the relationship or to their individual contributions to it. Emergent forms weave together their own practices and create their own realities. The reducing of relationship to the individuals who compose it works best with premises of methodological individualism, which are valid only as analytical artifice.

19. The role of mythic segments of temporality (perhaps teleological) constitutes a distinct problematic.

20. Yet as Kracauer (1969: 130) notes: "The belief that the widening of the range of *intelligibility* involves an increase of *significance* is one of the basic tenets of Western thought. Throughout the history of philosophy it has been held that the highest principle, the highest abstractions, not only define all the particulars they formally encompass but also contain the essences of all that exists in the lower depths." The history of field-research anthropology in the twentieth century may be understood as an unresolved struggle with this premise.

References

Abbott, Andrew. 1992. "From Causes to Events: Notes on Narrative Positivism." *Sociological Methods and Research* 20: 428–455.

Barth, Fredrik, ed. 1978a. *Scale and Social Organization*. Oslo: Universitetsforlaget.

———. 1978b. "Conclusions." In *Scale and Social Organization*, 253–273. Oslo: Universitetsforlaget.

Bateson, Gregory. 1972. *Steps to an Ecology of Mind*. New York: Ballantine.

Biersack, Aletta. 1989. "Local Knowledge, Local History: Geertz and Beyond." In *The New Cultural History*, ed. Lynn Hunt, 72–96. Berkeley: University of California Press.

Bourdieu, Pierre. 1977. *Outline of a Theory of Practice*. Cambridge: Cambridge University Press.

Chartier, Roger. 1982. "Intellectual History or Sociocultural History? The French Trajectories." In *Modern European Intellectual History: Reappraisals and New Perspectives*, ed. Dominick LaCapra and Steven L. Kaplan, 13–46. Ithaca, NY: Cornell University Press.

Clifford, James. 1988. *The Predicament of Culture*. Cambridge, MA: Harvard University Press.

Collingwood, R. G. 1957. *The Idea of History*. New York: Oxford University Press.

Darnton, Robert. 1985. "Workers Revolt: The Great Cat Massacre of the Rue Saint-Severin." In *The Great Cat Massacre and Other Episodes in French Cultural History*, 75–104. New York: Vintage Books.

———. 1986. "The Symbolic Element in History." *Journal of Modern History* 58: 218–234.

Davis, Natalie Zemon. 1975. "Women on Top." In *Society and Culture in Early Modern France*, 124–151. Stanford: Stanford University Press.

———. 1984. "Charivari, Honor, and Community in Seventeenth-Century Lyon and Geneva." In *Rite, Drama, Festival, Spectacle: Rehearsals Toward a Theory of Cultural Performance*, ed. J. J. MacAloon, 42–57. Philadelphia: Institute for the Study of Human Issues.

de Certeau, Michel. 1984. *The Practice of Everyday Life*. Berkeley: University of California Press.

Egmond, Florike, and Peter Mason. 1997. *The Mammoth and the Mouse: Microhistory and Morphology*. Baltimore: Johns Hopkins University Press.

Ermarth, Elizabeth Deeds. 1992. *Sequel to History: Postmodernism and the Crisis of Representational Time*. Princeton, NJ: Princeton University Press.

Evans-Pritchard, E. E. 1961. *Anthropology and History*. Manchester: Manchester University Press.

Evens, T. M. S. 1995. *Two Kinds of Rationality: Kibbutz Democracy and Generational Conflict*. Minneapolis: University of Minnesota Press.

Fernandez, James. 1988. "Historians Tell Tales: of Cartesian Cats and Gallic Cockfights." *Journal of Modern History* 60: 113–127.

Friedland, Roger, and Deirdre Boden. 1994. "NowHere: An Introduction to Space, Time and Modernity." In *NowHere: Space, Time and Modernity*, ed. Roger Friedland and Deirdre Boden, 1–60. Berkeley: University of California Press.

Garbett, G. Kingsley. 1970. "The Analysis of Social Situations." *Man* (n.s.) 5: 214–227.

Geertz, Clifford. 1965. *The Social History of an Indonesian Town*. Cambridge, MA: MIT Press.

———. 1973a. "Thick Description: Toward an Interpretive Theory of Culture." In *The Interpretation of Cultures*, 3–30. New York: Basic Books.

———. 1973b. "Deep Play: Notes on the Balinese Cockfight." In *The Interpretation of Cultures*, 412–453. New York: Basic Books.

———. 1980. *Negara: The Theatre State in Nineteenth-Century Bali*. Princeton, NJ: Princeton University Press.

———. 1983. *Local Knowledge: Further Essays in Interpretive Anthropology*. New York: Basic Books.

———. 1989–1990. "History and Anthropology." *New Literary History* 21: 321–335.

———. 1995. *After the Fact: Two Countries, Four Decades, One Anthropologist*. Cambridge, MA: Harvard University Press.

Gell, Alfred. 1992. *The Anthropology of Time*. Oxford: Berg.

Ginzburg, Carlo. 1989. *Clues, Myths, and the Historical Method*. Baltimore: Johns Hopkins University Press.

———. 1993. "Microhistory: Two or Three Things That I Know about It." *Critical Inquiry* 20: 10–35.

Gluckman, Max. 1958. *Analysis of a Social Situation in Modern Zululand*. Manchester: Manchester University Press.

———. 1961. "Ethnographic Data in British Social Anthropology." *Sociological Review* 9: 5–17.

———. 1967. "Introduction." In *The Craft of Social Anthropology*, xi–xx. London: Social Science Paperbacks.

Goffman, Erving. 1970. *Frame Analysis*. New York: Harper and Row.

Handelman, Don. 1976. "Bureaucratic Transactions: The Development of Official-Client Relationships in Israel." In *Transaction and Meaning: Directions in the Anthropology of Exchange and Symbolic Behavior*, ed. Bruce Kapferer, 223–275. Philadelphia: Institute for the Study of Human Issues.

———. 1978. "Bureaucratic Interpretation: The Perception of Child Abuse in Urban Newfoundland." In *Bureaucracy and World View: Studies in the Logic of Official Interpretation*, by Don Handelman and Elliott Leyton, 15–69. St. John's: Institute of Social and Economic Research, Memorial University of Newfoundland.

———. 1983. "Shaping Phenomenal Reality: Dialectic and Disjunction in the Bureaucratic Synthesis of Child-Abuse in Urban Newfoundland." *Social Analysis* 13: 3–36.

———. 1987. "Bureaucracy and the Maltreatment of the Child: Interpretive and Structural Implications." In *Child Survival: Anthropological Perspectives on the Treatment and Maltreatment of Children*, ed. Nancy Scheper-Hughes, 359–376. Boston: Reidel.

———. 1994. "Critiques of Anthropology: Literary Turns, Slippery Bends." *Poetics Today* 15: 341–381.

———. 1998. *Models and Mirrors: Towards an Anthropology of Public Events*. New York: Berghahn.

Himmelfarb, Gertrude. 1989. "Some Reflections on the New History." *American Historical Review* 94: 661–670.

Hunt, Lynn, ed. 1989. *The New Cultural History*. Berkeley: University of California Press.

Jayawardena, Chandra. 1987. "Analysis of a Social Situation in Acheh Besar: An Exploration in Micro-History." *Social Analysis* 22: 30–46.

Kapferer, Bruce. 1972. *Strategy and Transaction in an African Factory*. Manchester: Manchester University Press.

———. 1987. "The Anthropology of Max Gluckman." *Social Analysis* 22: 3–21.

Kracauer, Siegfried. 1969. *History: The Last Things Before the Last*. New York: Oxford University Press.

LaCapra, Dominick. 1988. "Chartier, Darnton, and the Great Cat Massacre." *Journal of Modern History* 60: 95–112.

Lee, Dorothy. 1959. "Codifications of Reality: Lineal and Nonlineal." In *Freedom and Culture*, 105–120. New York: Prentice-Hall.

Lévi-Strauss, Claude. 1966. *The Savage Mind*. London: Weidenfeld and Nicolsen.

Lowenthal, David. 1985. *The Past Is a Foreign Country*. Cambridge: Cambridge University Press.

Mah, Harold. 1991. "Suppressing the Text: The Metaphysics of Ethnographic History in Darnton's Great Cat Massacre." *History Workshop Journal* 31: 1–20.

McFeat, Tom. 1974. *Small-Group Cultures*. New York: Pergamon.

Mihata, Kevin. 1997. "The Persistence of 'Emergence." In *Chaos, Complexity, and Sociology: Myths, Models, and Theories*, ed. R. A. Eve, S. Horsfall, and M. E. Lee, 30–38. Thousand Oaks, CA: Sage.

Mitchell, J. Clyde. 1956. *The Kalela Dance: Aspects of Social Relationships among Urban Africans in Northern Rhodesia*. Manchester: Manchester University Press.

Motzkin, Gabriel. 1992. *Time and Transcendence: Secular History, the Catholic Reaction, and the Rediscovery of the Future*. Dordrecht: Kluwer Academic Publishers.

Muir, Edward. 1991. "Introduction: Observing Trifles." In *Microhistory and the Lost Peoples of Europe*, ed. Edward Muir and Guido Ruggiero, vii–xxviii. Baltimore: Johns Hopkins University Press.

Roberts, John M. 1951. "Three Navaho Households: A Comparative Study in Small Group Culture." Papers of the Peabody Museum of American Archaeology and Ethnology, Harvard University, Cambridge, MA, 40, no. 3: 1–88.

———. 1964. "The Self-management of Cultures." In *Explorations in Cultural Anthropology: Essays in Honor of George Peter Murdock*, ed. Ward Goodenough, 433–454. New York: McGraw-Hill.

Roseberry, William. 1982. "Balinese Cockfights and the Seduction of Anthropology." *Social Research* 49: 1013–1028.

Sharron, Avery. 1982. "Dimensions of Time." *Studies in Symbolic Interaction* 4: 63–89.

Shermer, Michael. 1995. "Exorcising LaPlace's Demon: Chaos and Antichaos, History and Metatheory." *History and Theory* 34: 59–83.

Sider, Gerald, and Gavin Smith. 1997. "Introduction." In *Between History and Histories: The Making of Silences and Commemorations*, ed. Gerald Sider and Gavin Smith, 3–28. Toronto: University of Toronto Press.

Turner, Victor W. 1957. *Schism and Continuity in an African Society*. Manchester: Manchester University Press.

Veeser, H. Aram, ed. 1989. *The New Historicism*. London: Routledge.

Velsen, Jaap van. 1967. "The Extended-Case Method and Situational Analysis." In *The Craft of Social Anthropology*, ed. A. L. Epstein, 129–149. London: Social Science Paperbacks.

Walters, Ronald. 1980. "Signs of the Times: Clifford Geertz and the Historians." *Social Research* 47: 536–556.

Weber, Max. 1964. *The Theory of Social and Economic Organization*. New York: The Free Press.

Wilcox, Donald. 1987. *The Measure of Times Past: Pre-Newtonian Chronologies and the Rhetoric of Relative Time*. Chicago: University of Chicago Press.

Chapter Two

THE PAST IN THE PRESENT
Actualized History in the Social Construction of Reality

Christian Giordano

Having been trained as both a sociologist and an anthropologist, I have in my research consistently been oriented toward the present. While carrying out fieldwork projects, however, I have often been confronted by opinions, questions, answers, convictions, reasoning, reflections, and concrete forms of social behavior that cannot be untangled and articulated exclusively in terms of the "here and now." It would be all too easy to develop a tendency to underestimate the past by viewing it as a dead hand upon the present, rather than an active, operating force. There is, however, more to the presentist orientation in social research than that. For this orientation is an expression of the epistemological and methodological bipolarism that has divided the social sciences and historiography for almost two centuries.

It is well known that the relationship between historical research and the social sciences has virtually to the present day been characterized by a reciprocal lack of recognition, if not outright antagonism. This has brought about a clear division of labor between history as a *science du passé* and the social sciences as *sciences du présent*. This was discussed very explicitly at the beginning of the twentieth century by a disciple of Durkheim, the sociologist Simiand. For him, the difference between history and the social sciences did not consist merely in a different relationship to time; it was also based on a profound methodological distinction, which Kant had acknowledged by contrasting the principles of homogeneity (*Homogenität*) and specification (*Spezifikation*) (Simiand 1903; Lévi-Strauss 1949: 363ff.; Cassirer 1985: 12). It was Simiand who insisted that the task of the social sciences is comparison and generalization, and that

References for this chapter begin on page 70.

history should be based on the monographic method. From a comparable point of view in the opposite camp, the historian Croce was fond of contrasting the "strong individualisation" of the historical method with the "pale abstractions" arrived at through social analysis (Croce 1970: 298). This dichotomization has been taken over almost to the letter by anthropologists, especially if one thinks of the chief theoretician of British functionalism, Radcliffe-Brown, who borrowed the terminology of the neo-Kantian philosopher Windelband in order to distinguish between nomothetic anthropology and idiographic history (Radcliffe-Brown 1976: 4ff.).

One can, then, plausibly maintain that since the nineteenth century there has been a progressive sectorization between history and the social sciences, even on the part of those authors who have been least disposed to accept methodological straitjackets, such as the classics of the interpretive and phenomenological schools of thought, from Schütz to Berger and Luckmann. It is interesting to note that these social scientists attribute relatively little importance to the relationship between experience and history in their analyses of the *Lebenswelt* or the social construction of reality (Schütz and Luckmann 1979: 119ff.; Berger and Luckmann 1979: 119ff.). Even they have adapted to a certain style of sectorization that, in spite of recent attempts to abandon it, is still a very widespread topos and is often simply taken for granted. Were this not the case, Wallerstein's excellent book, *Unthinking Social Science* (1991), would not need to have been written. The clichés of methodological bipolarism that separate history and the social sciences are still deeply rooted in both scientific communities, and the resistance to change is great. My impression is, however, that we social scientists are even farther away than historians from a paradigm change, that is, from accepting the historicization of social analysis.

Let me give an example. When one speaks with social scientists—especially with sociologists—on the subject of clientelism and corruption in Italy or nationalism and ethnicity in East-Central Europe, the notion of historicity is employed to understand or explain these phenomena only with many "ifs" and "buts." The questions that are posed during such debates have a similar tone, and it is difficult to convey the idea that the present-day political culture of Italy or the current ethnic discourses in postcommunist societies are linked to precise historical experiences that have been lived by past generations and revisited, modified, or even reinvented—sometimes intentionally—by present generations. Those who think in terms of the sectorization of the social sciences often point to the most immediate and immanent causes, such as the characteristics of the Republican political system in Italy or the lack of material and ideological resources after the fall of socialism in East-Central Europe. The question is whether history is really necessary to understand the present situation or if it is sufficient to look for causes inherent in the system.

In spite of praiseworthy efforts to focus attention on the potential of historical anthropology to bridge disciplinary gaps, the interpretation of the present through the past is still an anomalous way of proceeding in the social sciences, the practitioners of which remain convinced that the present can be decoded exclusively in its own terms.

The History of the Historian and That of the Anthropologist

As noted above, Wallerstein has spoken out against the sectorization that has plagued the human sciences since the nineteenth century. He has, furthermore, proposed a search for a new paradigm that transcends the divisions between the social sciences and history and has made suggestions for their future unification (Wallerstein 1991). The somewhat unusual name he has given to his program is "historical social sciences," and it is worth pausing briefly to ask what this means. Reading Wallerstein attentively, I have become convinced that his goal is not to reduce history and the social sciences to a kind of flattened average but to break down certain barriers that make a fruitful theoretical and methodological exchange difficult. To include history in anthropology and vice versa is, therefore, the real aim of historical social science. If my impression is correct, some of the conceptual peculiarities of the two parent disciplines would be maintained, but they would no longer be in direct opposition to one another; rather, they would be aspects of a more holistic interpretation of reality. The goal is not to create a monolithic conception of history but to call attention to the complementary aspects of the different points of view. There are probably some useful differences between the history of the historian and that of the anthropologist, which should be examined independently of the iconoclastic impulses of those who would like to obliterate them. Taking these differences as given, I shall now provide a brief characterization of each, with an emphasis on the anthropologist's view of history.

Even those historians who have repudiated what Braudel has called *l'histoire événementielle* and have opted instead for *l'histoire pensée* are primarily concerned with the reconstruction of past epochs, with processes in past socioeconomic cycles, or with long-term trends in daily life and in the collective consciousness. In all of these cases, real and concrete time is of central importance. It is, in fact, Braudel who magisterially illuminates this point when he notes that even those historians who draw upon anthropological research—in the form of village studies, for example—must organize their approach, from beginning to end, in terms of a phenomenon that is "mathematical," "exogenous," and, therefore, external to the human being, namely, time (1977: 77). The observation of Braudel seems to me to be very significant, since it is verified by the practice of even those historians whose approach to dating is most like that of the social scientists. We rarely find a lack of precise time references in the books of historians, and even those scholars who work with materials to which it is difficult to assign a reliable date, as in ancient and medieval history, do not, for this reason, question the importance of accurate dating. This tendency is clearly evident even among historians who are not chained to the temporal course of events, for example, Le Roy Ladurie, Le Goff, or Duby. To realize the fundamental importance of time for historians, it is enough to read the titles and subtitles of their works, in which the time factor regularly appears, more or less explicitly.

The social scientist and, consequently, the anthropologist who takes the historical dimension of the subject being studied into consideration is much less worried by time. Time, although not of secondary importance, is much less concrete, much more endogenous, and, thus, condensed in the individual viewed as a social actor. This specific conception of time is clearly linked to the anthropologist's view of history. As a fieldworker in the present, the anthropologist values the past especially as a force that conditions the present without mechanically determining it. I believe that the history of the anthropologist is, thus, nearly always actualized history—a past that is more or less intentionally mobilized in the present. This actualization or mobilization of the past is usually carried out with specific aims in mind—finding one's bearings in everyday life, signaling a sense of belonging or identity, transmitting a symbolic or metaphorical message to other social actors, stabilizing relations of power or of social disparity, rebelling against conditions that are considered to be unacceptable, and so on.

Let us look at some examples. After seven hundred years of independence, Poland was partitioned and occupied by Prussia, Austria, and Russia in three successive phases between 1772 and 1795. We know that the process of territorial division met with strong resistance in all parts of the country. This resistance culminated in the unsuccessful uprising led by Tadeusz Kościuszko (1794–1795), which was bloodily repressed, due in large measure to the harsh intervention of the Russian troops of General Suvorov. It is less well known that Kościuszko, with an army of enthusiastic but poorly armed peasants, managed to defeat the Russians in the Battle of Raclavice (4 April 1794), which must be considered the most glorious moment of the uprising. For the argument I want to make, it is important to remember that these peasants carried with them a banner with the words "Feed and Defend" stitched upon it. Almost two hundred years later, at the climax of the protest movement led by the trade union *Solidarność*—a few months before General Jaruzelski came to power (December 1981) and right at the moment when a Soviet invasion was feared—the rural wing of *Solidarność* organized a demonstration in Raclavice, during which the demonstrators appeared in historical costume—or at least in what they imagined to have been the peasant way of dressing at the end of the eighteenth century. And, as in the time of Kościuszko, the banner with the same motto appeared. Now, as an anthropologist, I am interested in the real battle of Raclavice only insofar as it helps to illuminate more recent developments. Almost two hundred years after the historical event in question, the rural section of *Solidarność* acted with the aim of making the following point: the present-day agriculturists—the most integrated part of society and the part least contaminated by socialism—are ready, as were the peasants of that time, to "feed and defend" Poland in the case of intervention by the customary invader, that is, the Russians. An analogous situation exists in Italy. Recently, the Federalist Party of the Lega Nord made reference to the celebrated oath of Pontida, a pact that was drawn up between the communities of Lombardy in the Middle Ages in order to ward off the invasion by Emperor Friedrich Barbarossa. For the Lega, Barbarossa personifies the corrupt and centralist government of Rome. During the *Risorgimento,* however, the oath of Pontida was interpreted in terms of contemporaneous conflicts with Austria and was one of the fundamental symbols of Italian unity.

If the anthropologist is primarily interested in actualized history, then the first questions to be posed are the following: How do specific social actors use past events in the present? In what way is history reinterpreted, manipulated, and even reinvented? Which facts are chosen and which others discarded? What are the reasons for such choices? A moment's reflection shows that in the case of actualized history the problem of time is less crucial, because the metaphors, metonyms, and allegories it employs jump over the ages. Thus, the concrete time of history, as defined by Braudel, loses its real dimension and, in a certain way, cancels itself out. Perhaps, then, the distinction between anthropological historiography and historical anthropology may be understood in terms of two different concepts of time, which have not yet been examined in depth. Below I analyze some aspects of this problem, with the aim of expanding upon the theme of actualized history as an anthropological field of research.

Actualized History and Founding Myths

The cohesion of every community is based, as Max Weber said, on *Gemeinsamkeitsglauben,* that is, on the belief of having traits in common (Weber 1956: 1:235ff.). Often, however, the traits in question are not seen by the members of the group as phenomena generated by the immediate present; on the contrary, the idea that the longer ago a common trait took shape, the more solid, unalterable, and perpetual it is, seems to be much more widespread. It is for this reason that many "identity managers" in the independent Lithuania of today are not against defining their people as the "dinosaurs of Europe," for in this way the grandeur and, even more significantly, the great age of their collectivity is emphasized. History proves itself to be an enormous quarry from which one can extract those stones that show how, "even then," the group constituted a unity. Naturally, the chosen facts are reelaborated and often so cavalierly manipulated as to appear to outside observers as inventions.

Since the publication of the seminal work by Hobsbawm and Ranger, the term "invention" has been given pejorative connotations and linked to notions of "falsehood" or "subterfuge"(Hobsbawm and Ranger 1983: 1ff.). For this very reason, Herzfeld (1991: 12, 46, 205) rejects the concept of invention, noting that, judged by this standard, all history would have to be viewed as contaminated or falsified. To me, this seems comparable to the obsession of the Anglo-Saxon Puritans with the capital sin of lying. There is, I would suggest, nothing scandalous in the invention of stories and traditions. It may be, in fact, a necessary performance that is, nonetheless, based on events that actually occurred in a nebulous or legendary past. Insofar as it is linked to the *Gemeinsamkeitsglauben* of a community, history must be continually reexamined and adapted to new situations. In this sense, actualized history is always also situational history. This becomes clear when one thinks of historical actors such as Jelacic in Croatia or the poet Sevcenko in the Ukraine, who, in the course of the twentieth century, have frequently been denounced and rehabilitated.

Actualized history is not a faithful reconstruction of the past; rather, it always contains something invented. This is especially evident in the founding myths of a group, that is, in those events that are believed to have given birth to the collectivity. Nowadays, almost all the communities that have come about as a result of a political pact—for example, the modern nation-states—derive their legitimacy, at least in part, from similar founding myths that are produced at certain moments and under particular circumstances, thanks to the actualization of history. An illuminating example is Switzerland, a country known abroad as a land without history. Until 1798, Switzerland was a quadrilingual, bidenominational Confederation composed of city-states, peasant republics, and colonized territories that, for one reason or another, were nearly constantly in conflict with one another. Contrary to what is believed today, harmony and stability were not earmarks of the first five centuries of this singular political community. In 1798, with the birth of the United and Indivisible Helvetic Republic, France made its first attempts to transform the old Confederation into a modern nation-state. But the real change came about only after the war of the so-called *Sonderbund* between Catholic and Protestant cantons (1847) and the drawing up of a new political pact—the federal constitution, which was approved in 1848. In this way Switzerland became a nation-state, which was, however, still in need of strengthening. This strengthening was achieved through the conscious, well thought out invention of a founding myth—an actualization of history.

Wilhelm Tell was, in a very real sense, a nineteenth-century hero who, until 1848, may have been better known to foreign writers and musicians such as Schiller and Rossini than to the Swiss themselves. But during this same period the Confederates' common fight for independence from the foreign domination of the Habsburgs was emphasized. The Habsburgs, paradoxically, came from a region that has always been in Swiss territory. Two or three insignificant battles, almost skirmishes, between the Helvetians and the Imperial troops thus took on a disproportionate importance, while the microhistorical divisions and differences, which had frequently put the existence of the Confederation at risk before 1798, were ignored. In this way, the impression that Switzerland is a country with a harmonious past, free of the troubles of other nations, was created.

The most interesting phenomenon of this nineteenth-century construction of the Helvetic founding myth is undoubtedly the invention of the national holiday of the first day in August, which, even now, is celebrated with a certain solemnity. This day commemorates the oath of Grütli (1291), that is, the pact of alliance between the three "primitive cantons." This is believed to be the founding act of the Confederation. In fact, the character and date of this holiday were the result of a skillful decision made by desk-bound politicians. The oath of Grütli was only one of several pacts of alliance that were drawn up in the Middle Ages within the territory of present-day Switzerland. Furthermore, it is neither the best documented nor the oldest. There were earlier alliances that, had they been chosen, would have made the Confederation some fifty years older, with all the obvious consequences for past, present, and future commemorations. But, from a territorial point of view, the oath of Grütli is the most centrally located and, consequently, the one best suited to represent, metaphorically speaking, the "heart" of the nation. Its exact date is unknown, but reliable documents speak of "a day in August." The choice of the first day of the month has its own rationale: the number one has, it seems, a certain charismatic aura; it symbolizes unity and perhaps excellence, as well. The political and intellectual elite of that period, however, linked as it was to secular, rational, and liberal milieus, could not have ignored the fact that the number one left much less space for numerological speculations than did other dates, such as the seventh, thirteenth, or seventeenth.

The case of Switzerland is particularly instructive, since it demonstrates the efficiency (Ricoeur 1985: 3:314) of the founding myths of a group, which in this case are the product of a deliberate actualization of history. In fact, the invention of founding myths and the skillful management of actualized history are vital components in the representation of the Helvetic community. Besides institutional mechanisms, which cannot be discussed here but whose importance must be acknowledged, the invention of adequate founding myths is undoubtedly an essential component of the success of the Swiss model, which has recently been held up as an example for regions torn by violent ethnic conflicts (e.g., the cantonization project in Bosnia).

Thus, invention through the actualization of history may be shown to be a necessary ingredient for the stability of a political pact, which cannot simply be reduced to a mystification of reality. One might add that if in the Helvetic case it is a matter of invention, then three cheers for invention! For, whether or not the invention is true, it is certainly welcome.

Managing Exemplariness by Bringing History Up to Date: Saints, Heroes, and Victims

A community in search of cohesion and therefore also in search of a collective identity will turn not only to the founding myths but also to the construction of exemplariness. Also in this case one is almost always dealing with an updating of history, as, if we leave aside the various personality cults put into action by the totalitarian systems in order to glorify the figure of a real leader and which are therefore still active in the present, exemplariness, as a complex of virtue to be admired and possibly to be imitated, is normally attributed to eminent characters from the past. Exemplariness is thus passed on by bringing history up to date.

It is clear, by looking particularly at the excellence of those who have marked or even formed the past of a group, that this community tends in this way to underline its superiority in the present. In this case the construction of exemplariness becomes an essential element in the fight for recognition of a social group. What seems particularly interesting to me, however, is not the insistence on the inevitability or necessity of turning to the exemplariness in the collective practical identities as much as making plausible the different ways of and specific reasons for the creation of virtuous characters in a given society. I would like to premise that the fabrication of exemplariness is usually based on the sanctification or the heroization of people belonging to history. But the criteria needed to be declared saints or heroes greatly varies from group to group, which also holds true for what we can define as the European context. There are therefore different ways of bringing history up to date and of conceiving exemplariness, especially if we compare Western Europe with Central and Eastern Europe, including the Balkans. One thing that strikes the Western traveler who visits the Russian or Balkan monasteries is the omnipresence of the images of the military saints, as, for example, those of St. George, St. Demetrius, and St. Theodore (Delehaye 1909). The repeated representations of war scenes such as battles and sieges also leap to the eye of the foreign observer. It is emblematic that in the Moldovita monastery in the foothills of the Romanian Carpathians, not so far away from the present-day border with the Ukraine, one can admire the frescoes of at least three military saints as well as a masterly representation of the seizing of Constantinople by the Ottoman armies.

This element leads us to believe that the construction of exemplariness in Central and Eastern Europe is based on a narrow relationship between ecclesiastical roles and acts of warfare. This is also shown by the architectonic structure of the old Russian monasteries, which were true and proper fortresses for the defense of the national territory against the real or presumed threats that came from the East or the West. The famous Golden ring, which was formed by a system of grand monasteries such as those of Sergijev Posad and Suzdal, is an incomparable military-ecclesiastical cordon intended to defend Moscow in the case of Mongolian or Polish-Lithuanian invasions. On the western border of present-day Russia one finds, however, a series of fortress-monasteries, such as the celebrated Troytski Monastir of Pskhov, whose function in the past was to block the Swedish invasions and those of the knights of the Teutonic order. But the narrow relationship between ecclesiastical roles and military roles also evokes the problem of the link between saintliness and heroism, the latter being understood as a complex of warlike virtue. Without wanting either to create artificial differences between the Eastern and Western Europe or specific Russian or Balkan stereotypes, it seems evident to me that in Central and Eastern Europe, far more frequently than in Western Europe, exemplariness, constructed in terms of saintliness, is still linked today with the heroic quality, that is, the military prowess of the historic characters in question.

There is no doubt that the epic Russian poems that celebrate the memorable fights between the Bogatyrs of Kiev against those who threatened the integrity of the legendary Land of Rus emphasize the heroic prowess of the protagonists, amongst which Ilya of Murom stands out. Although Ilya was never sanctified, his warlike charisma is related to a miraculous recovery that took place at the symbolic age of thirty-three and to his extraordinary sense of morality, which made him carry out terrifying and cruel acts only when it was really necessary, making one think of a latent and natural saintliness. Looking, however, at other historical figures who have always been considered founding heroes of the Russian Motherland, one observes that they were effectively sanctified and have, in fact, maintained their historic exemplariness until today. In these cases of bringing history up to date there is a combination of saintliness, heroism, and masculinity. In other words, in order to acquire the status of saint, it is practically necessary to be primarily a heroic warrior. This is certainly not the only way of constructing saintliness in Russia, but it represents an important possibility that has not yet lost its relevance.

In this sense the most symbolic case is undoubtedly that of Alexander Nevski, who is rarely seen as a saint by Westerners but rather as an implacable and courageous warrior who was capable, in prohibitive conditions on a frozen lake, of defeating the powerful armada of the knights of the Teutonic order who came from the Baltic territories. On the contrary, in both the hegemonic discourses and those subalterns that developed after the fall of the Soviet Union, Alexander Nevski is also, and above all, St. Alexander of the Neva—the man who fought heroically and successfully for the survival of his native land under threat from foreigners and to whom is dedicated a famous and much frequented monastery in St. Petersburg. Obviously analogous characters also exist in Western Europe, but it is symptomatic, for example, that El Cid, the Western hero, who is most comparable to Alexander Nevski, has never been led to the honor of the altars, while the saintliness of Joan of Arc is to be attributed more to her martyrdom than to her warlike virtues.

If we would now like to further strengthen our observations on heroic, warlike and essentially masculine saintliness, we could cite the quite widespread tradition in East-Central Europe of bestowing the dignity of sainthood on many sovereigns distinguished for their military skill. It is well known that the recent attempt to sanctify the last tsar, Nicholas II, at first failed miserably. In my opinion, the initial although temporary lack of success of this project is not a matter of chance but is because the exemplariness of this last Russian monarch is considered to be deficient, not only by the majority of the orthodox ecclesiastical hierarchies but also by the people. In fact, it is not so easy to use heroic and virile attributes to legitimize the saintliness of Nicholas II.

We do have both kings and princes in Western Europe who have achieved the dignity of sainthood. Here, however, if we leave aside isolated exceptions of the Middle Ages, regal exemplariness, which can lead to sainthood, is constructed with other criteria to those so far mentioned. The great French historian Marc Bloch in his masterly book on "thaumaturgic kings" teaches us that already in France as well as in England in the Middle Ages, the exemplariness of those sovereigns, who, it is worth noting, were only very rarely sanctified, was based on the supernatural abilities to carry out miracles by curing people affected by debilitating illnesses (Bloch 1983). The charisma of these powerful people thus came to be defined not so much by their military prowess as by their therapeutic ability. One is therefore dealing with a mystic or miraculous regality rather than a heroic one (Bloch 1983: 19ff.). But let us return to Alexander Nevski, who is understood as a prototype of warlike, heroic, and masculine sanctity, partly because this protagonist of Russian history was not brought up to date when communism fell in that country but was perfectly integrated in the Soviet pantheon, as Sergy Eisenstein's film of 1938 clearly illustrates. This adoption can seem somewhat surprising at first in a state that declares itself to be atheist even, if Lenin in the famous decree of 1919 recommended that antireligious activities were not exaggerated in order not to offend the sensibilities of the masses who were able to seek comfort in fanaticism. Certainly Alexander Nevski was silently deconsecrated but never in any radical manner. In fact, on the central panel of Pavel Dimitrievic Korin's famous triptych of 1942 he is purposely portrayed next to the banner of Christ. And this is because Stalin, at that time threatened by the German armies, played on the religious sensibilities of the Russian people in his mobilization for the patriotic war. In this way the Soviet dictator gave back to Alexander Nevski, at least for that moment, his vest of *Homo religiosus* and saint. It does, however, seem obvious to me that the virtues described here, which were intrinsic to the exemplariness and saintliness of these characters, facilitated their integration into Soviet mythology. It would have been more arduous for the communist power to confer exemplariness on one of the many saints devoted to merely religious activities even if they were not always peaceful or marked by tolerance. But it probably was not only the warlike or virile virtues of the protagonists that facilitated their acceptance into the Olympus of Soviet heroes but also the fact that Alexander Nevski was a victorious hero, that is, a true hero such as those of the Russian fables analyzed by Vladimir Propp (1970) or those of the Nietzschean-Marxist project of someone like Maxim Gorky or Anatoly Lunacharsky, where there is no room for victims and antiheroes are the representatives of an "unsound principle" (Günther 1993: 84ff., 144ff.). And here is another possible reason for the laborious sanctification of Nicholas II: the last tsar was not a hero also because he was a loser all along the line.

The recurrent bringing up to date of historic characters, whether they be saints or heroes, by way of a winning exemplariness, makes us think at the same time of the opposite case or in other words of a losing exemplariness. Tzvetan Todorov in his last book, *L'homme dépaysé*, makes two interesting observations about this. The first is as follows: "The collective memory usually prefers to keep two types of situations in the past of the community: those where we have had either victorious heroes or innocent victims" (1996: 70ff.). And in regard to the United States he adds: "Politicians and actors have themselves understood that it is not enough to appear as victors but that they must be associated with the cause of victims. This is certainly one of the most fascinating changes which have taken place in the American mentality over recent years: the replacement of the heroic ideal with the ideal of the victim" (ibid.: 216). Obviously Todorov's assertions have a certain pertinence as, since the Vietnam War, one has witnessed in the United States a real and proper crisis of American heroism, so very well managed above all by Hollywood with its marines, deliverers of liberty and its sheriffs, guarantors of justice. But does the dichotomy between heroes and victims implicitly formulated by Todorov really have such a general validity as supposed by the author? If we think of the above-mentioned examples, which belong mostly to the Russian world, it seems that Todorov is absolutely right. If we think, however, of the Balkans, the state of things is very different. In fact, it is surprising that Todorov proposed this polarity between the ideal of the hero and the ideal of the victim as he is originally from Bulgaria, a quintessential Balkan country where a strong dialectic if not an outright fusion between the two ideals can be observed. The construction of exemplariness in this country, as in the neighboring ones, in truth, follows a specific dramaturgy according to which the hero or the saint, whether he be holy or a layman, is at the same time an innocent victim of an unbearable power that has imposed a secular yoke. The model of the Balkan hero-victim was personified by both Vasil Levski, the Bulgarian hero par excellence (an orthodox deacon who is now viewed as a saint, though not officially recognized as such), and Christo Botev, the great patriotic poet and laical saint (who was particularly glorified by the socialist rhetoric), since they paid for their revolutionary prowess against the Turkish occupiers with martyrdom. But even all those ambiguous and partly anonymous characters, halfway between rebel and bandit, who inhabited the impassable mountains between Bulgaria and Macedonia at the beginning of the twentieth century, can be considered as both heroes and victims. In fact, these men, who caught the imagination of the great reporter John Reed in his book *The War in Eastern Europe* (1916), fought against the residue of the Ottoman Empire in Europe, losing, more often than not, their lives. One can suppose, with truthfulness, as the example of Jane Sandanski teaches us, that these warriors, feared but also esteemed for their cruelty, are in fact considered heroes just because they are victims.

Naturally, there are many cases of winning exemplariness that exist alongside this losing exemplariness. The most significant representatives of these are certainly the Albanian national heroes, the Champion of Christ George Castriota Skanderbeg and the Magyar-Romanian hero Hunyadi Janos/Jon

Hunedoara, who in certain ways resembled Alexander Nevski (Castellan 1991: 81ff.). However, in spite of this very different pantheon of heroes and saints, losing exemplariness, personified above all by hero-victims, is in the Balkans an essential component of the national identity and of the consequent definition of "us" and "them."

If now toward the end of this chapter one seeks an explanation of how on earth in Central and Eastern Europe, far more than in other parts of the continent, one finds oneself faced by the construction of heroic, warlike, and masculine saintliness, while in the Balkans losing exemplariness has such an incontestable fascination whether it be in the hegemonic classes or in the subaltern ones, one must not let oneself be seduced by facile cultural arguments. By explaining culture through culture we are only contributing to the perpetuation of old stereotypes and prejudices, for example, "these are essential elements of an irrational world such as that of the Byzantine Russian orthodox, where," as the Hungarians of Transylvania add with a certain disrespect, "illuminism, having never got past the Carpathians, has never arrived." Somewhat more plausible, however, than the cultural argument would seem to me to be the historical-anthropological argument, that is, the assumption that bringing the past up to date, as we shall see in a following chapter, is the result of a cognitive process based on the historic experience of a community. One could then rightly ask if heroic, warlike, or masculine saintliness would not be better put in relation to the chronic instability of the borders in Central and Eastern Europe, which, from time immemorial, have been defined and redefined. One would thus be dealing with a saintliness of border or, more precisely, a political saintliness inherent to communities scourged by the variable geometry of their territories. Losing exemplariness based on the idea that the hero-victim binomial is inseparable would then be an expression of the "vision of the defeated" (Wachtel 1977), that is, of the vision of those who, after centuries of living through oppression and perceived injustice, as shown by the example of the Balkan societies, consider themselves to be the historically betrayed (Giordano 1992). Just as a result of this, more in-depth historical-anthropological research should be initiated. And this, I feel, is only the first piece of ground that needs to be covered more deeply in an anthropological-historical perspective that takes the strict relationship between present and past into account.

The Destruction of the Past and the Reversibility of Events: Two Elementary Forms of Actualized History

Two common ways of actualizing history are (1) the destruction of the past, that is, the systematic elimination of facts, symbols, and social practices that are linked to ages considered to be barbaric, obscure, or degenerate; and (2) the reversibility of events, that is, the project of getting back to how things were before, with the aim of overcoming a near past that has proven to be a fatal error.

The institutional elites of the countries of East-Central Europe seem, for example, to have used and to continue to use history as a formal and manipulative instrument of deceit. But perhaps such elites were, and are, also victims of their own illusions. As Matvejevic has aptly stated, socialist regimes tried to move history and to push it forward with all means at their disposal—and this holds true for all former Eastern bloc countries, from the GDR to Bulgaria, with a few exceptions and some deviations (1992: 38). The chief advocates of this endeavor did not shrink from the systematic destruction of the past, which was presented as the oppressive legacy of a corrupt and degenerate epoch of despotism, poverty, exploitation, and alienation. In this regard, it is instructive to see how the Bulgarian rulers dealt with land registration after the agrarian reforms of 1946. Driven by the conviction that the dark era of small land ownership was gone forever, the local communist authorities destroyed the land records during the course of collectivization. In such cases, one should never underestimate the symbolic meaning of such actions, for it is precisely by means of the destruction of such records that the unacceptable past can be eliminated. The criteria by which the reconstruction or restoration of the historic monuments of the former GDR was undertaken display some interesting parallels. Consider, for example, the treatment of the central areas of Berlin and Dresden. One can hardly avoid coming to the conclusion that the cultural resource management of the GDR was intended to erase German history before 1945 through inadequate care and downright destruction of architectural symbols. In contrast, the institutions responsible for the protection of monuments in the *Bundesrepublik* distinguished themselves by careful attention to the preservation of historic buildings, which, for an Italian observer, seems to have been exaggerated and overplayed. Attitudes toward history and the management of cultural resources in the GDR changed only when the regime was in its final death throes. The attempt to destroy the unpleasant aspects of history can also be seen in the socialist restructuring of Bucharest, where, above all, the "degenerate" evidence of bourgeois construction was supposed to be eliminated. One can easily cite many similar cases of this iconoclastic rage against history. It must be remembered, however, that socialist regimes were based more upon a view of reality "as it should be" than on reality itself (Matvejevic 1992: 41). Matvejevic's observation holds true not only for the socialist perspective on the present and the future; it is also valid with regard to the past.

In this sense, the past was destroyed and, at the same time, replaced by a "how-it-should-have-occurred" construction of history. Socialism, therefore, did more than simply deny or negate history; in fact, socialist discourses about the past may be regarded as processes of historicization, though the historicization in question was of a distinctly teleological sort. In the socialist countries, the manipulation of the past was the responsibility not only of politicians and official writers but also of social and cultural scientists, including the practitioners of the prevailing national ethnology. This is especially evident in the fixation of ethnologists on a peasant-based folk culture. The farmers of southeast

Europe had, in fact, been dispossessed and were either proletarianized by their entry into the agricultural collectives, urbanized by their migration into the cities, or systematized by means of centralized measures. Nevertheless, the image of a virgin and noncapitalistic folk culture was propagated by the state and party and cultivated and administered by ethnologists.

This systematic invention of tradition served, in the so-called peasant and worker states—the People's Democracies of East-Central Europe—to legitimate numerous political measures. Once again, Todor Zivkov's Bulgaria is a good example. The invention of a monoethnic Bulgarian folk culture is no doubt closely connected with the policy of forced Bulgarization or expulsion of the Turkish minority between 1960 and 1989 (Silverman 1992: 269). The fiction of a primeval Romanian folk culture that was suppressed and eclipsed by neighboring groups also facilitated Ceaușescu's repressive policies in Transylvania.

The transition of 1989 radically altered this view of history. The socialistic interpretation of the past was suddenly declared to be made up of lies that served the interests of the regime. At the same time, socialism itself was denounced as a fatal historical mistake. If, however, the socialist discourse about history was based on the selective destruction of the past, then the postcommunist construction of history takes as its point of departure the premise of the reversibility of events. The first discourse rests on a prospective model, while the second is based upon a retrospective view. By the reversibility of events, I mean the idea that the burdensome past can and should be undone. According to the logic of this model, it is necessary and desirable to re-create the conditions of the presocialist era, as if socialism never existed—or as if it existed only outside of the flow of history. This endeavor was strikingly described to me by many interviewees who compared socialism to a dead-end street: "When one wants to come out of a dead end, one must return to the original point of entry," they claimed.

In my view, most of the economic, political, and social reforms of the postcommunist era are being conceived in accordance with the principle of the reversibility of events. For in a variety of cases—in establishing the criteria for Latvian nationality, in the restitution of urban real estate in the former GDR, and in the many instances in postcommunist societies where statues of Lenin have been torn down and street names have been changed—the agencies responsible for carrying out the reforms refer to a glorious presocialist past, which is seen as the basis for the transformation of the present and the determination of the future. A similar tendency is clearly evident in the design and execution of the agrarian reform law passed in Bulgaria in 1992. This law provides for the return of land to its former owners in accordance with the "correct" property relations that existed in 1946. To this end, committees were formed throughout the country and charged with a task indispensable for the reversibility of events, namely, the reconstruction of presocialist property rights. In this regard, the socialist period is treated by legislators as a historical black hole. They ignore processes such as urbanization and the occupational reorganization of rural strata, which fundamentally altered the social structure of Bulgaria over the last forty-five years.

Actualized History as a Form of Knowledge

Up to now, I have emphasized the strategic use of the past through the actualization of history. But this view, important as it is, carries the danger of limiting one's vision to the intentional and rational aspects of social behavior. It is obvious that actualized history is not born out of nothing; rather, it emerges from a very precise context, which the German historian Koselleck has defined as the sphere of experience or *Erfahrungsraum* (Koselleck 1979: 349ff.). This "sphere" may be experienced directly or in a mediated form, which can then be transmitted to others. In any case, it is unthinkable that the actualization of the past be realized without the prior knowledge of what has gone before. Those who refer to the past, consciously or unconsciously, have recourse to a selective knowledge that is condensed and stratified. From the perspective of historical anthropology, one can say that every collectivity has, in regard to its own past, a kind of cognitive capital that represents the basis of a particular consciousness or historical sensitivity (Geertz 1983: 175).

Why is there such an evident difference in the attitudes of the Italians and the Spaniards toward the war in Bosnia? The explanation may appear at first sight to be banal: the Italians have not sent any UN troops to the area, while the Spaniards are represented by an important military contingent. But reflection upon the language used in official discussions, television reports, and even in everyday conversations reveals another possible explanation, which, of course, does not exclude the first. The Spaniards seem to be more sensitive to the events in the former Yugoslavia—in particular, the war in Bosnia—because they associate them with their own civil war. The Italians, on the other hand, have never been confronted with the same type of armed conflict, and they experience the same events with much less intensity. It is obvious that the siege of Sarajevo does not have the same meaning for Italians as it does for Spaniards, who see it in terms of the analogous dramas of Toledo and Segovia. Different forms of knowledge or cognitive capital have thus given rise to different kinds of historical sensitivity, which then crystallize in different attitudes toward the same events.

As this last example shows, actualized history does not consist of objective facts, even if it is based upon them. It is derived instead from what Husserl called "internalized history," *innere Geschichte* (Husserl 1962: 9:381). This internalized history, which may subsequently be actualized, represents a precious resource for social actors, who use it to interpret the future and project themselves into it. Every individual, as a member of a particular collectivity, constructs his or her own horizon of expectations by means of the past future. This is not the title of a science fiction film by Steven Spielberg but Koselleck's striking formulation, which sets the sphere of experience, that is, the perceived past, in direct relationship to the "horizon of expectations," *Erwartungshoriz-ont*, that is, the projected future (Koselleck 1979: 349ff.).

In order to clarify my argument, I would like to refer briefly to my field experience in Mediterranean societies, especially in Sicily. Many people in Mediterranean societies understand themselves to be the objects rather than the subjects of history. Conversations with ordinary people as well as with members of the regional or national intelligentsia indicate that history is perceived not in terms of progress but as an interminable series of defeats and frustrated hopes. History is a kind of collective trauma, and the past is interpreted as a continual betrayal. From this point of view, it is the foreign or distant elites that determine the destiny of the oppressed and ban them to the margins of their own society. Of course, for "history's betrayed" (Giordano 1992) there are not only traumatic but also glorious moments, moments of epic splendor, e.g., the Egypt of the pharaohs, the Greece of the Hellenes, the Sicily of the Normans, and the Morocco of the Almoravids; but these spheres of experience are perceived as primordial and unrepeatable events. At a particular point in time, it is thought, history somehow "went wrong"—an irreversible development that is reproduced in the present and will continue to be reproduced in the future. In these societies one may note a generalized atmosphere of skepticism, which is linked to the notion that the future is an inevitable repetition of the past. Thus, the sphere of experience coincides almost exactly with the horizon of expectations. Under these conditions, practically every externally proposed reform—for example, agrarian reforms or projects of industrial or community development—is received with incredulity and suspicion, as the case of Sicily shows (Giordano 1992: 35ff.). This skepticism is combined with an attitude of refusal toward the state, which is seen as an instrument of oppression in the hands of those foreign and invading elites who succeed one another in an endless cycle of domination. In the eyes of "history's betrayed," the flaws of a state based on the maxim "the weak with the strong and the strong with the weak" justify social practices such as banditry, rebellion, clientelism, and, last but not least, mafioso behavior.

For observers from northwestern Europe, such attitudes and behaviors may appear to be expressions of an antisocial character, amoral familism, fatalism, or unbridled individualism. From the anthropological point of view, however, they may be understood as the product of the historical knowledge derived from the particular sphere of experience of those who feel betrayed by history. It is, thus, valid to conclude that actualized history, as a form of knowledge generated by particular spheres of experience, is a significant component in the formation of cultural systems, that is, coherent wholes that include *Weltan-schauungen*, value systems, rules, and social practices.

Scale Reduction: A Real Problem?

In my own research on actualized history, I have not made use of scale reduction. I have never done fieldwork in a single village or group of villages for an extended period of time, though in principle I am not opposed to such a research strategy. On the contrary, it seems that the reduction of scale can, in many cases, be a suitable way of proceeding, if used with due caution. It is, at any rate, important to remember that historical-anthropological research should be focused on a problem and not on a place.

There may, however, be other problems with scale reduction. It is possible that research carried out in a microcosm may become too comfortable and reassuring for the researcher. It is, after all, personalized and allows for close contact and facility of orientation inside a well-defined social space. These are advantages that should not be underestimated, but they may also be a fatal trap, if they lead one to view the village as a miniature reproduction of the global society. This was the illusion of many previous anthropologists, especially those who belonged to the British school of functionalism—consider, for example, Malinowski, Radcliffe-Brown, or Firth and their predilection for islands. The village, on the contrary, is a structure that is encapsulated in a much larger and hierarchically organized social reality, and it is only the last link in this larger order.

An overemphasis on research in villages may encourage the omission of important sectors of society such as political and intellectual elites at the regional and national levels. Due to their position of power, however, these actors are the most significant producers of actualized history. Following the lead of Pareto, Mosca, and Michels—the great theorists of elites—I am suspicious of efforts to analyze the actualization of history through scale reduction. If, however, scale reduction is linked to history from below or to the study of history as a weapon of the weak, it can be a most useful way of proceeding. But in such cases researchers no longer treat the village as an autonomous and isolated reality; rather, they look "beyond the community" (Boissevain and Friedl 1975) in a way that may be recommended for all those who work in the field of historical anthropology.

Concluding Observations

1. The difference between anthropological history and historical anthropology consists in the anthropologist's interest in various kinds of actualized history. The anthropologist takes the past into consideration only insofar as it is significant for understanding the management of the present or projections into the future.

2. History is of interest to the anthropologist as a form of knowledge that informs the collectivity's savoir faire and its sense of the "here and now." This specific "knowledge" may, of course, be based on actual occurrences, but even in this case they are products of conceptualization, as we have learned from Kant. Actualized history, considered as an object of historical anthropological investigation, is a conceived, imagined, or even invented product.

3. History for the anthropologist does not only consist of objective events or processes; it is, above all, a constantly reelaborated and reinterpreted internalized history.
4. Actualized history is internalized history in use. It is characterized by its own array of symbols, myths, constructions, and inventions. It may serve as an instrument of dominion, a strategy for resistance, an object of identification, an element of social cohesion, or a detonator in collective conflicts. Actualized history is, therefore, an essential component in the basic social processes in which the members of a collectivity are involved.
5. The method of scale reduction is only a partially suitable way of proceeding in historical anthropological research. It is useful in many cases, but it is not absolutely necessary.

References

Berger, P., and T. Luckmann. 1979. *The Social Construction of Reality*. Harmondsworth, UK: Penguin Books.

Bloch, M. 1983. *Les rois thaumaturges. Etudes sur le caractère surnaturel attribué à la puissance royale particulièrement en France et en Angeleterre*. Paris: Gallimard.

Boissevain, J., and J. Friedl, eds. 1975. *Beyond the Community: Social Process in Europe*. The Hague: European-Mediterranean Study Group.

Braudel, F. 1971. "Geschichte und Sozialwissenschaften. Die 'longue durée.'" In *Schrift und Materie der Geschichte. Vorschläge zur systematischen Aneignung historischer Prozess*, ed. C. Honegger, 47–85. Frankfurt am Main: Suhrkamp.

Castellan, G. 1991. *Histoire des Balkans (XIV–XX siècle)*. Paris: Fayard.

Cassirer, E. 1985. *Der Mythus des Staates. Philosophische Grundlagen politischen Verhaltens*. Frankfurt am Main: Fischer-Verlag.

Croce, B. 1970. *La Storia come pensiero e come azione*. Roma-Bari: Laterza.

Delehaye, H. 1909. *Les légendes grecques des saints militaires*. Paris: Libraire Alphonse Picard et fils.

Geertz, C. 1983. *Local Knowledge: Further Essays in Interpretive Anthropology*. New York: Basic Books.

Giordano, C. 1992. *Die Betrogenen der Geschichte. Überlagerungsmentalität und Überlagerungsrationalität in mediterranen Gesellschaften*. Frankfurt am Main and New York: Campus Verlag.

Günther, H. 1993. *Der sozialistische Übermensch. Maksim Gorkij und der sowjetische Heldenmythos*. Stuttgart and Weimar: Verlag J.B. Metzler.

Herzfeld, M. 1991. *A Place in History: Social and Monumental Time in a Cretan Town*. Princeton, NJ: Princeton University Press.

Hobsbawm, E., and T. Ranger, eds. 1983. *The Invention of Tradition*. Cambridge: Cambridge University Press.

Husserl, E. 1962. *Phänomenologische Psychologie*. Vol. 9. The Hague: Husserliana.

Koselleck, R. 1979. *Vergangene Zukunft. Zur Semantik geschichtlicher Zeiten*. Frankfurt am Main: Suhrkamp.

Lévi-Strauss, C. 1949. "Histoire et ethnologie." *Revue de Métaphysique et de Morale* 54: 363–391.

Matvejevic, P. 1992. *Otvorena Pisma*. Zagreb: n.p.

Propp, V. 1970. *Morphologie du conte.* Paris: Seuil.

Radcliffe-Brown, A. R. 1976. *Method in Social Anthropology.* Chicago and London: University of Chicago Press.

Reed, J. 1916. *The War in Eastern Europe.* New York: Charles Scribner's Sons.

Ricoeur, P. 1985. *Temps et récit.* 3 vols. Paris: Seuil.

Schütz, A., and T. Luckmann. 1979. *Strukturen der Lebenswelt.* Frankfurt am Main: Suhrkamp.

Silverman, Carol. 1992. "Peasants, Ethnicity, and Ideology in Bulgaria." In *Die Volkskultur Südosteuropa in der Moderne,* ed. K. Roth, 295–308. Munich: Selbstverlag der Südosteuropa-Gesellschaft.

Simiand, F. 1903. "Méthode historique et science sociale." *Revue de synthèse historique* 6: 1–22, 129–157.

Todorov, T. 1996. *L'homme dépaysé.* Paris: Seuil.

Wachtel, N. 1977. *La vision des vaincus.* Paris: Gallimard.

Wallerstein, I. 1991. *Unthinking Social Science.* Cambridge: Polity Press.

Weber, M. 1956. *Wirtschaft und Gesellschaft.* 2 vols. Tübingen: J.C.B. Mohr and Paul Siebeck Verlag.

Chapter Three

FIGURATIONS IN HISTORICAL ANTHROPOLOGY
Two Kinds of Structural Narrative about Long-Duration Provenances of the Holocaust

Hermann Rebel

I

The danger of transforming consequences into their own causes dogs any attempted history, but particularly one whose final objects of interest are as overwhelming as the orgies of murder that took place in East-Central Europe during the 1940s, altogether constituting those experiences and memories of insane horrors that we have come to call the Holocaust.[1] This has become a more acute logical problem as the historical field where we are currently "free" to look for the Holocaust's provenances has steadily narrowed, even as it appears, however coincidentally, that the very global corporate and financial entities on which we all depend daily have long been, and presently still are, fully complicit in perpetrations of holocaust-forms. From this perspective, we might recall Daniel Goldhagen's cramped and circular German anti-Semitism argument, which seemed at odds with and yet, from another perspective, also obviously helped erase simultaneous, coincidental revelations about the genocidal banking operations by which the so-called international community, through its Swiss accountants and agents, once held Nazi Germany to making at least some of its debt payments with, among other things, Auschwitz gold.

It is an irony that Ranke might have appreciated had he seen how, in an effort to construct repressively displacing, that is metonymic, histories (where "outcomes" perpetually swallow all of their "causes," even the holocausts), we have, largely unwittingly, rewritten the Holocaust as comedy, as but one

---

Notes for this chapter begin on page 83.

more in a series of conflictual, even traumatic, but always finally completed and resolved episodes in our bumbling advance toward finding security at last in achieved, civilized humanity.[2] The ceaseless present proliferations of holocaust-forms, evident in eruptions of genocidal predations on a global scale, combine, however, to reveal the bad faith in any of the current comedic resolutions for the Nazi Holocaust, including Goldhagen's (1996: 582). When we read, by contrast, the work of a survivor such as Jiří Weil, who had the courage actually to narrate the Holocaust *directly* as comedy, we can only watch his experimental intention falter as he cannot but turn toward an emplotment that fits none of the classic categories that Hayden White's (1973) metahistorical schematics lay out for us. Weil's tale gives up on a resolution long before it collapses into ending by telling in irredeemable detail the torture and murder of two resistant children.[3]

Demonstrably, the task of constructing Holocaust narratives stretches White's possible emplotment models past their breaking point. At the same time, one has to note that his discussion of Ranke's intellectual relationship to his teacher Wilhelm von Humboldt (White 1973: 178–187) offers an opening for such histories that elude classic emplotments but that yet have to be told. While we certainly have to pass through some aspects of the historian's task as White sees it—as when "the historian confronts the historical field in much the same way that the grammarian might confront a new language"—we ought not to stay overly long in this mode, particularly when he takes us into a somewhat less than adequate (i.e., a grammarian's) reading of metonymy in which he in effect displaces the displacing qualities of metonymic linkages and overplays the integrative (as opposed to the revelatory or differentiating) qualities of synecdoche (White 1973: 34–36, and passim). It may well be for this specific misrecognition acting as parameter inside White's arguments that he tries to stuff Humboldt back into the comedic frame next to Ranke by emphasizing the high theory of Humboldt's idealist utopianism combined with his Aristotelian-aesthetic metahistory, by which ideas only endlessly struggle with brute matter to be realized (White 1973: 182–185). White is aware, nevertheless, that Humboldt's breakout from the comedic, and indeed from all of the classic emplotments, occurs in the method by which he follows this ideal-material dialectic as it assumes, consumes, and discards historical forms. White paraphrases Humboldt: we never grasp the successes and failures of these actualizations in any single form that we can discern but rather by "the imposition of provisional, middle-range, formal coherencies" strung together in synecdochal linkages capable of representing, of revealing the "'form of events' and the 'inner structure' of the whole set of events contained in a narrative ... in which all events are conceived to bear a relationship to the whole which is that of microcosm to macrocosm." Achieving a representation of this relationship is a creative act of the historian, with the actual mimetic reproduction not that of a copy but of a "figuring of its 'inner form' ... [providing] *a model* of the proportion and symmetry of it" (White 1973: 180, emphasis in original).

"Figuration" in this sense is the historian's creative apperception of correspondences in the contents of archival materials, an imposition of a *finally recognized* "figure" that is intrinsic to and yet also more than, and in that sense also outside of any actual historical moments to which these materials speak. What one might call a "figural narrative" derives from readings of historical evidentiary materials and is always an instrument of the historian's intent to disclose as yet untold linkages and crossings in the historical processes from which these materials derive. Figurations simultaneously sustain and undermine, that is, move across and between the displacing separations and boundaries that sustain the narrow range of options for recognition that logician-grammarians (like White) would claim are all our historical labors have to work with.

Norbert Elias's historical sociology of a "court society" figure (Elias 1983: 17–24, chap. 4, and passim; see Wolf 1977: 28–35) takes apart archival materials relevant to the actual court life of Louis XIV only then to transcend this particular historical object even as he discloses it by examining the multiple, often conflicting, on occasion even necessarily self-destructive roles that the various "actors" have to assume when they need to act out this historically constructed "courtier" society in order to realize, daily, the risks and rewards of their hegemonic projects. This is also to perceive and analyze figurations as historical processes of language formation, not simply in the sense of naming actions—a figure least often appears as "itself"—but rather in the sense of perceiving what actings-out are related to what textualized formations, to "what the word figures" (McLaughlin 1990: 86). In the Holocaust narrative I outlined in 1996, I followed different moments of dispossession and their historical forms and intertwining trajectories as these actualized a repeated but never fully acknowledged, yet in all instances arguably necessary, "dispossession figure" that one can call up from the most diverse sources.

Recognizable social-textual figurations contain considerable powers of connectivity, of hermeneutic convertibility, of trans- and, indeed, of multiple temporality, to none of which any central or classically limited emplotment motif can stick for long. This need not prevent us from accepting at least that part of the Rankean historical project—including particularly its comedic strategy—that wants to convert inscrutable, simultaneously disclosing and suppressing metonymics in historical texts and actions into the recognizing, transformative strings of synecdoche. With this turn toward the relative freedom of the middle-range precincts of archivally derived figural narratives, a different kind of Holocaust history becomes possible.

II

There have been previous attempts by practitioners of anthropological history to formulate explanations linking Nazi forms with structural features that appear to recur in the long duration I outlined in a 1996 *Focaal* essay.

To distinguish historical anthropology narrative from this anthropological history approach we need, first, to be clear about the often unwitting figural complicities and implications of the latter in the "logical" relationships among the paradigmatic forms that it intends to analyze and, secondly, to contemplate what we might retain from this approach, and what we might as a result do in analytical practice to bridge the two sides in the so far unwageable debate.

Since to wage a debate means to take sides, I want to begin a process of possible reconciliation of the two approaches by first rejecting certain powerful and pervasive constructions—represented here by the anthropological histories of Victor Turner and Marshall Sahlins—concerning the relationships between historical "events" and "structures" and the allegedly illusory temporality arising from our experiences of what Turner, in particular, perceives as merely our "personal" passions and strivings that on occasion reach historicity by triggering rituals of reintegration.[4] We can agree with Turner's phenomenology of time, which marks history as "human cultural time"; however, for Turner such time is created only in special moments of "social drama" that, paradoxically, are a kind of anti-time when the rhythmic repetitions of ritual arrest the flow, suspend the incessant succession of events taking place in what he sees as historically empty everyday life, and reconjure a sense of the timelessness of the before-time that underlies and renders trivial the human tribulations that have produced the present crisis (Turner 1985: 227–228, and passim). Sahlins's version of this is that changes can finally only feed structures, and his deceptively simple formula for a synthetic breakthrough designed to tame and absorb history for anthropology is that "event is the empirical form of a system." It is on this ground that he feels he can propose "that Maitland's famous dictum should be reversed: that history will be anthropology, or it will be nothing" (Sahlins 1985: 153ff.; cf. also Sahlins 1981: 8).

Without belaboring the logical and emplotment flaws in such conceptualizations, one can point out, first, that for Sahlins's synthesis to work he has to slide back into philosophical realism by deftly transposing event into a "happening" that is "under the burden of 'reality': the forces that have real effects, if always in the *terms* of some cultural scheme." Second, we need to point to Turner's chosen grounding in Durkheim's metonymic historicities that even at the best of times always teeter on the brink of absurd self-parody by which "law needs crime, religion needs sin, to be fully dynamic systems."[5] As was suggested at the beginning of this essay, our present concerns require us to reject categorically any metonymic constructions in that comedic emplotment that redeems the violence of crime with the positively integrating forces it presumes to release in return.[6] Instead, they require us to turn to the dangers of these processual and mechanistic neutralizations of our everyday experiences of historical time by testing them against the demands of writing a cultural history of the Nazi Holocaust that understands the Holocaust itself as a form of melancholia, an unredeemed, unspoken, and interminable sorrow that only

knows to resist closure by flight into repetition, "an unspeakability that orga-
nizes the field of the speakable" (Butler 1997: 186; Rose 1966).

There are any number of anthropological historians who have taken to the
Turnerian symbolic actionist model, and it is no surprise that they have been
absorbed in histories of ritual and performance.[7] However, the uncomfortable
place that the Holocaust occupies in modern history as the still most visible
and undeniable, rationally intended and yet thoroughly insane instance of
official, state-organized violence that, for all its "legality," strove to remove its
operations from plain view and to retain, for all its manifest terrorist presence,
a design for deniability, presents a tougher challenge to what we have called,
for the purpose of the present debate, anthropological history.[8] To illustrate
this we note, first, that there are materials and even prior anthropological histories at hand that readily lend themselves to a symbolic actionist construction
of the Holocaust, and it is instructive to see where these lead us and what kinds
of satisfactions they can provide.

III

In the course of teaching surveys of German history, my attention has been
drawn to work by Arnold Price concerning what he calls "warrior club [*Weihebund*] settlements" emerging from the Marcomanni wars of the second century, developing during the centuries of so-called *Völkerwanderungen*, the
migrations of peoples, and segueing, finally, into the institutions of the Bur-
gundian-Frankish state during the sixth and seventh centuries from where
the form was exported by Anglo-Saxon migrants to England.[9] Some aspects
of Price's marshaling of facts seem forced, unnecessarily awkward, internally
incommensurable, and straining at the bounds of inference, but there are
aspects of his central story, based on etymological and archaeological evidence
too complicated to present here, that I find sufficiently convincing to explore
as a possible basis for an experimental anthropological history and, barring
that, as one possible narrative thread in a historical anthropology, that is, in a
genealogical, "figural" reconstruction of the dispossession figure at work in the
deeper provenances of the Holocaust.

Price proposes to model specific two-tiered Germanic societies in which
the empowered, inheritance-transmitting communities of recognized tribes
and clans hive off communities of dispossessed males who, if they do not
organize themselves to join the gangs and armies of migrants, remain to form
"suburban" communities attached to and in simultaneously conflicted and
cooperative relations with the main communities of heirs. At the core of these
separate but still attached communities of the dispossessed were military associations bound into membership through sacral oaths and initiation ritual,
who "ate together" (with the assistance of the main communities' contributions) but who also developed marginal agricultural settlements and family

life by (presumably ritualized) raiding of and abducting (probably marked) women from the central clan communities. Members of these associations bore the burden of numerous signs of exclusion and inferiority in return for their effectual attachment to the communities of heirs. The payoff for the latter came in the form of a resident and armed boundary police simultaneously guarding against invasions by "foreign" migrant armies while also empowered with officially unrecognized obligations to engage in specific acts of policing of the main communities themselves. Price's contribution to a possible anthropological history of German holocaust-forms lies in this apparently possible identification of a recurrently persistent form of religious-organizational practice that empowered dispossessed but attached offspring to organize in oath-bound military formations and to engage in extrajudicial "visitations" of violence, even to the point of death, against both intruding "foreigners" or identifiable but otherwise legally immune transgressors within. For Price, the warrior clubs as such disappeared into the *posse comitatus* of the Frankish state, and he refrains from speculating about the subsequent "long-duration" historical life of these and similar kinds of "warrior" associations. His very suggestive idea remains a fragile historical construct and he is right not to overburden it. Nor do I want to do that with the experimental construction I am about to put on it by linking it first to a narrative I will try to discount and avoid but then also by drawing it, if only by implication, into a different (i.e., my) story about the long-term provenance of the Nazi Holocaust.

Carlo Ginzburg, in one of his best and most eye-opening essays, warns us that "in some quarters research into extended cultural continuities is … inherently unacceptable because it has been controlled for so long … by scholars more or less tied to the culture of the right" (Ginzburg 1989: 126). His particular focus is on the appearance in 1939—out of the classicist and pre–Cold War anti-totalitarian milieu surrounding Marcel Mauss's Collège de Sociologie—of Georges Dumézil's epochal *Mythes et Dieux des Germains*. Dumézil saw a living mythology practice throughout German history culminating in the Nazis' youth and paramilitary brigades, a practice that reached into the mythological-scholarly grab bag to construct, periodically, formations of sacral warrior bands, modeled on variously imagined prehistoric forms, whose release of berserker rage restored order so that a good king could redistribute wealth away from an evil, usurious king. This does, at first sight, appear to have some family resemblance to Price's historical sociology of what he calls "warrior clubs," whom he, too, identifies with cultic rage and with forms of collective property holding (escheat). It alerts us to determine more precisely whether or not there is something more to his version than what the intellectually exhausted and politically compromised narratives by Dumézil and his forerunners can offer.

Dumézil's envisioned historical process of consciously reinvented mythic forms was built on the classicist Nazi ideologue Otto Höfler's and on his student Lily Weiser-Aall's structural-functionalist readings of Germanic men's and youth societies as entities that were, periodically and consciously, brought to life to be harnessed for communal revitalization.[10] Although Price avoids any direct formulation of a long-duration relationship between what he sees as warrior clubs and their possible Nazi re-creations, his work does owe something to works written under that sign. While Höfler gets only one footnote, Weiser-Aall appears far more frequently, and in one instance Price indeed identifies the warrior clubs with the groups discussed by her (Price 1981: 190). Moreover, his direct use of motifs from the *Nibelungenlied* suggests that he might see, however unclearly, the warrior clubs bearing, in later medieval versions, a nearly identical resemblance to their "originary" or "basic" characteristics. His is a sociology that might easily serve structuralist anthropological histories.

Periodic reinventions and ambiguous empowerments of the Germanic warrior clubs' acting out before, during, and after the Holocaust of structurally programmed versions of communal, simultaneously internal and external boundary policing, and of the attendant, violent "ritual" forms are all as if tailored to Turner's enclosure of historical time into the "ritual dances" of cultures. The members of these organizations are identified, by their physical and social spaces, as what Turner calls "liminal *personae*," as "threshold people," living a kind of social death "as though they are being reduced or ground down to a uniform condition to be fashioned anew and endowed with additional powers." They are a counterstructure, *communitas* outside of but attached to structure and, inside their aura of "lowliness and sacredness," they constitute "an unstructured … and relatively undifferentiated *comitatus*" under "the general authority of the ritual elders" (Turner 1977: 95–97). To derive intellectual satisfaction from this metonymic conversion of the ineffable, abetted-as-long-as-unrecognizable violence (which could conceivably, in its "intentional" construction, include Auschwitz) of perpetually reenacted warrior club forms into the "regenerative abyss of *communitas*" is objectionable because it invites the historian into complicity not only with Turner's personal, dated, and vitalist theology of redemption (Turner 1977: 139, 246; in this connection see perhaps Strohm 1998) but also with intellectual genealogies that furnish, in the past as well as in the present, the exonerative constructions that simultaneously authorize and deny mass murder.[11]

The flaw in a demoralizing anthropological history that can, when it chooses, rewrite holocausts as necessary comedic collapses into the regenerative, redemptive violence of *communitas* is that the historical motor driving this structure, more precisely the apparently *necessary dispossession* that forces some into liminality, remains an untheorized, misrecognized act of expulsion—in itself a repressed violent motion further repressed by and redeemable only in the dispossesseds' allowing themselves to be recruited for violently defensive or punitive acts construed as rituals of reintegration. It remains a central, life-threatening but unspeakable experience of exclusion that is inherent in everyday life and that is, for that very reason in the Turnerian conception, outside of time, outside of and below historical experience. It is here that we can recover aspects of Price's work to illuminate the experienced and remembered violences that reside within and speak to the violence and to turn them, perhaps, toward a second kind of "structural narrative" aiming at a figural-historical anthropology of the Holocaust.

In an article that takes up Richard Koebner's hypothesis that Germanic forest taboos might have retarded the clearing of woods and the expansion of arable lands, Price departs from Justus Möser's "realist" understanding of medieval royal forests as traceable continuations of pagan forest restrictions to make the point that when the medieval records "refer to such royal forests ... they do not mean woodlands as such, but rather a special system of restrictions that can be instituted upon an area and that also may apply to nonwooded areas" (Price 1965: 377). Without using the word, Price has a sense of the sacral "German forest" not as a physical-cultural "reality" but as an abstract "figure"; moreover, his is a figure that does not simply represent itself, that is, the forest that is out of bounds, but "figures" something else (McLaughlin 1990), in this case an as yet not analyzed taboo. Of the various explanations he ventures, the most promising would appear to be his recognition that forest taboos figured separations, exclusions, boundaries between tribal entities and that they might be conceived as the figural ground for Germanic migrations driven by a search for *culturally* arable land.[12]

With regard to the warrior clubs, Price seems less willing to depart from the realist, symbolic-actionist constructions by which they have maintained a historical presence, but his evidence enables a figural reading—it always being the historian's choice (and risk) of what to call "figure"—by which the warrior clubs figured instead the specific management, by means of a contract authorizing "masked" and, therefore, deniable, unofficial violence, of the socially threatening conflicts inherent in moments of inheritance and dispossession in a particular historical location. The contract between "the dispossessed and then asymmetrically re-connected" (Eric Wolf, correspondence, 18 January 1997) and the "heirs" is revealed by, among other things, differences in funerary forms, by the main communities' subsidizing of the warrior clubs' common table (a metonymic collective inheritance portion that avoids individual accounting), by the warrior clubs' adherence to inheritance-negating escheat and by their practice of terminating the membership of one who came into an inheritance. In the light of these specific, differentiating perceptions we can draw a distinction between those forms of organized violence that we might or might not perceive as historical refigurations of the warrior clubs.

We can exclude the consciously retained and invoked memories of Germanic warrior associations that we find in the language surrounding German mercenary gangs (*Landsknechte*), police agents (*Schergen*), executioners' associations (*Henker*), paramilitary organizations (including the SA),[13] and so on—all of whom are, after all, "official" perpetrators of violence—and focus instead on the unofficial and yet ritualized (that is to say misrecognized, *unconscious*) forms that have their own historical life and that surface in the changing historicities of world-turned-upside-down rituals of late medieval and early modern urban and village life, to the village-political "houserunnings" and "deroofings" of the eighteenth and nineteenth centuries (Suter 1985; Blickle 1991; cf. also Sider 1986: 75–80, and passim; Davis 1975). Most interesting, of course, are the rein-ventions of these forms in the twentieth century where we find echoes of them in such resistance youth groups as the *Edelweisspiraten*, who had no difficulty converting their anti-Nazi activities during the Third Reich into resistances against the foreign occupation authorities after the war (Kenkmann 1996: 7). Finally, it is most remarkable that after the "great turn" of 1989–1990, we see yet another upsurge of such forms involving also youth gangs, tacitly abetted vigilante groups connected to neo-Nazi organizations, and, with significant influence on the national political process, gangs of incendiarists and terrorist bombers targeting asylum seekers and immigrants, for whom the murders at Mölln and Solingen have become an indelible sign.[14] We have to recall that these were not acts by isolated fanatics but were committed under the eyes of a passive police and were in effect (tacitly and therefore "deniably") orchestrated by communal, youth, apprentice, athletic, and other groups that were in turn clandestinely connected with and funded by official political party and media organizations (see *Der Spiegel* 47, no. 27 [1993]: 78–81).

IV

To draw these distinctions, we have to be careful not to equate "figuration" with "template" (Eric Wolf, correspondence, 18 January 1997), that is, with a definable form that is consciously imposed by historical actors to shape and give meaning to their actions. David Hunt's (1995) critical appreciation of Eric Wolf's *Peasant Wars of the Twentieth Century* alerts us to this danger in his discussion of the distinction Wolf draws, without fully realizing it in his analysis, between perceiving social and political formations in terms of either a "template" or an "engram." The latter, adapted from physiology and psychol-ogy, Wolf understood as, in Hunt's words, "not just a memory, but a term of process, an alteration of neural tissue occasioning the return of a buried image from the past." However, in his search for a prefiguration of peasant movements during the Vietnam War, Wolf, also in Hunt's view, "misses a treat-ment of plasticity in peasant thinking" as his text "switches from a language of movement ('engrams') to a static representation ... ('templates')" (Hunt 1995: 109–111). In this light, the themes Price explores create an engrammatic opening that is absent from the anthropological histories of Dumézil et al. To illustrate the difference between structural-grammatical and figural-rhetorical narratives, we note that for Price the warrior clubs are not always-already-present "templates" for repeated enactments of merely redemptive violence but are only one form ("engram") in a larger complex of such forms (memory) that orchestrate the, for many, deadly serious "social dance" surrounding the daily experiences and representations of inheritance and dispossession.

Nietzsche's perception about the historian's inevitable curiosity about where the remembered was while it was forgotten is reflected in Carlo Ginzburg's residual perplexity about "the *unconscious* continuity between Germanic myths and aspects of Nazi Germany ... as a phenomenon related neither to race nor to the collective unconscious" (Ginzburg 1989: 145). To solve the problem we can perceive figurations as the mechanisms of a social (i.e., not necessarily "collective") unconscious, with the warrior clubs appearing as only one form in which dispossession is simultaneously remembered and repressed, that is, in motion through occasionally touching timescapes between both sequential "real" time and contiguous memories in time.

Elias's modeling of this figural process as a social dance is not, as with Turner, one of overriding structuration but rather of multiple and, in terms of time and scale, open-ended and often overlapping and interacting micro-historical moments that allow us to model and compare specific, including *individual*, strategies capable of specific evolution. His is also a multilinear evolution model[15] by which the "variability of human connections" and their respective evolutions may be viewed as repetitions of figuration efforts (as in "court" formations or in formations for and of "dispossession") enacted in their historical uniqueness with differential results and implications (Elias 1983: 3, 9; cf. also Newmark 1988). This allows us to point in passing to some earlier themes of this essay and to enroll the multilinear evolutions of figurations in an analytical project for "infiltrating the defences of rightful meaning." By exposing and undermining the hegemonic presence in figured social actions, whose forms have been "worn smooth, made invisible" (McLaughlin 1990: 85–86), such a project aligns itself well with the resistances rhetoric offers against the naturalizing logics of both metaphor and of the grammars of metonymic displacements. It thereby helps us carry out that step in historical scientific analysis by which metonymic denial and distancing can be converted into and revealed as linked proxies, as synecdoche.

Norbert Elias's notion of a "figuration" perceives "cycles of violence" not as a temporary descent into the abyss of *communitas* but rather as a possible devolution, a "descent," into "reciprocal," perpetual, and terminal destructions among partners in a social relationship (Mennell 1989: 88–89). This perception of foundational social contracts and their possibly catastrophic historical unfolding opens a further space for a historical narrative about the experience—without any outright or necessary objectification—of an "originary" historical-experiential figuration of social relationships, or, more precisely, of dispossession, which I have sought to theorize elsewhere in terms of a "trauma of primary accumulation" (Rebel 1989: 364, and passim). Observing the dis- and rearticulations of figures that simultaneously perform and deny dispossession mechanisms and their auxiliary constructs allows us to override the current opinion that there is never a "moment of origin" and theorize instead a possible Holocaust history in terms of the undetermined structural play of the unfolding displacements of murderous practices of dispossession in Austro-German historical culture

playing out what began as the "determined form of the originary discrimination" (Greenblatt 1988: 7; cf. Farias 1989: 344–345) with *experiences* of "origins"
that may or may not then be constructed as such in history.

The figural narratives about dispossession that I outlined in the 1996 *Focaal*
essay and here in historical repetition of the warrior club forms are grounded
in such experienced origins, appearing as the violently conducted modal rearticulations between kin and tribute forms (in sixteenth- and seventeenth-century Austria, for example) by which tribute-producing family firms managed,
among other things, their inheritance strategies in such a way that a small
minority of heirs could participate in what I call elsewhere the franchise-bid-
ding and labor-hoarding markets of the empire[16] by accumulating, managing, and sheltering their enterprises' surplus, all at the expense of a growing
population of effectually dispossessed siblings and children and in conflict
with a "modernizing," predatory tribute empire. With a view toward opening
a new field of provenances for the Holocaust, it is possible to trace, in turn, the
figures of the social dance surrounding this "structurally necessary" dispossession through different spaces and discourses, that is to say, through the
historically intertwined levels of Austria's social and institutional hierarchies
devolving from a multiethnic tribute formation to a police province in a German fascist empire.

As my 1996 essay outlined, we encounter in this narrative endless metony-
mies, that is, language displacements of and repressive, silencing allusions
to fatal but necessary processes of dispossession. These constituted ironic,
pathetic emplotments in which languages of membership, care, and welfare
signified their opposites as they singled out and became attached to dispossessed persons who were on their way toward administered deaths. We find
a *concealed* duplicity inside publicly structured, even "ritualized," processes
by which certain figurations of language did double duty in simultaneously
identifying and concealing those structurally necessary but dangerous and
unspeakable performances that were purportedly necessary for the life of the
structure. This forces on us a more difficult project.

Viewing the prehistory of the Holocaust from the anthropological history
perspective, one could only ever claim to find merely a single line of structuration moving from historically empty everyday life through increasingly
"virulent" historical crises of collapse and reintegration. We have to agree with
Baudrillard that this threatens to fetishize the Holocaust as a simulation object
that merely conceals a single, originary, deeper trauma (Baudrillard 1994: 44–
45; also Rose 1966). Even if, to a degree, it does on occasion do exactly that, such
a view closes us in a circle where all historical action becomes merely emblematic, a self-redeeming parable. Writing the Holocaust as historical anthropology, on the other hand, perceiving it in terms of a duplicity of inheritance and
dispossession figures, requires a recognition of a structuration dependent on
multiple, interwoven microhistories in everyday life where "systemic" (i.e.,
systematically figured) collapses and reintegrations occur all the time, at any

given and, most often, privately and historically concealed moment. It is there that we will find certain "historically," that is, simultaneously mnemonically and obliviously lived figurations pointing toward organized forms of terminal exclusion and organized disposal. We can also, however, expect to find there attempts, no matter whether "successful" or not, to break out, if only discursively, of such repetitious enactments of organized, known but concealed, endlessly absorbed crimes, to resist the compulsions coming out of the modal-historical, moment-to-moment articulations of the hegemonic bloc as this latter's negotiators and architects select and call into action "ordinary people,"[17] that is, people "without" history, to act as the visible, accusable perpetrators of those widely perceived but staunchly misrecognized genocides that are among the defining moments of the past century as well as of this present age. A counterhegemonic historical anthropology requires a perpetual disclosure of those necessarily absurd and criminally written political economies that put forward and demand realization of hegemonic consensus figures, claiming exclusive possession of the ground of significant discourse, requiring the unquestioned domestic absorption of necessary sacrifices within "unhistorical" everyday social life and, when that threatens to collapse on a large scale, finding new life in culturally managed mass dispossessions, experienced as genocidal visitations by those so selected.

Notes

1. The account of how we came to this usage advanced by Finkelstein (1998: 87–100) points in the wrong direction and should not, in any case, dissuade us from acknowledging the unique qualities of concept, scale, and collective pathology that compel us to recognize this vast civilizational collapse in our collective historical experience as "the Holocaust."

2. And watching the human spectacle from our loges in the clouds of the *posthistoire*. For Rankean comedic emplotment I am following Hayden White's stimulating *Metahistory: The Historical Imagination in Nineteenth-Century Europe* (1973: 166–169, 176–178, and passim); for perspectives on the "posthistoire," see Roth (1995), and Niethammer's satisfying *Posthistoire: Has History Come to an End?* (1992).

3. Weil (1991); another recent attempt at a comedic Holocaust emplotment is Roberto Benigni's controversial and award-winning film *Life is Beautiful*.

4. "Ritual was at once a process of plural reflexivity ... at the social level it was an endeavor to purify relationships of envy, jealousy, hate, undue possessiveness, grudges." Elsewhere: "[T]he stage of Crisis, conflicts between individuals, sections and factions follow the original breach, revealing hidden clashes of character [!], interest and ambition" (Turner 1985: 232, 292). And never a word about the structured and "necessary" and even ritual qualities of the individual and collective breakdowns that constitute the historical (i.e., remembered and, in turn, denied) unfolding of everyday life.

5. Turner (1985: 292); cf. also White (1973: 166–167), and the previous discussion in this essay concerning Ranke's repudiation of the metonymic mode with its predictably mechanistic reversals that are empty of time and hence also of narrative, as witness Sahlins's banal

last words that "the historical process unfolds as a continuous and reciprocal movement between the practice of the structure and the structure of the practice" (1981: 72); translator Ann Smock comments on Blanchot's statement "Let us not believe we have said anything at all with these reversals" by pointing out that "Such expressions have a motionless instability. They reverse, turn back, re-turn without cease, but as though it were ceaselessly that they reached a point of no return" (translator's remarks to Blanchot 1986: viii–ix); and finally, that ultimate reversal requiring only our accepting without asking for explanation: "He gave also their increase unto the caterpillar, and their labor unto the locust" (*Psalms* 78:46).

6. To do otherwise leads to the confusions that mar Finkielkraut (1992: 26–30, and passim). At the outset of this essay I pointed to a current usage of historical discourses about the Holocaust that places *present* holocaust-forms "under erasure." Examining the comedic emplotments that serve such history-tellings, we see a passing recognition of past state-organized political mass murders, as occurred, say, in Pinochet's Chile, segue in a decade or two into framing narratives about redemptive economic and political "success" (*The Newshour with Jim Lehrer*, PBS, 17 April 1998). But as such displacing success stories constitute endlessly the metonymic reminders of the holocaust forms they eternally redeem, they also close off, permanently, any option for moving beyond mourning, for ever questioning the purported "necessities" that authorize and projectively redeem past as well as present genocides and, indeed, those waiting just below the horizon.

7. Some examples of this approach by historians may be found in Wilentz (1985); a historical "school" along these lines announced itself with Hunt (1989).

8. From within either discipline, making the choice between "anthropological history" or "historical anthropology" may appear to be difficult because either choice grants only one discipline the presumed privilege of being the noun, the main thing, and not merely the modifier. For a historian to throw in his lot with "historical anthropology"—as I do even as I attempt to bridge the two—may then appear as a turning away from my "own" profession and as a willingness to accept a subordinate role in an interdisciplinary migration. But the matter is not that simple. While the facts are that for my historical research program I found very few allies among historians and that the opportunities to clear a conceptual ground for it in print were given me by anthropologists, this accounts only in part for my participation in the present collective attempt to conceptualize a historical anthropology. More important is my growing sense that at the present time neither historical nor ethnographic work is generally and sufficiently grounded in the complexities of the different traditions of "philosophical anthropology" (see Habermas 1958), and my predilections may be explained by the fact that I occasionally find such a philosophically serious outlook among the anthropologists but not among the historians. I am thinking of Wolf (1974: 29–33, 47–49, 61, 84, and passim), who develops a specifically historical project that is grounded in Julian Steward's "multilineal evolution" (see Gould 1996) and upholds the creative over the "coded" dimensions of human experience by searching for the historicities of human designs. Finally, as far as the putative subordination of the adjectivized discipline is concerned, I can point to diplomatic historian A. J. P. Taylor's trenchant observation that "weaker" partners tend to control alliances since they can always threaten to collapse. This in turn leads to a resolution of the opposing statements by Maitland and Sahlins, mentioned a moment ago in the text, one that I can live with because, for an alliance between history and anthropology to work, we continue to require a separate historical discipline as a necessary condition. This is to say that anthropology will be historical or it will be nothing.

9. Price summarizes his early work and proposes a larger framework in "Early Places Ending in -*heim* as Warrior Club Settlements and the Role of Soc in the Germanic Administration of Justice" (1981). Among his earlier work we find "The Role of the Germanic Warrior Club in the Historical Process: A Methodological Exposition" (1980), "Die Nibelungen als kriegerischer Weihebund" (1974), "Differentiated Germanic Social Structures" (1969), and "The Germanic Forest Taboo and Economic Growth" (1965). I find the approach taken by

Hedeager (1992: 35, 46, and passim) offers some support for and further contextualizes the implications of Price's argument in a useful way.

10. Höfler apparently himself experienced the "proof" of his functionalist thesis when, in 1936, his work went out of favor with the post-SA Nazi Party as the latter downplayed its "ber-serker" posture (Ginzburg 1989: 140); in this connection, see the view developed in Elias (1996: 227–228).

11. It would be a relatively simple matter to implicate Turner's formulations (cf. Turner 1977: 244–245; cf. Niethammer 1992: 46–49) in the always popular kind of modernist antimod-ernism (pioneered by Rousseau) that would see the Holocaust as a typically "modernist" manifestation, that is, merely as a technologically and mass-culturally hyperextended dis-tortion of formerly balanced processes of cultural life and death.

12. Price (1965: 373–374); interesting along these lines is the conclusion in Weiner (1998).

13. Eric Wolf, correspondence, 18 January 1997. Eric Wolf raises a question in his letter about how to demonstrate the "use" of such groups (this presumably in connection with his then-forthcoming *Envisioning Power: Ideologies of Domination and Crisis* [Berkeley: University of California Press, 2000]. I cannot do justice in this note to the complexity of his questioning as he moves through references to works by Schurz, Lowie, Mühlmann, Wikander, Much, Von Schröder, and so on. which he perceives as grounded in the eighteenth- and nine-teenth-century creation of "a cumulative 'imaginary'" by "politicized literati" of the likes of Justus Möser and Felix Dahn.

14. A good and less well known case in point appears in the court proceedings that disclosed and produced guilty verdicts for the secret activities in 1992 of the town council of Dolgenbrodt when the latter funded several unemployed apprentices' firebombing of a migrant asylum.

15. See note 17 below; also the discussion in Rebel (1998: 199).

16. "German Peasants Under the Austrian Empire," manuscript in progress.

17. One historical instance of many being Police Battalion 101 "in action" in Bilgoraj, Poland, in July 1942; see Browning (1982).

References

Baudrillard, J. 1994. *Simulacra and Simulation*. Ann Arbor: University of Michigan Press.

Blanchot, M. 1986. *Writing the Disaster*. Lincoln: University of Nebraska Press.

Blickle, P., ed. 1991. *Landgemeinde und Stadtgemeinde in Mitteleuropa*. Munich: Oldenbourg.

Browning, C. 1982. *Ordinary Men*. New York: HarperCollins.

Butler, J. 1997. *The Psychic Life of Power*. Stanford: Stanford University Press.

Davis, N. Z. 1975. "The Reasons of Misrule." In *Society and Culture in Early Modern France*, 97–123. Stanford Calif.: Stanford University Press.

Elias, Norbert. 1983. *The Court Society*. New York: Pantheon.

———. 1996. *The Germans*. New York: Columbia University Press.

Farias, V. 1989. *Heidegger and Nazism*. Philadelphia: Temple University Press.

Finkelstein, N. 1998. "Reflections on the Goldhagen Phenomenon." In *A Nation on Trial: The Goldhagen Thesis and Historical Truth*, ed. N. Finkelstein and R. Birn. New York: Holt.

Finkielkraut, A. 1992. *Remembering in Vain: The Klaus Barbie Trial and Crimes against Human-ity*. New York: Columbia University Press.

Ginzburg, Carlo. 1989. "Germanic Mythology and Nazism: Thoughts on an Old Book by Georges Dumézil." In *Clues, Myths and the Historical Method*, trans. John and Anne Tedeschi, 126–145. Baltimore: Johns Hopkins University Press.

Goldhagen, D. J. 1996. *Hitler's Willing Executioners: Ordinary Germans and the Holocaust.* New York: Knopf.

Gould, S. 1996. *Full House: The Spread of Excellence from Plato to Darwin.* New York: Harmony.

Greenblatt, S. 1988. *Shakespearean Negotiations: The Circulation of Social Energy in Renaissance England.* Berkeley: University of California Press.

Habermas, J. 1958. "Philosophische Anthropologie. Ein Lexikonartikel." In *Philosophie,* ed. A. Diemer and I. Frenzel, 18–35. Frankfurt am Main: Fisher Lexikon.

Hedeager, L. 1992. *Iron Age Societies: From Tribe to State in Northern Europe, 500 BC to 700 AD.* Oxford: Blackwell.

Hunt, David. 1995. "Prefigurations of the Vietnamese Revolution." In *Articulating Hidden Histories: Exploring the Influence of Eric R. Wolf,* ed. Jane Schneider and Rayna Rapp. Berkeley: University of California Press.

Hunt, L., ed. 1989. *The New Cultural History.* Berkeley: University of California Press.

Kenkmann, A. 1996. "Die wilde Jugend in den Städten." *Die Zeit* 26 (April): 7.

McLaughlin, T. 1990. "Figurative Language." In *Critical Terms for Literary Study,* ed. T. McLaughlin and F. Lentricchia, 80–90. Chicago: University of Chicago Press.

Mennell, S. 1989. *Norbert Elias Civilization and the Human Self-Image.* Oxford: Blackwell.

Newmark, K. 1988. "Editor's Preface." In *Phantom Proxies: Symbolism and the Rhetoric of History,* ed. K. Newmark, iii–vii. New Haven: Yale University Press.

Niethammer, L. 1992. *Posthistoire: Has History Come to an End?* London: Verso.

Price, Arnold. 1965. "The Germanic Forest Taboo and Economic Growth." *Vierteljahrschrift für Sozial- und Wirtschaftsgeschichte* 52, no. 3: 368.

———. 1969. "Differentiated Germanic Social Structures." *Vierteljahrschrift für Sozial und Wirtschaftsgeschichte* 55, no. 4.

———. 1974. "Die Nibelungen als kriegerischer Weihebund." *Vierteljahrschrift für Sozial und Wirtschaftsgeschichte* 61: 199–211.

———. 1980. "The Role of the Germanic Warrior Club in the Historical Process: A Methodological Exposition." *Miscellanea Mediaevalia* 12, no. 2.

———. 1981. "Early Places Ending in -*heim* as Warrior Club Settlements and the Role of Soc in the Germanic Administration of Justice." *Central European History* 14: 187–199.

Rebel, Hermann. 1989. "Cultural Hegemony and Class Experience: A Critical Reading of Recent Ethnological-Historical Approaches. (Part Two)." *American Ethnologist* 16, no. 2: 350–365.

———. 1996. "Disposession in the Communal Memory." *Focaal—European Journal of Anthropology* 26/27: 167–189.

———. 1998. "Peasantries under the Austrian Empire, 1300-1800." In *The Peasantries of Europe from the Fourteenth to the Eighteenth Centuries,* ed. T. Scott, 191–225. London and New York: Longman.

Rose, G. 1966. *Mourning Becomes the Law: Philosophy and Representation.* Cambridge: Cambridge University Press.

Roth, M. 1995. "The Nostalgic Nest at the End of History." In *The Ironist's Cage.* New York: Columbia University Press.

Sahlins, M. 1981. *Historical Metaphors and Mythical Realities: Structure in the Early History of the Sandwich Islands Kingdom.* Ann Arbor: University of Michigan Press.

———. 1985. *Islands of History.* Chicago: University of Chicago Press.

Sider, G. 1986. *Culture and Class in Anthropology and History: A Newfoundland Illustration.* Cambridge: Cambridge University Press.

Strohm, S. 1998. *Die Gnosis und der Nationalsozialismus.* Frankfurt am Main: Suhrkamp.

Suter, A. 1985. *"Troublen" im Fürstbistum Basel, 1726–1740.* Göttingen: Vandenhoeck & Ruprecht.

Turner, Victor. 1977. *The Ritual Process: Structure and Anti-Structure.* Ithaca: Cornell University Press.

———. 1985. *On the Edge of the Bush: Anthropology as Experience.* Tucson: University of Arizona Press.

Weil, J. 1991. *Mendelssohn Is on the Roof.* New York: Farrar Straus Giroux.

Weiner, D. 1998. *A Little Corner of Freedom: Russian Nature Protection from Stalin to Gorbachev.* Berkeley: University of California Press.

White, Hayden. 1973. *Metahistory: The Historical Imagination in Nineteenth-Century Europe.* Baltimore: Johns Hopkins University Press.

Wilentz, S., ed. 1985. *Rites of Power: Symbolism, Ritual and Politics since the Middle Ages.* Philadelphia: University of Pennsylvania Press.

Wolf, E. 1974. *Anthropology.* New York: Nelson.

———. 1977. "Encounter with Norbert Elias." In *Human Figurations: Essays for Norbert Elias,* ed. P. Gleichmann, J. Goudsblom, and H. Korte, 28–35. Amsterdam: Amsterdam Sociologisch Tijdschrift.

Chapter Four

Beyond the Limits of the Visible World
Remapping Historical Anthropology

August Carbonella

When you go into the street, history begins. The headlines tie your hands and put you against the wall; or they arm you with little bottles of vitriol and tell you when to throw. Civil war in China. Starvation in Puerto Rico. Third day of the longshore strike. You are beyond the limits of the visible world now.

— Thomas McGrath, *This Coffin Has No Handles*

Introduction: Community as Claim

Anthropologists, it seems, return anew to the question of scale at least once in every generation. For illustrative purposes this question can be posed in a couple of ways. Should we study communities as isolated microcosms or as small replicas of national or global entities? To what degree, if any, do villagers represent larger class or social formations? These variants of the scale question, while sharply drawn, indicate a lingering tendency among anthropologists to tacitly attribute a remarkable degree of coherence and solidity to communities. Herein lies the problem. The way we pose the question automatically reifies both the locus and focus of analysis. A historically informed anthropology should begin with modes of inquiry that allow us to view communities as social constructions that involve varying degrees of tactical power, control over labor processes, cultural coherence, and openness and closure.

A more appropriate analytical starting point would view the community as a claim advanced to solidify and structure highly disparate processes within a single field of dominance.[1] Claims to community are almost always tied to wider sources of political, moral, and organizational power. It is in the connections between and among these relational fields that we find an adequate focus of analysis for a historicized anthropology and social history, not in some predetermined, bounded territorial unit.

Eric Wolf, who throughout his career steadfastly resisted the temptation to either draw artificial boundaries around communities or fix them as cases for taxonomic comparison, has developed the perspective advanced here most significantly.[2] This was clear even in his earliest attempts to elaborate a comparative typology of peasant communities. In numerous comments on closed corporate peasant communities, Wolf argued that they were historically constructed in the struggle between the colonial states' demands for labor power and the locally specific ways those demands were negotiated, accommodated, or refused (Wolf 1955, 1957, 1986). Central to his argument was the understanding that communal cultural traditions and institutions operated within multiple relational fields. To take a well-known example, communal institutions of reciprocal exchange in Mesoamerica were explored in terms of their embeddedness in religious fiestas that were revitalized, if not reinvented, by colonial states. These fiestas were the principal means of demonstrating membership in the community, and thus served to heighten localist affinities and identities. This cultural localism bolstered the geographical isolation of villagers forcefully settled into nucleated communities. At the same time, the exchange and redistribution of labor and services that took place during the fiestas contributed to indebtedness for some members of the community and enhanced wealth and prestige for others. Wolf linked this social differentiation to a spiral of dependence and authority through which tribute payments and seasonal labor for colonial mining and agricultural enterprises were secured. For Wolf, then, traditions in the closed corporate communities were a major locus of contradiction, serving both as mechanisms of incorporation into wider political and economic fields and as the forcing ground of a shared sense of *communitas*.

Even more, Wolf proposed that the resilience of communal traditions was only partly explained by the way they both sustained and masked relations of power. To reinforce this point, he contextualized and understood communal traditions within a particular geography of colonialism, as illustrated by his analytical interweaving of localism and isolation. Localist sentiments and affinities characteristic of the closed corporate community provided a mythic alter image to their enforced isolation. Isolation, in turn, reinforced villagers' subjection and dependence on the state by channeling and circumscribing their participation in wider commodity and labor markets. This constructed geography of colonialism, then, both expressed and structured the fundamental social relationships and orientation of community members.

Writing some thirty years before the renewed interest in spatial analysis in the 1980s, Wolf's seminal innovation in these early essays was to link the production of social geographies to the making of histories. While this linkage ultimately undermined his own search for typological comparison, because each community was formed and transformed within uniquely configured fields,[3] he did not retreat into a particularistic anthropology that treats communities as isolated microcosms. In a remarkably coherent body of work spanning forty years, Wolf scrutinized the wider webs of connection and power that shape a community's involvement with various forms of capital, state, and political organizations.[4]

In what follows I want to suggest the importance of Wolf's analytical framework for expanding the parameters of working-class studies within anthropology and social history, an expansion that I hope will simultaneously help move us beyond our mutual, lingering dependence upon reified notions of community. Many anthropologists and social historians focus on class cultures within particular communities. While it may be argued that the localized studies of working-class culture common to much social history and historical anthropology enable a 'bird's-eye' view of everyday resistance, our historical understanding will be greatly diminished if these studies are not tied to a more nuanced examination of the power-laden processes that produced these communities in the first place. Communities, I will argue, are mapped in constant relation to wider hegemonic projects, forms of rule, and/or oppositional movements. It is within and against these intersecting processes, operating across multiple relational fields, that local identities and differences are formed and reformed. Although I sympathize with the political impulse in historical anthropology and social history that continually energizes the search for local sites of resistance, I find the corresponding, if implicit, assumption (hope?) that the histories, cultures, and identities that sustain resistance are somehow outside of reigning hierarchies, ideologies, and incorporative pressures to be politically and theoretically disabling. What needs to be addressed, instead, is the contested production of particular geographies of power, and the possibilities for subaltern maneuver and resistance that exist within and beyond them (see Hardt and Negri 2000; G. Smith 1999).

Localism and Isolation: The Making of a Fordist Geography

We can begin by exploring the transformations of territory and tradition that sustained and naturalized Fordist social relations in the United Stated during the 1920s and 1930s. As Antonio Gramsci perceptively argued almost seventy years ago, the hegemony of Americanism and Fordism was established "by a skillful combination of force (destruction of working-class trade unionism on a territorial basis) and persuasion (high wages, various social benefits, and extremely subtle ideological and political propaganda)" (1971: 285). Significant here—but habitually overlooked in the literature—is Gramsci's identification of *force* with the construction of a particular geography of power. Many social scientists and historians have attributed the rise of a new culture of Fordism to the internalization of consumer values by the working class.[5] This argument short-circuits the historical struggles that were necessarily involved in establishing the integration of mass production, mass consumption, and the high-wage economy.[6] An anthropologically richer understanding of the transformation of working-class culture during the rise of Fordism is suggested by Gramsci's emphasis on the production of a new social geography. Gramsci's rather elliptical remarks can be clarified and deepened through a reading of some recent studies of the territorialization of power essential to the reconfiguration of community as a Fordist relation of production.[7]

The battle to install Americanism and Fordism opened with a series of strikes throughout the country that were provoked by industrialists in the late 1910s and early 1920s. Workers walked off their jobs *en masse* to protest monopoly capital's implementation of the American Plan, which was a series of fairly coordinated strategies to weaken or destroy autonomous unions.[8] From management's viewpoint, the American Plan could be regarded as highly successful. First, the open shop drive solidified corporate control over the labor process and eliminated the lines of communication and organization that linked dispersed working-class communities. The destruction of these geographical linkages isolated working-class communities and left workers with few resources to protest the increasing regulation of work, family, and social life.[9]

Second, the elaboration of localist ideologies and the idealization of purportedly traditional American community values by corporations and the mass media reinforced the isolation of working-class communities.[10] This ideological persuasion aimed to sublimate the recent history and memory of class warfare in many localities and to delegitimize the notion of class in popular discourse. At stake was capital's ability to control the absenteeism, blue Mondays, wildcat strikes, high rates of labor mobility, and other disruptive labor practices characteristic of the earliest stages of mass production. Although these forms of protest may have seemed like the result of a spontaneous anarchy to unsympathetic observers, they were in fact made possible by both the formal and informal networks and movements of laborers.[11] Despite their radically different philosophies, mixed locals of the International Workers of the World (IWW) and American Federation of Labor (AFL) regional networks of labor councils coordinated the movements of a mobile working class and helped create a distinct working-class political culture.[12] Although divisions and marginalizations certainly did occur within working-class communities and between regions, the political culture that united them posed major difficulties for corporate and state hegemony. The destruction of these informal and institutional networks was, therefore, crucial to monopoly capital's effort to make "the whole life of the nation revolve around production," to use Gramsci's apt phrasing (1971: 285).

While the American Plan represented a remarkable attempt to give unity and coherence to monopoly capitalists' varied strategies of labor control, it took on regionally specific textures and appearances as corporate managers and local media mythologized aspects of regional landscapes and history to consolidate their hold over particular communities. As Mike Davis discovered in the case of Los Angeles, a brutal and long-lasting campaign to destroy unionism by a cohort of the city's leading industrialists and businessmen was complemented by the elaboration of a romantic myth in which the city was represented as an enormous (Mediterraneanized New England) village devoid of racial and class tensions. Davis argues compellingly that this idealized utopia entered the "material landscape as a design for speculation and domination" (Davis 1991: 23). The design of working-class housing and the pattern of land use, for instance, reflected the powerful influence of this myth. This formula for inserting a middle-class sensibility into the most habitual experiences of everyday life captured the imagination of cultural critics across the political spectrum. Writers, journalists, and publicists that Davis associates with boosterism saw in the new Los Angeles a materialist pedagogy of democracy. On the other hand, Los Angeles's landscape has also proved an enduring source of leftist pessimism, prophetically framed by Horkeimer and Adorno as they surveyed with horror the bungalow-filled landscape in the 1940s, positing it as proof that the proletariat's "world historic mission" was now absorbed into a family based consumerism (Davis 1991: 48).

The mythic elaboration of the New England village provides another example of the unique configuring of communities during the implementation of the American Plan. As Margaret Crawford shows in *Building the Workingman's Paradise*, some Northeast industrialists collaborated with urban designers to build simulacra of picturesque New England villages as part of a wider effort to mythologize supposedly pre-industrial cultural values, such as individualism, industry, thrift, and middle-class familialism. Inscribing middle-class values into the social landscape simultaneously repressed working-class cultural and political forms, particularly the "un-American" collectivist practices and discourses associated with newly arrived immigrants and an emergent industrial unionism (Crawford 1995: 112). Nowhere in these new garden cities was there any space for union halls or labor-sponsored working-class gatherings. Moreover, the picturesque New England village became a central symbol of "American" values in manifold expressions of a new, mass-mediated, national popular culture (Löfgren 1995; Meinig 1979).

Similarly, absentee-owned mining and lumber companies in Appalachia were instrumental in constructing a folk myth that tied traditional mountain culture to craft production and "hillbilly" music. David Whisnant, in his wonderfully provocative *All That Is Native and Fine*, usefully contrasts an example of the corporate-sponsored construction of a "mountain folk" with forms of working-class cultural production that were forcefully suppressed:

> Instead of filling a "folk" museum with old-timey things from an era long since mostly disappeared, Commonwealth established a "museum of social change," to be filled with such things as lynch ropes, photographs of the idle rich at Atlantic City,

strike relics, and a "plush [Episcopalian] collection bag with gilt pole" promised by H. L. Mencken. Instead of the Victorian Christmas play produced at the folk school each year, playwright Lee Hays (a later organizer of the politically radical Almanac Singers) formed the Commonwealth Players to produce labor-oriented plays such as *One Bread, One Body* (1937). Meanwhile, Campbell Folk School students were writing and producing short "folk" plays. *Get Up and Bar the Door* (1935) was set in a one-room mountain cabin and featured Sal and Hickory Perkins ("By cracky, Sal, we had better roll the punkins under the bed, for they'll shore freeze in the hen-roost afore mornin'"). (Whisnant 1983: 177)[13]

As Whisnant's comparison suggests, all these mythologized traditions and landscapes omit a violent history of labor struggles, like the West Virginia Coal Wars of 1921—to take an Appalachian example—that ended with the killing of a few score miners by the U.S. Army and state militia and charges of treason for some 350 surviving miners (Brecher 1972: 101–143).[14] Indeed, an elaborate reworking of the past was central to the shaping of these disparate localisms, which, in turn, had a dramatic impact on class relations. They stifled class-based expressions of culture within specific localities and reinforced the cultural differences of workers from different regions.

The effort to transform working-class culture and politics did not end with the elaboration of these regionally specific localisms. Public space within communities was more tightly controlled, as corporate managers, social reformers, and police sought to make the streets and public meeting places safe for respectable pursuits and rational recreations.[15] In many communities, corporations or local governments colonized the educational, cooperative, and leisure activities that had been run by unions and workers. In a similar fashion, the private spaces of home and family life were increasingly the targets of corporate rationality. Corporate sociology departments, like that found in Ford's Highland Park factory, sent social workers and nurses to instruct workers and their families on the more rational way of conducting social and family life that was demanded in modern industrial society (Gartman 1986: 206–209; Meyer 1981). This instruction tied corporate notions of rationality to the core values of Americanism. In yearly "citizenship" competitions held in many localities, for example, citizens' committees that were frequently headed or sponsored by corporate managers rated the cleanliness and neatness of homes and yards.[16] The linkage of home ownership, "rational" family life, and good citizenship became a favorite theme of both the Hoover and Roosevelt administrations (Cross 1993: 169). Family, community, and patriotism were, therefore, elevated as the touchstones of a new corporate culture at the same time that alternative moralities, practices, and understandings were forcefully marginalized.[17]

New Deal labor legislation ultimately provided the political and judicial framework for the consolidation of the Fordist social system. This is well illustrated by the way the family was institutionalized as the key nexus of Fordist social relations (see, among others, Aglietta 1979). The 1935 Wagner Act effectively socialized the wage contract for workers in the core mass production industries by linking wage gains to increases in social productivity. The elimination of arbitrary wage competition reduced the deflationary pressures on wages and gradually integrated the core working class into the culture of mass consumption.[18] Consequently, family wage payments, although for many years more ideological than actual, situated the socially and politically reconstructed family at the center of Fordism as the integrating link of production and consumption (Clarke 1991: 96).

More significantly, perhaps, the Wagner Act created a codified system of decentralized labor relations that solidified the political and geographical isolation of different sectors of the working class. This potential was made clear in the debates that preceded the final drafting of the bill. Congressman Gildea, the democratic representative from Pennsylvania, succinctly captured the mood of many opponents of Wagner's initial proposals: "The amendment (Wagner-Coonery disputes bill) strikes a damaging blow against unions which labor through its own efforts has created and degenerates into an extension of the Government-union idea, one union for each plant" (quoted in the epigraph to Clark 1989). Even conservative labor leaders seemed keenly aware of the dangers of the government-sponsored legislation. AFL president William Green stated his objection early in 1934:

> Elections in individual plants supported by the National Labor Board should not be confused with real collective bargaining. We must recognize that over and above the National Industrial Recovery Act and the National Labor Board, there is a need for organizations of workers on a basis at least as wide as the organization of employers in trade associations for code making and code enforcement. In the long run we must look to independent organizations of workers on a national or international basis for real collective bargaining. (Quoted in Tomlins 1985: 124–125)

Despite these objections, the Wagner Act's passage created the legal infrastructure for the decentralization of labor relations by industry and community. The procedures of collective bargaining and union representation were all tied to local-level negotiations and elections (see Herod 1998). At the economic level, monopoly firms increasingly manipulated this system to play one locality off another in their attempts to secure higher productivity and control, if not lower wages. At the political level, a primary effect of decentralization was the often profound indifference of workers in one location to the plight of workers in other localities. The homogenizing tendencies inherent in the socialization of the wage contract, at least for core workers, thus had the ironic effect of increasing territorial divisions and antagonisms.

The articulation of new state-sanctioned forms of labor organization with corporate cultural campaigns produced a rather distinctive geography, which continues to limit the span of working-class action to this day. It is important to note here the historically brutal spatial isolation or *ghettoization* that the working class and poor people of color were increasingly subjected to within this

Fordist geography (see Davis 2000; Horne 1997a; Marable 2000). Indeed, the impact of the racial, political, and geographical isolation of different segments of the working class produced during the reign of Fordism is now increasingly apparent as capital investment is moved from one location to another, at often dizzying speeds, by firms looking for the most advantageous business and labor-management environments. Ironically, organized labor's inability to develop an adequate response to post-Fordism's "furious mix of different forms of exploitation" (Negri 1996: 164) and marginalization can be partially explained by its continued containment within this Fordist geography.[19]

Our prevailing theoretical models of class formation render opaque the historical and social construction of this landscape of power. Ira Katznelson's (1993) stimulating and ambiguous attempt to link spatial analysis to the history of class formation, for instance, winds up reifying both space and class through his identification of a necessarily expressive relationship between the nineteenth-century class-segregated city and working-class politics. Similarly, Frederic Jameson's important discussion of the rise and fall of Detroit's League of Revolutionary Black Workers in the 1960s assumes the homologous unity of working-class politics and the city form itself, which leads him to attribute the decline of this dynamic organization to its leaders' misguided, in his view, efforts to "accede to a larger spatial plane" (Jameson 1991: 414).[20] This unproblematic linking of class formation and locality obscures the shifting historical and geographical matrices of working-class culture and politics. Furthermore, it inadvertently naturalizes what has been a critical mode of political incorporation during the modern age: the construction of identities tied explicitly to a particular locality—identities, to put it differently, that deny the idea of a *class belonging* across several places and identities.[21] A more flexible approach is therefore required to move us beyond the bounded geography of communities to the multiple, connected spatialities of class.

The Isolated Mass Worker Revisited

As we have seen, the construction of a Fordist geography simultaneously channeled and circumscribed the actions of different segments of the working class and increased the opportunities for capital accumulation. This power-laden geography centered on the enforced isolation of dispersed working-class communities, which involved the elimination of a whole chain of communicative and organizational networks within and between localities. Continued reproduction of the Fordist social system and of a Fordist working class depended crucially on this command of space.[22]

Enforced isolation of the working class has not been unique to the United States. Rather, as Goran Therborn (1983) reminds us in his comparative study of class in different national contexts, it is a central hegemonic process. Therborn's evidence suggests that the study of class formation should include an analysis of the political and cultural power brought to bear in securing the isolation of different working populations. It may be fair to say, though, that historical anthropologists and social historians are generally less interested in how power works than in detailing resistance to it.[23] Many contemporary studies of class simply bracket out the mechanisms involved in installing and maintaining hegemonic projects. Consequently, isolation is often mistaken for autonomy and posited as the basis of working-class resistance and militancy.

Kerr and Siegel first theorized the relationship between isolation and militancy in the early 1950s. Working within the paradigm of modernization theory, they developed the concept of the isolated mass worker to explain the persistent militancy in certain working-class communities, particularly those inhabited by miners, loggers, and longshoremen. They viewed militant workers as not fully modern, by which they meant not sufficiently "middle-class." According to Kerr and Siegel (1954), the continued isolation of workers in communities with their own cultural codes, myths, and forms of association accounts for this incomplete socialization. Isolation simultaneously insulated these communities from middle-class institutions and ideological pressures, and facilitated a vigorous culture of opposition to colonial-like authorities and employers. This perspective raises many questions. Can longshoremen working in the busy international port of San Francisco realistically be seen as isolated from dominant social institutions? Even more, can the concept of an isolated mass worker best explain the geographically discontinuous and historically variable relationship between local working-class communities and what Raymond Williams has called "the high working class tradition, leading to democracy, solidarity in the unions, socialism" (quoted in Sparks 1996: 99). I will deal with these questions more adequately below. For the moment, I want simply to emphasize the hidden but rather striking correspondence between this classic use of modernization theory and the moral economy approach so prevalent in contemporary social history and anthropology.

Similarities between the theory of the isolated mass worker and moral economy arguments are most apparent in James Scott's ethnography of plantation workers in Malaysia (1985: 321).[24] Indeed, the language is almost identical. Scott argues that the plantation workers often live outside the cities where the "agencies of hegemony" are located, enabling the creation of cultural practices and narratives that sustain resistance to the dominant culture. Like Kerr and Siegel, Scott equates geographical isolation with cultural and discursive insulation and, by extension, the potential for militancy. Moral economy arguments are not limited to such peripheral settings, however. Notions of cultural insularity and isolation are frequently used to explain the experience of urban industrial workers. In this case, it is often the residual rural traditions of newly proletarianized workers that are posited as the basis of resistance to capitalism. Herbert Gutman, one of the most eloquent proponents of this viewpoint, argued that the "pre-modern" cultural values and communal loyalties of immigrant workers served as the basis of resistance to exploitation and the harsh conditions of industrial labor (1977: 1–78). Roy Rosenzweig (1983), in an influential study of working-class leisure practices in a New England industrial community, similarly maintained that local immigrant groups drew upon a coherent ethnic consciousness and culture to keep an emergent consumer culture at arm's length.

There is much to admire in the often-nuanced analyses of moral economists. Scholars working within this tradition frequently provide detailed accounts of the local subaltern traditions and customs (kinship structures, neighborhood associations, and mutual aid networks). Yet a couple of criticisms can be advanced here. First, moral economy interpretations of the thickness and multiplicity of ties within working-class communities are often framed within the oppositional premodern/modern couplet. Where modernization theorists equated the supposedly premodern with backwardness, moral economists frequently equate it with resistance. In both instances, culture is reduced to a bounded, static possession of a particular group, whose members remain always outside of the hierarchically organized forms of modern culture and ideology. Not surprisingly, neither paradigm has been able to adequately explain historical change.[25] Second, moral economy's focus on the social ties of community frequently comes at the expense of an investigation of their shifting relationship to that "high working class tradition" that Raymond Williams has identified as crucial to an understanding of the working class. The point here is not to privilege supralocal forms of class affiliation over local class cultures, but to argue that local working classes necessarily exist in a state of continuing tension (relationship, influence, and possibly antagonism) with larger class formations. It is this tension between the local and supralocal that is frequently targeted for attack or exploited by new hegemonic projects. It thus provides a window into the larger fields of force that shape and transform working-class cultural forms.

Remapping Working-Class Cultures and Histories

Eric Hobsbawm's (1984) attempt to map the spatial/temporal matrices of English working-class formation provides an opening for a more relational and processual historical anthropology.[26] Hobsbawm's engagement with E. P. Thompson's classic work, *The Making of the English Working Class* (arguably the definitive moral economy text), inserts the issue of territorialization into a cultural Marxism concerned almost exclusively with historical processes and metaphors. Although Hobsbawm's formulations cannot be appropriated for the U.S. context without some revision and expansion, his exploration of the historical geography of class is of great theoretical consequence. Specifically, it allows the study of class to be placed within a wider framework of hegemonic power.

Simply stated, Hobsbawm argues that the modern English working class was "made" after 1870, not in the first decades of the nineteenth century, as

E. P. Thompson would have it. More is at stake here than a disagreement over periodization. A brief review of Thompson's argument is, therefore, necessary to contextualize Hobsbawm's critique. Thompson stressed the residual but active presence of artisanal and agrarian community values and traditions in the shaping of an emergent working class's experience and consciousness. He argued that these cultural traditions enabled emergent working classes to critically evaluate their new conditions and to struggle against them. It was within this process of evaluation and struggle that the working class *made* itself, to use Thompson's richly evocative phrasing. Tradition, in Thompson's usage, is an active force in the shaping of class consciousness. This reworking of the notion of tradition, from a passively inherited cultural trait to an active social force, has been enormously useful both for anthropologists concerned with historicizing their discipline and historians looking to uncover the cultural dynamics of class formation. However, Thompson's formulation of tradition and, by extension, class consciousness as the lived experience of community points to a major methodological shortcoming. Although Thompson's own historical evidence points to the tentative emergence of a sense of class belonging across several places and identities, his implicit assumption that a single community is a small replica of a class and can be studied in isolation marginalizes forms of supralocal affiliation and association.[27]

This is the point of entry for Hobsbawm's critique. Hobsbawm argues that the study of class formation should aim to show how workers in discrete communities are able (or not) to overcome their isolation or provincialism, as he prefers, and form themselves into a class. This, he claims, was not possible during the early nineteenth century. For Hobsbawm, the world of early-nineteenth-century labor was constituted by a collection of largely isolated and self-contained "microcosms" that were unable to transform themselves into a national phenomenon. The transformation of segmented working populations into a national class became possible only at the end of the nineteenth century, as a result of the growing concentration of both capital and labor, the rise of an interventionist state, and the corresponding widening of mass politics and trade unionism.

While Thompson captures brilliantly the historicity of class, Hobsbawm contextualizes the making of class within both time and space. The English working classes of the early nineteenth century certainly experienced the effects of capitalist exploitation, and they elaborated their demands for a more just society in the language of communal and artisanal traditions. But, according to Hobsbawm, class formation—the making of *a* working class—became possible only later, with the growing geographical linkages of trade unions and the Labour Party in the last quarter of the century. Hobsbawm's emphasis on the webs of connection among and between localities directs our attention to two intersecting components of class: a *local dimension*, manifest in particular working-class cultures; and a *wider spatial dimension,* manifest in supralocal lines of affiliation and association. This immediately forces us to think about the historically specific ways that these two dimensions of class become articulated or disarticulated.

Hobsbawm himself does not explore this question. Although Hobsbawm identifies the relationship between the growth of national labor organizations and the transformation of working-class culture, he does not further interrogate how this connection may be broken or mediated by capital and the state. Nonetheless, his identification of this articulation provides a historical perspective capable of posing such questions. It enables us to think about class as a continual process of formation and reformation—centered on the construction and destruction of political cultures—within a web of constraint and possibility.

Two ethnographic studies may serve to expand and deepen this point, while picking up the thread of the earlier discussion of localism and isolation. David Cohen's "The Production of History" (1994) and William Pilcher's *The Portland Longshoremen* (1972) offer sharply divergent perspectives on the politics of historical memory and forgetting in two working-class communities. Yet taken together, they suggest the importance of the wider spatial dimension of class in shaping discrete working-class cultures.

Cohen's study is a wide-ranging discussion of historical memory and forgetting in the textile city of Lawrence, Massachusetts. Cohen's reconstruction centers on the family history of Camella Teoli, who, at the age of thirteen, was scalped while tending a cotton thread-making machine, causing her to be hospitalized for several months. Shortly after Camella returned home, a citywide strike closed down Lawrence's textile mills for two months. The 1912 textile strike, as it was called, immediately captured national public attention. The arrests of the IWW poet Arturo Giovannitti and labor organizer Joe Ettor on false murder charges provoked massive support demonstrations in many cities. Travelling "Wobbly" lecturers toured the country, spreading news of the strike through their talks on the labor council circuit.[28] Press coverage of the strike was also constant. Mass-mediated images of the city's children being shipped out of town on trains to safer havens, and the rough interventions of the police in this mass juvenile exodus, fostered intense national interest in and discussion of the strike. Concentrated scrutiny of the treatment of children in the city's mills followed. All eyes, it seemed, turned to thirteen-year-old Camella. She was summoned to testify before Congress on the abuses of the child laborers in the city. As a result of her appearance before Congress, Camella immediately became a media sensation; her picture and story were featured in national newspapers and magazines. Camella's ensuing notoriety is the leitmotif that anchors Cohen's story of historical forgetting, a story that is at once enormously suggestive and false: suggestive because it foregrounds the pressures and privations to which working-class memory is subject; false, because Cohen mistakes enigmatic and reticent responses with actual forgetting (see Sider 1996).

Cohen's story actually begins in the 1970s with the arrival in Lawrence of noted *Village Voice* journalist Paul Cowan to gather material for an article on working-class electoral politics. Cowan's interest was piqued by George Wallace's apparent success among descendants of the 1912 textile strike. Cowan was well known for his ability to create expansive historical metaphors from the experiences of a single person, family, or neighborhood.[29] Cowan's search for a fitting metaphor to frame the story of Lawrence led him to Camella, or rather to her daughter Josephine, since Camella had died a number of years before. To his professed shock, Josephine supposedly informed Cowan that she knew nothing of her mother's congressional testimony or of her injury, for that matter, despite the fact that Josephine supposedly combed her mother's hair into a bun to cover the scar and bald spot every morning until she died. This ritualized, and possibly invented, interaction between mother and daughter supplied the perfect metaphor for the story Cowan wanted to tell about the erasure of the past.

In recasting Cowan's story, Cohen sets out to interrogate the relationship between private memory and public representation, and its implication for the transmission of working-class experience and memory from one generation to the next. These are crucially important questions. But Cohen—like Cowan before him—starts with a purely psychological notion of memory or, in this case, forgetting. In this reading, the historical memory of the 1912 textile strike as well as Camella's injury, congressional testimony, and notoriety were lost to a psychological repression occurring within her family as much as within the dominant society. This familial repression is viewed largely as a reaction to an ascendant discourse of Americanism and the subsequent shame felt by descendants of immigrants in their own culture. Underlying this reading is a celebratory, if qualified, invocation of the historian as a redeemer of a pristine historical memory, a memory that leads eventually to a "popular uprising" of history production.

But Cohen's own evidence supports another interpretation, one that gets at the stultification of political energies following the textile strike of 1912. First, the IWW, which organized the strike and provided its chief spokespersons, left no institutional presence in Lawrence once the strike ended. Although the reasons for this are not clear, the subsequent organizational vacuum was quickly filled by a cohort of Catholic priests, local industrialists, and politicians, who constructed a repressive localist discourse and culture. In the weeks and months following the strike, the dominant cohort organized public demonstrations against the radical and "atheistic" leaders of the strike. Cohen approvingly quotes Cowan's interpretation of these demonstrations: "most of the strike organizers and most of the journalists had left town. Local people, abandoned by the outsiders, were forced to choose between the IWW and God, between being regarded as patriots or as un-Americans. And suddenly, the insurgents, not the conditions in the mills, were the main issue in Lawrence" (Cohen 1994: n.p.).[30]

Cohen's whole analysis is based on the assumption that working-class residents of Lawrence ultimately accepted this choice, though it is not at all clear why the city's undoubtedly large concentration of Italian anticlericals, to take an obvious example, would accept this interpretation. What can be assumed from this very public process of defining communal "insiders" and "outsiders," however, is the active marginalization and suppression of the means, forms, and outlets for workers to construct and sustain an alternative social vision. Without an alternative discursive framework, the memories of the 1912 strike were no doubt subject to extreme pressures and privations. This does not mean that they were forgotten, but that there was no working-class institutional space in which they could be made culturally and politically available. Josephine's reticence to speak about her mother's accident and notoriety to Cowan—a stranger—is, thus, readily understandable. She had not *forgotten* her history, as Cohen suggests. A number of remarks Josephine made to Cowan indicate that she was painfully aware of it. Rather, she had no way to *talk* about it, that is, no way to proudly claim it.

William Pilcher's ethnography, *The Portland Longshoreme* (1972) demonstrates how essential was a vibrant political culture, sustained and reproduced by its organizational ties to working classes in other port cities, to the social production of memory among the city's dockworkers. Working within the framework of the community studies tradition in anthropology, Pilcher's main concern is with the institutional mechanisms of social cohesion. Nonetheless, he offers a persuasive account of the intimate relationship between history, geography, and politics among Portland's dockworkers in the 1970s. According to Pilcher, the key institution of this "dispersed community" was the local union of the International Longshoreman's and Warehousemen's Union (ILWU). The cohesive capabilities of the union were given by its control of hiring and work practices on the docks, and by its role as the political and cultural center of the community. Union control over hiring, for instance, enabled jobs to be handed down from father to son to grandson. The union was thus deeply implicated in what Pilcher called "widely ramified kinship networks" that served to reinforce a sense of collective identity.

The connections between union and generational history were tied together through frequent repetitions of origin myths and legends and in a yearly commemoration of the longshoremen killed on "Bloody Thursday" during the wildcat strike of 1934, in which dockworkers protested both employer abuses and the conservatism of their union. The strike of 1934 had a profound effect on its participants, according to Pilcher, providing them with the sense of having "made" history. But that history was not *lost*, as it was for Camella's children and other working-class people of Lawrence. Instead, their *sense of history—their past*—was continually restated and reworked into a collective history in the *present*. Stories of the heroic deeds of the 1934 strikers, especially the *flying squads* who battled up and down the West Coast to reclaim the docks from police and company guards, were recounted often in hiring halls and lunchrooms. Through these stories, the values of unionism and collectivism were thus rehearsed regularly.

The Bloody Thursday commemoration elevated these stories to the level of public spectacle in a yearly remembrance of one of the strike's key battles. On 5 July 1934, an employer drive to reopen the West Coast docks was countered by a series of pitched raids mounted by the flying squads. Their rapid movement from one dock to another posed an acute control problem for the police and private militias, who ultimately started shooting at the strikers. Several strikers were killed and many more wounded in cities along the Pacific coast. In a massive show of support that helped turn the tide of public opinion, tens of thousands of dockworkers and their supporters marched through the various port cities the next day to protest the killings. The employers conceded defeat, as did the conservative leaders of the union. Out of this struggle emerged the most radical union in the United States, whose lasting power rested on its ability to coordinate the actions of its members all along the West Coast and its control of hiring and work practices in various port cities.[31]

The union's ability to command space was ritually demonstrated every year on 5 July, when all the ports from Washington to California were shut down as dockworkers took part in the commemorative parades and memorial services. The union's "bloody" origins were thereby ritualized and committed to collective memory. These legends and rituals were not simply the mechanisms through which historical memory was transmitted from generation to generation. They were also dramatic demonstrations of a working-class movement's assertion of power through the command of space. They were rituals, then, not just of local history but of a class in formation. As the massive yearly shutdown of Pacific coast docks demonstrates, these class dramas were possible because of the union's strong organizational links between communities.

Concluding Remarks

The importance of localism and isolation to hegemonic projects should now be clear. They are the twin axes around which certain claims to community, history, and morality are advanced and sustained over others. They are the forcing ground of a collective misrepresentation in which partial truths become totalizing and certain possibilities are denied. This is evident from the very different political legacies of Portland, Oregon, and Lawrence, Massachusetts. Therefore, anthropologists and social historians should not reproduce this misrepresentation in their investigative methods or through their analytical frameworks. If we return to Wolf's analytical framework, we discover a focus for anthropology that directs us to the webs of connection between particular social units and actors, and to the networks of power and influence that shape discrete historical outcomes. It is an approach that forces us to reconstruct the influence of multiple relational fields in our efforts to tell a "single" story.

Notes

I have many colleagues and friends to thank for their help and suggestions in the preparation of this essay. Don Kalb, Michael Blim, Michael Hanagan, Jane Schneider, and Gerald Sider carefully read earlier versions of this piece and provided extremely useful comments and suggestions for fleshing out my argument. I have not always taken their advice, as they will undoubtedly note, but I have often done so and with much appreciation. Sharryn Kasmir has a remarkable ability to make the right suggestion at the right time. One of those suggestions was on the importance of Hobsbawm's engagement with E. P. Thompson for rethinking the historical anthropology of the working class. I remain grateful. I am especially grateful to Patricia Musante for the stimulating conversations, editorial advice, and, most importantly, the codevelopment of many of the ideas presented here under my name. It goes without saying, of course, that the blunders remain mine.

1. The notion of community as claim draws on two sources of inspiration: Eric Wolf's use of the concept of society as a claim (1988: 757) and Derek Sayer's parallel use of the concept of the state as a claim (1994: 371). See also Ashraf Ghani's (1995) useful discussion of Eric Wolf's conceptual framework for analyzing power relations.
2. I have taken this point from William Roseberry's (1995) comprehensive overview of the corpus of Wolf's ideas and concepts.
3. This point was first made by Roseberry (ibid.).
4. The essays by Jane Schneider and Ashraf Ghani in the recent tribute to the work of Eric Wolf nicely trace the continuities of his conceptual approach. See Schneider and Rapp 1995.
5. This argument spans different theoretical and disciplinary perspectives, but exhibits a remarkable historical continuity. See Edsforth 1987, Ewen 1976, and Lynd and Lynd 1929.
6. The linkage of these three elements is considered the foundation of Fordism. In addition to Gramsci 1971, see Aglietta 1979, Davis 1986, and Harvey 1989a for informative analyses of the political economy of Fordism.
7. For present purposes, I have found Daniel Nugent's framing of community relations particularly apt, if necessarily incomplete. To quote: "The emergence and transformation … of affinities and identities oriented to a specific locale and related to organization of the labor process underline the way a community may figure as a relation of production" (Nugent 1993: 150).
8. For historical accounts of the American Plan, see Levine 1988 and Montgomery 1987.
9. I also elaborate this point in greater detail in an earlier essay (Carbonella 1992).
10. There is a growing anthropological literature on this topic. See, in particular, Davis 1991, McQuire 1991, Nash 1989, and Pope 1942.
11. Paul Buhle (1995) notes that the articulation of economic, political, and cultural struggles characteristic of the 1910s produced the most singular expression of a revolutionary modernism in the twentieth century. It was during this decade that, as Henri Lefebvre (1991 [1974]) notes, the manifold forms of particularistic power inscribed in space were shattered largely by the forceful entry of the working class onto the global political stage.
12. Useful discussions of these networked mixed locals or labor councils are provided by Kimeldorf 1989, Salerno 1898, and Scontras 1985.
13. Commonwealth refers to Commonwealth College in Polk County, Arkansas, an experimental educational learning environment for working-class students that forged a close link with many southern and national groups such as labor unions, radical student and political alliances, cooperatives, and agricultural reform organizations. The state of Arkansas charged the school's administrators with sedition and closed the school in 1940.
14. Denise Giardina's (1987) novelized account of "the battle of Blair Mountain" provides rich ethnographic insight into the Coal Wars.

15. The transformations of public space are detailed in Carbonella 1992, Clarke 1991, and Pries 1986.

16. Citizens' committees were representative of a growing alliance between corporate managers and local middle classes. See Carbonella 1998.

17. June Nash (1989) examines the historical processes in which these key terms came to express the values of a new corporate hegemony in Pittsfield, Massachusetts.

18. Davis (1986: 112–113) provides a useful discussion of the articulated effect of New Deal legislation and Fordist collective bargaining procedures.

19. During the 1980s, for example, local chapters of the UAW were forced into vigorous wage- and benefit-cutting competitions in an effort to save jobs. See Mann 1987. On the increasing marginalization of the black working class during this period, see Horne (1997a, 1997b) and Marable (2000). The marginalization of Puerto Ricans in the United States from the 1940s to the present is detailed in Davis (2000: 103–110).

20. For a riveting account of this extremely important radical movement, see Georgakas and Surkin 1998.

21. Jacques Ranciere (1994) brilliantly deconstructs the reified spatial logic underlying much social science and historical writing.

22. This section draws on David Harvey's manifold elaborations of a spatialized politics. See, in particular, Harvey 1989a, 1989b, 2000. See also Lefebvre 1991, N. Smith 1990, and Soja 1989.

23. Exceptions do, of course, exist. Eric Wolf's entire corpus of work has been dedicated, as Ashraf Ghani (1995) suggests, to "writing the history of power." Sidney Mintz's (1985) *Sweetness and Power,* Peter Linebaugh's (1991) *The London Hanged,* June Nash's (1979) *We Eat the Mines and the Mines Eat Us,* William Roseberry's (1989) *Anthropologies and Histories,* and Gavin Smith's (1999) *Confronting the Present* all meticulously detail manifold articulations of global and local power and their effect on local working populations. The historical anthropologist Gerald Sider (1996) is concerned with uncovering the variety of ways in which power infiltrates workers' daily lives and then drawing political lessons from that process of discovery. Finally, Don Kalb's (1997) *Expanding Class* examines the variety of ways that "Philipsism"—a Dutch version of Fordism—shaped the experience of the North Brabant working class.

24. Scott also condenses a wide range of historically and geographically differentiated agricultural workers into the single historical category of "peasant," thereby further clouding the issue of historical change. It should be noted that the moral economy approach is highly diverse. See the foundational historical studies of Herbert Gutman (1977) and E. P. Thompson (1966). One might usefully compare the cultural geography of Allan Pred and Michael John Watts (1992) and the German everyday life school to get a sense of the different emphases that obtain within the moral economy literature. For the latter, see Alf Ludke's edited volume, *The History of Everyday Life* (1995), and Eley 1989. Although distancing itself from moral economy approaches by drawing inspiration equally from Foucault and Geertz, the new cultural history re-creates a similar problematic in its search for micro-sites of resistance. See Hunt 1989. Similarly, the liberation ecologies of Arturo Escobar or Richard Peet and Michael Watts draw equally upon the culturalism of James Scott, the literature on place-based social movements, and the terminology of traditional ecology to posit a hazily sketched *local* as the premier site of resistance to globalization. See Escobar 1996 and Peet and Watts 1996.

25. Gareth Stedman Jones (1983: 76–89) usefully explores the tendency of both modernization theorists and the new historians to fall back on ideas of biological or psychological breakdown when explaining historical change.

26. My interpretation of Hobsbawm's critique draws heavily upon Jerry Lembcke's understanding of class formation as constitutive of and constituted by the processes of uneven spatial development and the insights he draws from this for the study of the two dimensions of class that I examine here. See Lembcke 1988.

27. Evidence for an emergent sense of class belonging across several localities and identities surfaces in the inaugural scene of Thompson's book. The first sentence of chapter 1 begins with the "first of the leading rules" of the newly chartered London Corresponding Society: "That the Number of our Members be unlimited." This immediately identifies class as a community of the present and the absent, in Jacques Ranciere's (1994: 92) phrasing. The tension between this expanded sense of class and the idea of class consciousness being rooted in the lived experience of community is never resolved, perhaps explaining the frequently noted difficulty in recouping usable theory from Thompson's historical masterpiece. On this point, see Johnson (1979: 216).

28. In Maine, attendance at talks by these Wobbly lecturers overflowed well beyond the capacity of local labor council halls. See Scontras (1985: 129).

29. I remember a 1970s story in the *Village Voice*, for example, that concentrated on the experience of a small group of orthodox Jews in Manhattan's Lower East Side, which came to represent, in his telling, the Jewish experience in America.

30. I worked from a typescript version of Cohen's study that was distributed to the Fifth International Roundtable in Anthropology and History meeting in Paris, 2–5 July 1986.

31. Very good historical accounts of the strike can also be found in Kimeldorf 1988 and Nelson 1990.

References

Aglietta, Michel. 1979. *A Theory of Capitalist Regulation: The US Experience.* New York: Verso Press.

Brecher, Jeremy. 1972. *Strike: The True History of Mass Insurgence in America from 1877 to the Present.* San Francisco: Straight Arrow Books.

Buhle, Paul M. 1995. *A Dreamer's Paradise Lost: Louis C. Fraina/Lewis Cory (1892–1953) and the Decline of Radicalism in the United States.* Atlantic Highlands, NJ: Humanities Press International.

Carbonella, August. 1992. "Historical Memory, Class Formation, and Power: A Central Maine Community, 1920–1988." *Focaal—European Journal of Anthropology* 19: 36–57.

———. 1998. "The Re-imagined Community: The Making and Unmaking of a Local Working Class in Jay/Livermore Falls, Maine, 1900–1988." Ph.D. diss., City University of New York.

Clark, Gordon. 1989. *Unions and Communities under Siege.* New York: Cambridge University Press.

Clarke, John. 1991. *New Times and Old Enemies: Essays on Cultural Studies and America.* London: HarperCollins.

Cohen, David. 1994. "The Production of History." In *The Combing of History*, 1–23. Chicago: University of Chicago Press.

Crawford, Margaret. 1995. *Building the Workingman's Paradise: The Design of American Company Towns.* London: Verso Press.

Cross, Gary. 1993. *Time and Money: The Making of Consumer Culture.* London: Routledge.

Davis, Mike. 1986. *Prisoners of the American Dream.* New York: Verso Press.

———. 1991. *City of Quartz.* New York: Vintage Books.

———. 2000. *Magical Urbanism: Latinos Reinvent the U.S. Big City.* New York: Verso Press.

Edsforth, Ronald. 1987. *Class Conflict and Cultural Consensus: The Making of a Mass Consumer Society in Flint, Michigan.* New Brunswick, NJ: Rutgers University Press.

Eley, Geoff. 1988. "Labor History, Social History, *Alltagsgeschichte*: Experience, Culture, and the Politics of the Everyday." *Journal of Modern History* 61: 297–343.

Escobar, Arturo. 1996. "Constructing Nature: Elements for a Poststructural Political Ecology." In *Liberation Ecologies: Environment, Development, Social Movements*, ed. Richard Peet and Michael Watts, 46–68. London: Routledge.

Ewen, Stuart. 1976. *Captains of Consciousness: Advertising and the Social Roots of Consumer Culture*. New York: McGraw-Hill.

Gartman, David. 1986. *Auto Slavery: The Labor Process in the American Automobile Industry, 1897–1950*. New Brunswick, NJ: Rutgers University Press.

Georgakas, Dan, and Marvin Surkin. 1998. *Detroit: I Do Mind Dying*. Updated edition. Boston: South End Press Classics.

Ghani, Ashraf. 1995. "Writing a History of Power: An Examination of Eric R. Wolf's Anthropological Quest." In *Articulating Hidden Histories: Exploring the Influence of Eric R. Wolf*, ed. Jane Schneider and Rayna Rapp, 31–48. Berkeley: University of California Press.

Giardina, Denise. 1987. *Storming Heaven*. New York: Ivy Books.

Gramsci, Antonio. 1971. "Americanism and Fordism." In *Selections from the Prison Notebooks*, ed. Quintin Hoare and Geoffrey Nowell, 277–318. New York: International Publishers.

Gutman, Herbert. 1977. *Work, Culture, and Society in Industrializing America*. New York: Vintage Books.

———. 1987. "Historical Consciousness in Contemporary America." In *Power and Culture: Essays on the American Working Class*, ed. Ira Berlin, 395–412. New York: Pantheon Press.

Hardt, Michael, and Antonio Negri. 2000. *Empire*. Cambridge, MA: Harvard University Press.

Harvey, David. 1989a. *The Condition of Postmodernity*. Oxford: Basil Blackwell.

———. 1989b. *The Urban Experience*. Baltimore: Johns Hopkins University Press.

———. 2000. *Spaces of Hope*. Berkeley: University of California Press.

Herod, Andrew. 1998. "The Spatiality of Labor Unionism: A Review Essay." In *Organizing the Landscape: Geographical Perspectives on Labor Unionism*, ed. Andrew Herod, 1–36. Minneapolis: University of Minnesota Press.

Hobsbawm, Eric. 1984. "The Making of the Working Class, 1870–1914." In *Workers: Worlds of Labour*, 194–213. New York: Pantheon Books.

Horne, Gerald. 1997a. "The Political Economy of the Black Urban Future: A History." In *Globalization and Survival in the Black Diaspora: The New Urban Challenge*, ed. Charles Green, 247–268. Albany: State University of New York Press.

———. 1997b. *Fire This Time: The Watts Uprising and the 1960s*. New York: Da Capo Press.

Hunt, Lynn, ed. 1987. *The New Cultural History*. Berkeley: University of California Press.

Jameson, Frederic. 1991. *Postmodernism: or, The Cultural Logic of Late Capitalism*. Durham, NC: Duke University Press.

Johnson, Richard. 1979. "Three Problematics: Elements of a Theory of Working-Class Culture." In *Working-Class Culture: Studies in History and Theory*, ed. John Clarke, Charles Critcher, and Richard Johnson, 201–237. New York: St. Martin's Press.

Kalb, Don. 1997. *Expanding Class: Power and Everyday Politics in Industrial Communities, The Netherlands, 1850–1950*. Durham, NC: Duke University Press.

Katznelson, Ira. 1993. *Marxism and the City*. Oxford: Oxford University Press.

Kerr, Clark, and Abraham J. Siegel. 1954. "The Interindustry Propensity to Strike: An International Comparison." In *Industrial Conflict*, ed. A. W. Kornhauser, R. Dubin, and A. M. Ross, 189–212. New York: Arno.

Kimeldorf, Howard. 1988. *Reds or Rackets? The Making of Radical and Conservative Unionism on the Waterfront*. Berkeley: University of California Press.

Lefebvre, Henri. 1991. *The Production of Space*. Oxford: Basil Blackwell.

Lembcke, Jerry. 1988. *Capitalist Development and Class Capacities: Marxist Theory and Union Organization*. New York: Greenwood Press.

Levine, Rhonda. 1989. *Class Struggle and the New Deal: Industrial Labor, Industrial Capital and the State*. Lawrence: University Press of Kansas.

Linebaugh, Peter. 1991. *The London Hanged: Crime and Civil Society in the Eighteenth Century*. New York: Penguin Books.

Löfgren, Orvar. 1995. "Being a Good Swede: National Identity as a Cultural Battleground." In *Articulating Hidden Histories*, ed. Jane Schneider and Rayna Rapp, 262–274. Berkeley: University of California Press.

Lynd, Robert, and Helen Lynd. 1929. *Middletown: A Study in Modern American Culture*. New York: Harvest Books.

McGuire, Randall. 1991. "Building Power into the Cultural Landscape of Broome County, New York, 1880–1940." In *The Archeology of Inequality*, ed. Randall McGuire and Robert Paynter, 102–124. Oxford: Basil Blackwell.

Mann, Eric. 1987. *Taking on General Motors: A Case Study of the UAW Campaign to Keep GM Van Nuys Open*. Los Angeles: University of California, Center for Labor Research and Education, Institute of Labor Relations.

Marable, Manning. 2000. *How Capitalism Underdeveloped Black America: Problems in Race, Political Economy, and Society*. Updated edition. Boston: South End Press Classics.

Meinig, Donald W. 1974. "Symbolic Landscapes: Some Idealizations of American Communities." In *The Interpretation of Ordinary Landscapes*, ed. Donald W. Meinig, 164–194. Oxford: Oxford University Press.

Meyer, Stephen, III. 1981. *The Five Dollar Day: Labour Management and Social Control in the Ford Motor Company, 1908–1921*. Albany: State University of New York Press.

Mintz, Sidney. 1985. *Sweetness and Power: The Place of Sugar in Modern History*. New York: Penguin Press.

Montgomery, David. 1987. *The Fall of the House of Labor*. New York: Cambridge University Press.

Nash, June. 1979. *We Eat the Mines and the Mines Eat Us: Dependency and Exploitation in Bolivian Tin Mines*. New York: Columbia University Press.

———. 1989. *From Tank Town to High Tech: The Clash of Community and Industrial Cycles in a New England Town*. Albany: State University of New York Press.

Negri, Antonio. 1996. "Twenty Theses on Marx: Interpretation of the Class Situation Today." In *Marxism beyond Marxism*, ed. Saree Makdisi, Cesare Casarino, and Rebecca E. Karl, 149–180. London: Routledge.

Nelson, Bruce. 1990. *Workers on the Waterfront: Seamen, Longshoremen, and Unionism in the 1930s*. Urbana: University of Illinois Press.

Nugent, Daniel. 1993. *Spent Cartridges of Revolution: An Anthropological History of Namiquipa*. Chicago: University of Chicago Press.

Peet, Richard, and Michael Watts. 1996. ""Liberation Ecology: Development, Sustainability and Environment in an Age of Market Triumphalism." In *Liberation Ecologies: Environment, Development, Social Movements*, ed. Richard Peet and Michael Watts, 1–45. London: Routledge

Peiss, Kathy. 1986. *Cheap Amusements: Working Women and Leisure in Turn-of-the-Century New York*. Philadelphia: Temple University Press.

Pilcher, William. 1972. *The Portland Longshoremen: A Dispersed Urban Community*. New York: Holt, Rinehart, and Winston.

Pope, Liston. 1942. *From Millhands to Preachers: A Study of Gastonia*. New Haven: Yale University Press.

Pred, Allan, and Michael John Watts. 1993. *Reworking Modernity: Capitalisms and Symbolic Discontent*. New Brunswick, NJ: Rutgers University Press.

Ranciere, Jacques. 1994. *The Names of History: On the Poetics of Knowledge*. Minneapolis: University of Minnesota Press.

———. 1995. *On the Shores of Politics*. London: Verso Press.

Roseberry, William. 1989. *Anthropologies and Histories: Essays in Culture, History, and Political Economy*. New Brunswick, NJ: Rutgers University Press.

———. 1995. "The Cultural History of Peasantries." In *Articulating Hidden Histories: Exploring the Influence of Eric R. Wolf*, ed. Jane Schneider and Rayna Rapp, 51–66. Berkeley: University of California Press.

Rosenzweig, Roy. 1983. *Eight Hours for What We Will: Workers and Leisure in an Industrial City, 1870–1920*. New York: Cambridge University Press.

Salerno, Salvatore. 1989. *Red November, Black November: Culture and Community in the Industrial Workers of the World.* Albany: State University of New York Press.

Sayer, Derek. 1994. "Everyday Forms of State Formation: Some Dissident Remarks on Hegemony." In *Everyday Forms of State Formation: Revolution and the Negotiation of Rule in Modern Mexico*, ed. Gilbert Joseph and Daniel Nugent, 367–377. Durham, NC: Duke University Press.

Schneider, Jane. 1995. "The Analytical Strategies of Eric R. Wolf." In *Articulating Hidden Histories: Exploring the Influence of Eric R. Wolf*, ed. Jane Schneider and Rayna Rapp, 3–30. Berkeley: University of California Press.

Schneider, Jane, and Rayna Rapp, eds. 1995. *Articulating Hidden Histories: Exploring the Influence of Eric R. Wolf.* Berkeley: University of California Press.

Scontras, Charles A. 1985. *Organized Labor in Maine: Twentieth Century Origins.* Orono: The Bureau of Labor Education, University of Maine.

Scott, James C. 1985. *The Weapons of the Weak: Everyday Forms of Peasant Resistance.* New Haven: Yale University Press.

Sider, Gerald M. 1996. "Cleansing History: Lawrence, Massachusetts, the Strike for Four Loaves of Bread and No Roses, and the Anthropology of Working-Class Consciousness." *Radical History Review* 65: 48–83.

Smith, Gavin. 1999. *Confronting the Present: Towards a Politically Engaged Anthropology.* London: Berg.

Smith, Neil. 1990. *Uneven Development: Nature, Capital, and the Production of Space.* Oxford: Basil Blackwell.

Soja, Edward. 1989. *Postmodern Geographies: The Reassertion of Space in Critical Social Theory.* New York: Verso Press.

Sparks, Colin. 1996. "Stuart Hall, Cultural Studies, and Marxism." In *Stuart Hall: Critical Dialogues in Cultural Studies*, ed. David Morley and Kuan-Hsing Chen, 87. New York: Routledge.

Stedman Jones, Gareth. 1983. "Class Expression versus Social Control: A Critique of Recent Trends in the Social History of Leisure." In *Languages of Class: Studies in English Working-Class History*, 76–89. New York: Cambridge University Press.

Therborn, Goran. 1983. "Why Some Classes Are More Successful Than Others." *New Left Review* 138: 37–56.

Thompson, Edward Paul. 1966. *The Making of the English Working Class.* New York: Vintage Books.

Tomlins, Christopher. 1985. *The State and the Unions: Labor Relations, Law, and the Organized Labor Movement.* New York: Cambridge University Press.

Whisnant, David. 1983. *All That Is Native and Fine: The Politics of Culture in an American Region.* Chapel Hill: The University of North Carolina Press.

Wolf, Eric R. 1955. "Types of Latin American Peasantry." *American Anthropologist* 57: 452–471.

———. 1957. "Closed Corporate Communities in Mesoamerica and Central Java." *Southwestern Journal of Anthropology* 13: 1–18.

———. 1982. *Europe and the People Without History.* Berkeley: University of California Press.

———. 1986. "Vicissitudes of the Closed Corporate Community." *American Ethnologist* 15: 752–761.

———. 1988. "Inventing Society." *American Ethnologist* 15: 752–761.

Chapter Five

"Bare Legs Like Ice"
Recasting Class for Local/Global Inquiry

Don Kalb

Few serious social researchers would deny the inescapability of pondering the conundrum of class—a conundrum because, while steadily contested, politically compromised, and conceptually inflated, the unsettling suspicion keeps surfacing that class involves inequality, power, culture, exploitation, accumulation, struggle and action, being in history and the making of history, being in place and the making of space, all in the same moment. Class, power, time, and space together form a huge program that has haunted social inquiry since Marx. Disciplined social science, on the other hand, has been a recurrent escape from its embrace, and understandably so, since it is hardly manageable in an orderly way. Nevertheless, in combination with other huge programs, such as those of state formation and legitimate leadership derived from Weber (and Marx), or the question of modernity and morality anchored in Smith, Durkheim, or Simmel (and Marx), or the issues of modern power and the self taken from Elias, Heidegger, or Foucault (and Marx), the big suspicion called class keeps creeping in, while issues of gender, race, and nation have become inseparably inserted.

In the preceding two decades of growing inequalities worldwide, escalating violence in spite of the hoped-for "peace dividend" after the fall of the Wall, and a tremendously accelerating global capitalism, class as an overriding conundrum has again lost its magnetic quality for Western critical scholarship, as the revolt of the 1960s and 1970s was incorporated and academia was "disciplined" once again. Except for the proverbial faddishness of social science concepts, this collapse was also caused by unsolved internal problems of teleology, essentialism, and reductionism in the materialist tradition. Classes have often been represented as actual, self-understood collectivities when they rarely were; and social structural position has been treated as an overwhelming, one-to-one, *stante pede*, determination of consciousness and action.[1] Three nonexclusive forms of response have emerged: proposing intermediate "class locations"; reducing the scope of structure's hold on consciousness via intermediate domains, above all political process and its timing; and reconceptualizing structure as just an effect of income- or work-related interests on individual consciousness, among other such effects. These reframings generally remained within the orbit of a methodological materialism while complicating the causal links and abandoning the Marxist theory of history. Class as a determinative factor was cut down to a size applicable to positivist procedures of establishing its weight among other factors. A thin materialism was the outcome, unresponsive to Antonio Gramsci's basic insight that "the different dimensions in any specific society do not move in sealed, logically determined orbits ... but interconnect in a single historical rhythm" (Katznelson 1992: 71). Small wonder that more ambitious analysts rapidly began to seek alternative ways of getting at that rhythm.

It was precisely at this point that anthropology's culture concept offered itself as an escape from the trappings of the thin-materialist enclosure and its unwieldy alternatives, above all in the form of Clifford Geertz's "thick description." It was rapidly appropriated by fields that had pioneered the most promising explorations of the class conundrum in the 1970s, the new social history and the new urban sociology, and they did so in ways that fostered its full abandonment by embracing "the new cultural history" (Bonnell and Hunt 1999; Hunt 1989) or a cultural studies program devoid of its initial British critical acumen and based in a sui generis reading of Foucault's notion of discourse. It helped to move attention away from the actual production of everyday life by emphasizing the radical nonreducibility of subjectivities (for example, Joyce 1991, 1994; Reddy 1984, 1987), by weakening the project to envision and explain structural change through time, by promoting flat empiricism or outright idealism, and in general by preventing a purposeful rethinking of classical materialist methodological trappings. Anthropology, above all, was appropriated to liberate meaning from any solid fix. Discourse or culture became the key.

In a recent discussion of class and/versus culture approaches, social historians Geoff Eley and Keith Nield recapitulate the history of this debate as well as the dilemmas (Eley and Nield 2000a: 1–30).[2] More than in earlier work, and in synchrony with other social historians such as Bonnell and Hunt (1999), they show themselves to be aware of the need to acknowledge the sheer existence of the social and not to fully reduce social existence to a semiotic happening. It is at this point that class is given some respect. But not much so, and in the end the big conundrum remains effectively silenced. Class, they say, echoing Patrick Joyce, is just one discursive form among other forms, a possible self-understanding amid other self-understandings, based in wider popular discourses of identity (Eley and Nield 2000b, esp. 82). But yes, they concede, class has taught us that underneath dominant discourses of identity there do exist local notions of injustice and the good life, subaltern identities anchored in dense fabrics of neighborhood, family, and work, which can inform struggle and mobilization and do sometimes enforce negotiation and concession on the part of political and economic elites. A full turn to the history of ideas is thus not warranted, they imply, *pace* such converted historians as Gareth Stedman Jones, Patrick Joyce, and Joan Scott. Despite this little criticism of the "cultural turnists," the complex conundrum clearly is reduced ad infinitum. What is left is merely the recognition of the possibility of local and largely hidden subaltern meanings. This, combined with the populist pulse of the social historian, does transform it into a manageable background verity for theses in social history departments, but it hardly chips away at the culturalist dogma that the overruling reality of human life is a semiotic and lexical one.

There is an issue of scale here. Sure class does always connote a local structure of feeling and experience that fails to fully comply with hegemonic prescriptions, simply because being a wage dependent worker or family unprotected by the securities of the comfortable middle classes implies that everyday life is differently lived, interests, on the long and short term, are differently structured, and hope and personal becoming play in a different register. But does it actually make sense to separate these local subaltern meanings from the larger envelopment of capitalism in time and space, or for that matter from what is happening to these same middle or ruling classes? Can we really understand such meanings if we fail to locate them in a specific relational nexus and recognize them as products of particular timings and spatializations of a much more universal social process? Class without capitalism must make little sense. We need to engage the whole relational, historical, and spatial conundrum and refuse to choose sides between an equally misguided old-style deductionism and determinism or a postmodern-style local idiography.

There is also an issue of hegemony, its status, and how to study it. Eley and Nield's merely localized concession to "the social history of the seventies" (with E. P. Thompson as totem) springs from their continued struggle against reductionism (ibid.). But that, to me, seems an old fight. Clearly, discourse, political culture, and religion have won full recognition in contemporary political practice and analysis. And although a critical tradition prefers to study such systems as imperfect, partly semiotic and partly institutional weapons in concrete human actions rather than as manicheic coherencies on paper, these public signifying forces will not easily be overlooked in today's social inquiries. Indeed, they are the material from which the expressive part of hegemonies is made and must therefore be integral to any analysis of power and exploitation. But hegemonies never fully saturate the human capacity to experience, bodily and relationally, the actual events of everyday life and history (see Gupta and Ferguson 1997 for a useful reminder). They never fully colonize memory (Sider and Smith 1997). While they may mystify, rationalize, invert, and block crucial learning moments of experience, unsettling thoughts and incoherent streams of awareness keep disturbing the most solid ego in her or his engagements with the "real" (yes) world. Eley and Nield recognize this to the extent that they allow for subaltern meanings among local groupings of the unprivileged. But with just a local take to it, they will not be able to analyze the why and how.

Moreover, "discourse," in spite of Foucault's intentions, often only describes the expressive and cognitive aspects of hegemony.[3] It rarely opens onto the relational and institutional interactions that actually happen to do the silencing and, by recursive operation and enforced habituation, the repressing of alternative relations and associated heterodox insights. Above all, discourse often fails to come to terms with one of the basic building blocks to a critique of the shortcomings of classical Marxism and liberal modernism alike, even though it was a basic Foucaultian project to reveal it: that modern worlds hardly function on the basis of natural individualism and calculated self-interest but rather through intricate social relations and institutional complexes that call for, and sanction, orthodoxy, instill motivation, and channel loyalty and voice, while preventing "the return of the repressed" in practice. It is at these relations and institutions, and their never fully successful silencing work, including the less articulate heterodoxies based in as yet unrealized relational possibilities, that my method aims. And this is the clue: these relations cannot be understood on "just" a local level.

So much more important now than continue to fight the strawman of reductionism[4] seems our capacity to grasp the complexities, contingencies, struggles, and subjectivities of actual place making, the making of local realities and modes of human becoming, in the face of a universalizing history of modern projects of which capitalism is a hardly negligible engine. How and by whom are specific places carved out from the forces of large-scale abstract processes such as global capitalism, state and empire formation, and the consequent forging and fracturing of hegemonies? And how are they expressive of the power relationships that spring from the meeting of the local and the global, that is, the conjunction of prior local histories and social structures with new global requirements and networks of accumulation? What are their liberating moments and their debilitating ones? And for whom? In other words, who becomes enabled to express which projects and interests? And who is silenced? Surely these are new framings of old questions that bring the big conundrum back into view and refrain from making nominalistic and arbitrary distinctions between something called the economy or work and something else called culture, discourse, or signification. We need to discover active contingency within overwhelming abstraction rather than continuously recycling a sanitized idea of discourse against a vulgarized notion of interest. Are the antinomies of the "category producing class" of the 1980s and 1990s not finally exhausted?

Contrary to Eley and Nield, I use the micro method not as a vehicle for articulating local populist truths about injustice, nor as a testing ground for abstract hypotheses that could have been tested anywhere. I take it as a well-framed window from below on the mechanisms, consequences, and emergent possibilities and contingencies of large-scale historical and spatial change as it envelops prior histories, previously engraved landscapes, and embodied human experience. It interrogates the big universalizing forces of modernity, driven by capitalism, as they become linked up with, and nested within, or, vice versa, disembedded from, concrete, human communities, relationships, activities, and understandings that do have a prior history of their own as well as a possible future not necessarily fully coterminous with the logic of large-scale forces. That is, I am proposing to approach class and the local through an alternative anthropological pedigree: one that focuses on historical and spatial linkages, on critical junctions in time and space.

The alternative anthropological pedigree I want to articulate is one that builds on Gluckman's situational analysis (1958), Boissevain's (1974) and Blok's (1974) network analysis, Gerald Sider's (1982, 1993) superb understanding of place making *avant la lettre*, and above all Eric Wolf's anthropology of the modern world (1964, 1969, 1982, 1999, 2001). It is also respectful of Appadurai's (1996) and Hannerz's (1991, 1996) anthropology of globalization, but seeks an approach more robustly rooted in a critical materialist tradition. And it reflects both in its formulation and in its inspiration the global fluctuations, turbulences and injustices that have marked the late twentieth century and will continue to rock our life arrangements in the new millennium.[5]

It is important to emphasize that without this spatial perspective of a dialectics of local and global histories it is not even possible to think about capitalism at all, nor even about a working class (cf. Cooper 2000; Kalb 2000; Stein, 2000). It is the conjunction of local production with translocal accumulation, organization, and marketing in space that defines capitalist process as well as any concrete labor (a concrete abstraction, as Marx aptly coined it) performed within its networks, and the alienation and mystification that it engenders. This also specifies its hegemonic requirements as well as the limits thereof.

The particular nature of any single node or locale must then be seen as having been produced by a threefold bundle of connectivity that always operates in, but never fully describes, whatever happens in situ: (1) the moment and prevalent mode of insertion into more universal processes such as capital accumulation, state formation, or cultural modernity; (2) the particular dynamics and sequences of its linkages with the global; and (3) the power resources that key actors within these linking networks can mobilize to change or shift the modes of linkage and therewith the nature of local life.

But in order to make the critical junctions perspective work in what I have elsewhere called the relational materialist mode (Kalb 1997), another basic anthropological insight must be recaptured: one on internal social relations within any locale as they are patterned to produce *couleur locale* or local specificity. This specificity, indeed, does not so much derive from a macro cosmos of culture that makes a locality culturally distinct (see the introduction to this collection), but rather from a multistranded set of human relationships, multistranded in a *particular* way, embedded in an overlapping set of connections between work, family, civil society, and other local institutional fields. Such internal connections are articulated, as Eric Wolf (1982, 2001) has insisted, around dynamic "key relationships" of production, reproduction, and accumulation, which lend a certain "structured coherence" (Harvey 1989: 125–165) to any territorial human arrangement. Our task is to precisely identify these structuring relations and the nature of the coherence that they produce. These cannot be separated from the specifiable and nonrandom networks of extraction, exchange, coercion, and signification that link locales and territories to higher levels of the global system(s). These are dynamic and multilevel *ensembles.* These higher levels in the chain, on their turn, continuously generate pressures and incentives for local reshuffling, discontinuity, and outright dislocation. Class, thus, becomes a program of local-global inquiry. It also turns into a modest analytical and methodological tool. It becomes an encouragement for actual discovery instead of an a priori idea of determination of consciousness by the relation to the means of production (as in "the social history of the seventies") or a mechanical allocation of sites to cores or peripheries with predestined logics of development (as in early world systems theory), or just a descriptive concept for registering local feelings of deprivation, as in Eley and Nield.

Note finally that my approach to place making and (counter) hegemonic struggle as happening within the interactions between local and global histories competes with visions advocated in anthropology by Arif Dirlik (2001) on the one hand and Arjun Appadurai (2000) on the other. While Dirlik sees the local as a site for authentic, antihegemonic creativity against global homogenizing forces, confirming Eley and Nield's reading of the continued importance of class as a local subaltern structure of feeling, Appadurai radically locates the capacity for critical understanding on the global plane (see also Smith 2002). While this essay does not explicitly engage with these positions, I want to point out that they do form a subtext to the present discussion on class. Indeed, I am aiming at a more dialectical alternative, which is not to be understood as a middle ground.

Flexible Familism: A Case Study

The rest of this essay develops a case study in the spirit of this program. It is located in the electrical city of Eindhoven, the Netherlands, in roughly the first half of the twentieth century.[6] It starts off with a long interview, which I held shortly after I felt I had discovered the "key relationship" that had shaped local destiny and individual biography between circa 1850 and 1950. I subsequently called this key relationship "flexible familism." It described a situation in which the region was turned into an export platform for labor-intensive light consumer goods in textiles, cigar making, and ultimately electrical production under the auspices of the Philips corporation. Without a sufficient home market or a polity intent on expanding its industrial production and investing in the necessary infrastructure, large-scale manufacturers from the 1850s onward tapped into the labor reserves of semiproletarian families in the region. These families had long been accustomed to occupational multiplicity and income pooling, and had increasingly linked part of the household labor supply to external, increasingly international sales markets. Merchants and employers were above all interested in the labor of local daughters. Daughters enabled them to limit costs and sustain a highly flexible labor force that could be substantially reduced in slack times without endangering local livelihoods or generating protest, and could also be rapidly expanded in good times. It solved the dilemma of any large-scale flexible labor force: combining discipline, dedication, and precision with being disposable and expendable. These essential properties were sustained by turning parental control over earnings, families, and general propriety into an external and implicit, though crucial, instrument of personnel management.

This was done in direct or indirect ways. Families could continue small-scale agriculture as a prime occupation and hire out daughters' labor to manufacturers. But as the access to land was getting harder in the course of the second half of the nineteenth century, fathers, too, increasingly sought industrial employment. Fathers who brought in several productive daughters were rewarded with status-conferring supervisory or service tasks and with higher household earnings and greater status in the community. Certainly as industry was becoming more complex and divisions of labor more elaborate, fathers with wage-earning daughters benefited in the local labor market. And while their families as a whole became more secure, their daughters were exploited within increasingly despotic mass production regimes. In this way, flexible familism gradually turned into the key dynamic of this area. It linked relations between generations and sexes with industrial growth, shaped key decisions in enterprises as well as families, determined the quality of the local public sphere and the concerns of local policy makers and moral authorities, and ultimately laid down its urban form and the potential social dynamics of association and identification. Flexible familism allowed Philips to conquer emergent international markets in advanced electrical consumer goods and to build an industrial base that came to count among the most capable in twentieth-century Europe.

While historical research had already demonstrated the quantitative salience of female labor in the area, an exploration of the actual relationships and subjectivities that were involved was lacking, as was a systematic idea of the role these relationships had played in both the events of local history and in popular experience and memory. Which trajectories of social becoming had been opened? Which had been shortcut? My concept of flexible familism promised to bring these issues together in a meaningful way. The purpose of the case study is to illustrate how a materialist critical junctions perspective can open up promising routes toward analyzing territorialized cultural process. I will start with a micro exploration and then rise up to higher levels in the chain and to further sequences in time.

"An Awfully Dumb Person"

It was my second encounter with the Van de Velde family (July 1992).[7] The first time, half a year earlier, I had interviewed the husband, Hennie, now I wanted to talk with his wife Maria. They lived in a neat Eindhoven middle-class suburb, built in the 1970s, furnished with heavy brown leather chairs. They appeared to enjoy my unannounced visit. It had been a good interview the first time, and they seemed to like talking about their lives and history with an informed outsider like me. They cordially invited me in. Hennie called for his wife to come and see who had entered.

Still standing in the corridor, I told Maria that I would like to interview her on the memories of her youth. Last time I had questioned her on her experiences as a young girl at Philips but, I told her, we had not yet addressed her relationships with her family. I said I was particularly interested in how much of her income she had to give up to her parents and how such things were generally arranged and talked about in her family. She had shown herself to be an open informant with a very detailed memory, so I did not expect problems. I had decided to reveal the point of my visit right at the outset, so as to optimally focus our talk.

Consequently, I was ill prepared when she showed serious doubts. She paled and wanted to move to the kitchen in order to prevent Hennie from trying to persuade her. But Hennie, in his relaxed and friendly manner, threw an arm around her and argued that there was no reason not to start the interview, since she could always stop it when she wanted to. She probably trusted me just enough to give me the chance.

When we were seated (Hennie was preparing tea) she explained her wavering. She had been ill some years ago and her youth and family had played a large part in that. She had been nervous and anxious and had suffered from insomnia. She was plagued by painful reminiscences of her adolescent years. It was hard for her to talk about it, she said, because she did not want to denounce her own family. These people were still her very own folks, she said. There had also been many moments of pleasure.

In spite of her initial hesitation and concern for the integrity of her family, it took less than a minute for her to start narrating without interruption. She quickly got irritated when Hennie intended to intervene. Everything she told me fully satisfied my incipient hypotheses on the complexity of father-daughter relations in the region. I had been ready to pose a whole lot of specific questions, but Maria needed no prompting. During short pauses she exclaimed: "It's hardly believable nowadays, but this was how it was.... What's the use of all this today? My children keep saying, 'Shut up, Mother, the past is the past and today is today'.... It's my own history but it is worthless."

I started the interview by asking how much she had earned as a girl of fifteen in the early 1950s (born in 1936), and how much she was expected to hand over to her parents. She still knew it exactly: She had made about twenty-three guilders a week, had given it all to her parents, and had received two guilders and fifty cents in pocket money. She was the seventh of eleven daughters, and everyone above age twelve was expected to somehow contribute to household income. As a young girl, for example, she used to go along the streets selling sweets prepared by her mother. Her father worked in a stockroom of the Philips light-bulb factory. "He used to work always, always. He never came late to his job at Philips, not even a minute, not in thirty years. Shortly after his pension he died. And we too had to work always, even when we were ill."

Hennie interrupts and says that everyone had to hand over all their money to their parents but that he himself had been lucky. "I got twenty-five guilders pocket money a week." Maria becomes angry with the suggestion that Hennie had had a better time: "Okay, but you too were working like a dog. Even all your earnings from overtime were given to your parents." "Yes," Hennie says, "but I was making fifty guilders a week by then as a toolmaker, because of overtime of course, but also because I used to be 30 percent above the norm. But, in fact, I was simply lucky to be the youngest at home. The others had had less privilege. And my parents, Father being a building contractor, were much better off than yours."

Maria determinedly brings the subject back to her own youth. How hard she used to work! At age sixteen she was employed at the BATA shoemaking plant in the village of Best. She got up at 5:30 AM in the morning; set the table for everyone; and took a bus at 6:30 AM. She started to work at 7:30 AM. She worked well above the norm and arrived home again at 5:30 PM, tidied up the house, which was often a mess, and started peeling potatoes for dinner. She cleaned up the dishes afterward and went to bed totally exhausted. "But I have always been really dumb," she says. "They used to say I was just dumb. 'Bleu,' they said. I was obedient and I was my mother's dearest child. She was always lying in bed with her sicknesses, but she made pretty clothes for me. My oldest sister had left the household by that time. She could not stand it anymore. My father was often drunk and aggressive. Nellie, my second oldest sister, was in fact running the household. The other four older sisters had boyfriends and were withdrawing from their responsibilities. I had to do everything.

"When I left school at the age of twelve, Nellie sent me as a maid to a small farmer's family in the nearby countryside. My parents didn't know about it. The money was paid directly to my sister—I never saw any of it. I was treated badly there, especially by the farmer's wife. I wasn't allowed to sit at the table. She had five children, but madam just stayed in bed and I had to arrange everything. I was not permitted to go home during the weekends. I often wept. And at Christmas I ran away. But I did not know where I was. I got lost and was picked up by the police and brought home. Only then did my parents realize that I had been gone for some time. That's how it used to be in those days. You simply needed to get rid of a child! But I can tell you, such things are not easily forgotten.... And then my father ... well ... you were not supposed to say so ... but he was always drinking. Not that he took anything from his wage from Philips. No, he never did that. But he was serving at the pub of a sister of his. So he had money for himself. He threatened us and he used to beat my mother when he was drunk."

"Yeah, he was a sharp guy," Hennie intervened. It was silent for a moment. Maria abruptly shifted the emphasis. "But at a certain moment, he was sitting in his chair, softly stammering some words. Everyone must have thought he was drunk. Mother had called him twice for dinner. But he didn't come. It turned out he had had a stroke! And later in the evening he was hit once again. Some weeks later he died. He had just retired, three months before. He had never been ill. But at that age, you wouldn't believe it, he still had the nerve to hang upside-down with his toes behind a high bar. And there he was, dangling for minutes! Looking around, grinning at the amazement all around."

Maria springs up: "But as little kids we also used to climb to the very top of a tree, catch frogs, roast them and eat their legs, or catch birds and cook them. We were also full of tricks! However, in his relationship with authorities Father used to be very obedient, too. When I was sixteen years old I was working at the bulb factory. To make more money the Belgians had tipped me to put small pieces of cardboard in the box. And so I did. But somehow someone must have talked. And the Belgians had probably pointed at me as the initiator of the deceit. After a few weeks of good earnings a calculator came checking my speed. 'You don't work so swiftly ... uh ... it does not quite match with the units you score.' I had to confess it all. But I didn't dare to betray the Belgians. They would have beaten me up at the gate! Then the department boss ordered my father to come. Father got very angry with me and I feared he would kick me. But still I did not tell the two of them about the Belgians. At home, however, I started to weep. Mother knew how honest I was. She often left small coins around in the house to check whether anybody would take them. But I never did, and she knew it well. It was decided that I should tell everything to the highest boss of the department. But still I did not dare. In the end I told everything. I said that whole row behind me was doing it, and the other one, too, and she also and she. Some were fired, others were fined, and I was moved to another department. I could even have started as a maid with Frits Philips. But I did not dare to ... or maybe my mother wanted to keep me home, so there was someone around ... she was always ill ... I don't know anymore."

Someone calls at the door. It is an ex-Philips scientist who needs Hennie for some private business. Maria and I are alone now. She starts to repeat much of what she has told. But in a low voice now, as if we were collaborators in some obscure affair. Then she turns to new stories.

"After Philips I went to work at BATA because the wages were better there. As a girl of sixteen I used to walk to all the factories, alone, looking for a better job. I walked hours doing so, because I never got any money for the bus.

I wondered why she did so since she had to give it all up. "They needed the money," she answered, "everyone had to work.

"When I was eighteen years old my mother made me a beautiful and narrowly fitting tweed suit. We very often went out. Each Sunday, but also on Saturdays. You couldn't afford nylons, so you went with your bare legs in high heels. There was no money to take a bus. We walked all the way to the dances at Stratum or Gestel. That could be more than an hour. Sometimes your legs were like ice.

"But in general it was no fun. It was work, work, and work again. Maybe it is true that I have always been dumb, like they used to say. I met Hennie at a dance. But I knew already him from stories. He could drink! He told my brothers-in-law that he would make me pregnant so I could leave home.

"I don't easily tell it … I've often been afraid of my father. When he was drunk you'd better look out for him. Because … he tried the kids to…. And incidentally, my friend, she's living in the next street, they also had twelve children, she's had a really disgusting youth. She was forced to go to bed with her father! Otherwise he would beat her up. And still she's one of the two normal sisters. The rest are wrecks. And she had to do it often enough! Your own daughters! But you do not have a mother anymore then, do you. As a mother you ought to drag him before court. Nowadays they'll do that. My father, too, when I saw him drunk, I kept away from him. Not when he was sober … no, no, not then."

"At the time I met Hennie we often used to go to dances. Many girls behaved like sluts, hanging on the bar and flirting. Me, too, sometimes. When you went to the toilets and came along the bar I was flirting, too. But I was always afraid of what would happen. I don't know…. I was of a special sort. I quickly got 'bleu.' Also when I had a fiancé. I had one before Hennie. But he never touched me, because I didn't dare to. Nowadays, when they know each other only for two days they just go to bed…. Is that true? Nowadays?… Well, in any case there will certainly be many who…. But that was totally different then. Although … it is true that also then there were many who…. We were simply not informed! We looked for babies under the cabbages in the gardens because we were told so! Is it not true then that I have been so awfully dumb? An awfully dumb person!"

"Worthless Histories"

In a dense narration of common events and circumstances of proletarian life in the region, Maria's story is deeply moving, above all for the intense tension it evokes between hostility and intimacy, fear and respect, trust and distrust that all social relations seem to have been imbued with. Maria, her husband now pensioned and her children independent, cannot in retrospect be unequivocal about any of the key relationships that have shaped her youth and person. Her history is "worthless" because each of the social relations she was entering into as part of the logic of gendered working-class life became at the same time precious as well as exploitative. The overarching experience, the memory of which brought her down thirty years after the relationships in which it was actually produced had vanished, was very well understood by her: her family, for all the fun and pride it had clearly given her, "wanted to get rid of a child" while it ruthlessly claimed the earnings of her relentless labor of body and mind. She was not sentimental about this: "Everyone had to work … they needed the money."

Ambiguity was overwhelming in relation to her father. By way of association with her friend's father, she deems him capable of rape, whether such things have happened in fact or not (we never learn). Her relationship with him was primarily one of fear. But when his character was criticized by her husband, she was immediately determined to highlight his funny *savoir vivre* and the little precious things she had learnt from him, which, she softly implies, helped to keep her going in spite of all the dark memories. His regular work was okay, and helped to sustain the household; but his irregular work enabled him to drink and tyrannize his family. However, his daytime activities for Philips also subjected him, in her eyes, to a domination that was hard to reconcile with his more independent skills and aspirations, for which, perhaps, his nighttime activities could have been a better training ground. While nighttime irregular earnings facilitated his recurrent drunken aggression, Maria somehow suspects that the source could well have been rooted in the humiliating obedience that Philips, being simultaneously employer, landlord, and lifetime social insurance for the whole family, exacted from him. Despite these insights, she is aware that his threatening presence played a central role in making her history "worthless." Nowadays, she imagines, men like him would perhaps be "dragged before court."

Her mother, likewise, is not represented by stable memories. Maria loved her, and was loved by her, but she did not trust her "illnesses," suspecting that they were an alibi for not taking responsibility for the household and not protecting her from exploitation by other sisters or violence by her father. In fact, the love for her mother made Maria willing to continuously exploit herself, as she seems to acknowledge. Unlike with her father, she does not suggest that her mother's failings could have been explained by the ungrateful roles she had to master in the wider class and gender relationships of the electrical city. She does not associate her "illnesses" with the eleven children she bore, nor with the exhausting task of running this large a proletarian household without an emotionally supportive husband. Maria was her favorite child, receiving fancy clothes to wear on Saturday nights. But in retrospect it could be no compensation. In the end, and again by association with her friend's situation, she was close to "having no mother."

Ultimately, the inextricable intertwining of exploitation and love made her deeply fearful of all intimacy. Her parents as well as her lovers, she suspected, would in the end not be that dissimilar. There is a remarkable logic of sequence in her story, where she moves back and forth between her father's imagined potential for violence, rape, and incest, her flirting with boys, her lack of insight in sexuality, and her lack of trust in intimacy. Her legs on high heels on Saturday night may have been provocatively bare, but they felt like ice. She did not trust her first lover to touch her for fear of betraying the love promise. Her next lover, who later became her dependable husband, was remembered as a famous drinker, not unlike her father. And she vividly remembers that he boasted to liberate her from her subjection by her family by appropriating her fragile sexuality, precisely what she feared her father could do. Ambivalences abound.

Maria was not representative in that her subjection was more multiple and her relationships with her parents more ambiguous than was probably the case with most other working-class girls. It made her feel she was "dumb." It led her to hate herself more than her aggressors. But in terms of the fundamental relationships at work, Maria was not at all exceptional. The tight interweaving of love and exploitation, of loyalty and abuse, somehow seemed to operate in the relationships of each adolescent girl with her family. Marginal and unskilled families surely tended to have more asymmetrical relationships than more "respectable" ones, even though their courting and leisure were less parentally regulated. But many female adolescents coped with a similar complex of ambiguities. The whole of regional culture was imbued with similar forms of oppression. While industrialization elsewhere tended to liberate youth, the specific pattern of export-led Southeast Brabant industrialization served to sustain and intensify "traditional" controls.[8]

In the early 1950s, Anna Vermeulen, twenty years old and once the nation's youngest primary school teacher, decided to leave home. She would enter a cloister, the one with the strictest reputation in the area, as she could no longer reconcile the dozens of futile and arbitrary restrictions at home with the public status conferred by her job. She was not allowed to, and the reasons given by her father were chilling: "The family was finally beginning to see some money from her [she gave up all her salary, which nearly matched her father's income as a lower civil servant] and he did not intend to let that go." This was a family of very good reputation, cherishing education and wisdom. Nevertheless, explicit instrumental and self-interested reasoning about children was not at all considered immoral. Note further that a cloister appeared to Anna as the most practical way out: it would even promise an intensification of self-restrictions, guilt, and punishment. And finally consider that Anna would later remember that she had loved her father dearly and that she had maintained an extraordinary intimate relationship with him. If it had not been for the memory of her husband and her sister, whom I also interviewed, amnesia would have spared Anna a painful and confusing part of her personal history.

"Spineless Spider"

The point is, of course, that flexible familism gave a particular meaning to circumstances that also occurred elsewhere. It is therefore important to read the minor differences closely. European industrialization until World War II generalized the family wage economy, in which grown-up children everywhere became earners for a general family pool of resources in a complex process of implicit or explicit negotiation (Andersen 1984; Seccombe 1995; Tilly and Scott 1978). Means from this pool were first of all allocated for household purposes and only secondarily for private ones. At the same time, the availability of independent jobs in individualized labor markets for young workers strengthened their negotiation position within the family. The best gross indication for this has been the general fall in the average age of marriage, indicating the actually increasing spaces of freedom that young people could claim vis-à-vis the parents' household, for both men and women. The other gross indication was the declining number of children.

On both scores, however, Eindhoven became an anomaly. The average age of marriage remained well above the national average, and more significantly so above the average of more "mature" industrial places such as Amsterdam or Rotterdam (Kalb 1997: 96; Boonstra 1993: 263). The average number of children did fall, but not nearly so sharply as elsewhere, and in fact got another hike in the early 1930s, which will be discussed later. These are all quantitative expressions of a kinship domain that had been drawn ever more firmly into the pressures of flexible familist accumulation, a relation in which the control by parents of children had become deepened rather than weakened. This happened while the country at large was moving in the opposite direction, which inevitably increased the tensions inherent in the arrangement. Familial love and care, as a consequence, became overlaid with complex feelings of exploitation and denigration and produced a fear of autonomy and intimacy that modernity, according to the classical accounts, was precisely said to undo.

Other domains of social life exhibited the same anomalous dynamic. While in the classical places of industry the concentration of the means of production in large factory complexes led to the concentration of workers, the Eindhoven area by the late 1920s was a sprawling, peasant worker-like, residential landscape around a highly concentrated core of capital-intensive manufacturing. Until the late 1950s, Eindhoven was composed of several strings of villages, separated from each other by small rivers and wetlands, connected by radial roads, which were jammed at rush hour with long columns of bicycles and buses, and linked to a set of huge factory outlays near its central station. Flexible familist export manufacturing in the first half of the twentieth century produced the most concentrated factory landscape in the Netherlands outside the Randstad conurbation and some of the largest industrial complexes of Europe. But wages in the area had never been meant to cover individual reproduction costs of unskilled workers. Moreover, for any young family with no children, or rather daughters, of wage-earning age, spending power was close to zero and would even fall as the first children were born, costs rose, and the mother's capacity to work outdoors was severely reduced. Incomes, consequently, were simply below the point at which either individuals or young families could migrate to the place. They were also too low for local taxes to be raised for necessary urban investments, or for adequate rents to be asked for decent housing. Infrastructure such as roads, sewerage, and bridges, as well as investments in working-class housing, consequently remained in systematic undersupply. As prices and congestion in the industrial and entrepreneurial core rose, workers moved outward to ever cheaper areas, undeveloped places preferably with some gardening opportunities available to grow vegetables or raise pigs and chickens. They would also cluster close to their family networks, given the importance of cross-generational or cross-sibling support. By 1930, the city had almost 100,000 inhabitants but did not look as such. Urban planners derogatorily spoke of its urban form as a "spineless spider," a narrow body throwing its legs clumsily and far into the underdeveloped peasant worlds of the surrounding countryside (Kalb 1997: 196–203). This was clearly not the urban modernity of the boulevard. But the planners and architects failed to see that it was modernity nevertheless.

However, something more complex was at stake than could be captured by the urbanist metaphor of the spider, although the prefix "spineless" may have hinted at it. The legs, indeed, were also the axes around which sharp working-class segregation was organized. Flexible familist production until 1910 was still relatively capital-extensive and featured very few production processes demanding formal skills. But as administrative and marketing departments started to grow, and especially after the Philips brothers went into ever more complex product lines with higher added value (such as glassmaking, the metal wire bulb, radar and wireless, complete radio sets) and started an independent and soon highly regarded facility for physics research, ever more specialized workers from elsewhere were brought into town. They could only be attracted if housing was offered to them, housing of a decidedly better and more urban quality than the dwellings available to local workers. From the 1910s onward big manufacturers started to build such company housing for skilled workers and educated families, mostly in fashionable expressionist Amsterdam School designs in neighborhoods that were inspired by the Garden City Movement. They were located close to the body of the spider, mostly in the direct proximity of the factories.

There emerged thus a readily perceptible grading of environments from the core to the outer neighborhoods, expressing steep income and status distinctions. This class grading, moreover, had until 1920 been formalized by actual political demarcations between municipalities. The six political units exhibited entirely different levels of taxation, totally different public investment ratios, different problems, and different policy concerns (Kalb 1997: 105–109, 196–203). They also nurtured their own associational life, in keen rivalry with the neighbors. On top of that, such status and political borders were further festered by religious difference. Educated and skilled labor, coming from the north and west of the country, was mostly Protestant or secularized (liberal and social democratic); local labor, in a response organized by an alliance of local clergy, shopkeepers and middle-class professions against immigration and the concentration of property among nonlocals, became ever more explicitly Catholic. These divisions were crystallizing themselves ever more sharply onto space. The "spineless spider" was not just a failed modern city; its parts were almost without exception also proudly parochial and inward looking. Flexible familism, at the point of production as well as in its public sphere, was intensely fragmented, socially and culturally. Ultimately, these class, confessional, and political borders separated capitalists and their core employees from, first, an inner ring of skilled workers, then a ring of unskilled local worker families who lived and were employed under flexible familist conditions, and finally a surrounding nonurban space of worker peasant families whose daughters' labor was ever more tapped into as big orders came in. A dense network of private and public commuter services linked the manufacturing core around the central station to an area with a diameter of some sixty kilometers, stretching all the way into Belgium.

Two systemic consequences sprang from this situation. The first was the absence of encompassing laborwide institutions and a related public sphere, the absence of ties between the various working-class segments, and the ensuing weakness of class discourses, critical politics, and labor protest (Kalb 1997: 121–136). The only strong and successful labor movement ever to emerge in Eindhoven was a male cigar makers' movement in 1907 under Catholic auspices, strongly sponsored by Catholic cigar manufacturers against some of their local liberal competitors. It mobilized more than 2,500 male workers who rallied against "liberal" employers who deviated slightly from established piece rates. A large Catholic female strike at Philips in 1909 against work on Sundays utterly failed because in the end too few local families were prepared to keep their daughters at home and to miss their earnings (or get a bad reputation with personnel management) for a cause that was widely perceived as mere identity politics. Nor did any support for the Catholic protest emerge from the young bachelor networks of skilled metalworkers in the Philips machine shop, who comprised the core of the local social democratic movement. These young workers in their twenties were newcomers from the north and west and their contacts with the local unskilled working girls in the mass production departments and outside the factory were few while their distaste for the Catholic Church was sincere. In their turn, they were left without any Catholic support in 1911 when they went on strike against Gerard Philips's refusal to allow them the privilege of a collective contract. Sharp segmentations, first of all of gender, but continuously overlaid with class and religion, thus were inherent to flexible familist manufacturing and were easily played into by the large manufacturers such as Philips or van Abbe. They thwarted all opportunities for a class movement in the largest manufacturing site outside the Randstad, and the site most crucial for the Dutch political economy in the decades ahead.

The second consequence was ultimately even more momentous. The flexible familist arrangement, while crucial to the growth of export-led labor-intensive manufacturing in the area, necessarily prevented urbanization from keeping up with capital accumulation. Given the low per-worker incomes, local housing rents were simply unaffordable for any family without additional wages from daughters' labor. Families with small children simply could not move to the city. Consequently, the local supply of daughters continuously declined relative to the growth of industry, as older local daughters married and retreated from work and a new stock of young girls was simply not available in the same numbers. Flexible familism, by separating the reproduction of its unskilled working class from the accumulation of its capital, ensured a disciplined labor force but also inevitably generated an exhaustion of its labor supply. The "spineless spider" not only served to deepen traditional patriarchy, and prevent urban modernity and working-class organization, in the end it also annihilated the demographic, social, and cultural preconditions of its own success.

Only large-scale investments in housing for unskilled worker families could have broken this perverse relation between industrial growth and the labor supply, certainly after Philips went into higher gear after 1924. The costs involved, however, were prohibitive and hard to calculate for decades to come, certainly in an emerging consumer industry for which the transnational markets were still very cyclical and highly capricious. Urban policy makers, too, were not enthused about the prospect of taking over responsibility for a large unskilled working-class that could well become unemployed in the first downturn and apply in large numbers for local social assistance or stage a labor protest. Moreover, while the Dutch social housing law of 1901 may have been famous for its facilities for state-sponsored housing investments, it was not meant to subsidize company housing. Only independent housing corporations were eligible and they were required to open their doors for everyone, not just for employees of X or Y. After 1924, when postwar markets took off again, and above all after 1927 when Philips was constructing the largest radio factory in the world, it could no longer avoid facing this dilemma so deeply engraved in the very territorial, social, and cultural landscape it had helped to produce.

Crisis

Until World War I, Philips Corporation had been a minor player in the emerging electrical market. In a general sense, Dutch twentieth-century industrialization depended largely on the growth of the German hinterland. Dutch players could not easily move on their own accord, except when operating on the colonial market. More importantly for our case, the knowledge base of each invention in the electrical industry, the Edison patents, were owned by General Electric of the United States, and shared with General Electric Corporation in the United Kingdom and AEG/Siemens in Germany. The Netherlands, however, did not yet recognize international intellectual property rights. The Dutch bourgeoisie was well connected, readily sent its sons abroad for study, and maintained at Delft a technical high school with international reputation. Philips emerged out of this spatial junction. Gerard Philips had discovered the practical potentials of the invention of the electron while studying in Scotland. His family, from Jewish background and located in an old mercantile town in the river country, near the Randstad, had long-standing connections with Eindhoven where they used to put out tobacco for processing it into cigars and where they had learned about the manufacturing potentials of the flexible familist arrangement. Those were the linkages that brought the Edison insights to Eindhoven, opened up huge international markets for local production, and ultimately put Eindhoven in a direct competitive relationship with Boston and Berlin and their respective outposts. However, given the small home market in the Netherlands and the exclusion from the Edison monopolies, it was only because of the locational advantage of cheap and flexible but surprisingly disciplined and precise labor in situ that the corporation could actually have survived. By concentrating on a small range of easily marketable consumer products, continuously rationalizing its production methods and fine-tuning them with the flexible familist arrangement, a minor player in a small country succeeded in gradually conquering substantial shares in an emerging international market of vital economic importance originally controlled by monopolists.

As Philips acquired critical mass and invested its surpluses into an autonomous research capacity, its position of international dependency gradually shifted. The real breakthrough came when Philips decided to become a prime mover in the emerging market of radio for household use in its Eindhoven outlays, from 1927 onward. Unprecedented quantities of capital were poured into the making of an impressive array of new industrial premises, equaling in size the largest European examples such as in Coventry, Wolfsburg, or Torino, and equipped with house-designed production technologies. However, by failing to solve its dilemma of the supply of unskilled labor, the expansions ultimately served to destroy precisely what had been crucial for its success and survival: the flexible familist arrangement.

In the two years between the late summer of 1927 and the autumn of 1929, the number of unskilled workers at Philips increased from some 7,500 to more than 18,000. A majority now came to the town as lodgers or commuters, the former by 1929 amounting to some 15,000 persons (Kalb 1997: 159–172). Radio production thus called a young and mobile proletariat into being, a novelty for the region. This had complex consequences. To begin with, young lodgers and commuters, outside the sphere of direct parental control, started to use urban space in new ways. They flocked into the city center after work and indulged in the newly emerging urban pleasures of courting, fashion, jazz, and cinema. Clearly, their claim on their own earnings had become firmer, as well as their claims on relationships, time and leisure.

This quick shift in urban culture immediately challenged the fixed gender images of flexible familist manufacturing. Catholic social workers agreed that Eindhoven in these years had rapidly achieved the highest proportion of "fallen youth" in the country. They admitted that this "fallen youth" was beyond the reach of moral activists or priests, who harvested more contempt than respect.

Before long, the town was known as "Dutch Brussels" (Kalb 1997: 166). The decline of patriarchal authority was well visible in the police statistics: compared to 1926 the number of recorded offenses in 1929 was three times as high, while the incidence of "recalcitrance" against officers had increased by a factor of five (ibid.: 165). Surely, this was also the result of heightened policing, as moral panic swept through the city's respectable circles. Local belles-lettres of the time produced two remarkable but little-known novels that wallowed in the moral morass of a supposed massive shift from tradition to cultural modernity. Feverishly and fearfully, both narratives explored the meaning of "light blouses," "short skirts," and "above all, legs, legs, legs…. O what a miserable plumage and coquetry" (ibid.: 167), and saw old values of honor and deference being destroyed at once.

The revolution in juvenile culture and adolescent power was of course not limited to nighttime or the urban pleasure zones. In fact, it put into question the whole regional hegemony of patriarchy as it was rooted in the flexible familist production arrangement. Philips management saw a "bad spirit" rising among its unskilled workers. The share of females in the production departments of the radio factory had been falling rapidly and managers failed to uphold the usual segregation between the sexes over different production lines. Productivity declined rapidly, as other indices, such as absenteeism, illness, and general labor-turnover, were peaking. While the largest stocks of capital ever to flow into manufacturing in the Netherlands were being amassed, it was the consequent wholesale transformation of class, urban, and family relationships in Eindhoven that immediately endangered their valuation.

"Social Policy" and the Managerial Revolution

Just three years later, in the middle of the crisis following the crash of the New York Stock Exchange, the Eindhoven cityscape had been significantly transformed, and flexible familism, as a hierarchical and gendered patriarchal culture, as a social form of production and as nonurban urbanity, was firmly restored by a managerial revolution from above. This transformation, and its sequencing, has as yet been little understood. A perspective on class as detailed here allows for discovery of the key processes and their interrelationships.

It started in late 1927 with Philips, now the pride of Dutch industry, alarmed at its apparent inability to facilitate the reproduction of its local labor force in ways that kept its cultural properties intact starting to lobby effectively with the Dutch state for help. The Dutch state, run by the conservatives, found the necessary resources in the framework of a large resettlement program targeted at several underdeveloped Dutch regions in crisis. These funds were now used to cover 80 percent of the costs of a huge housing program and allowed Philips to regain hegemony over its local human factor, first of all daughters' labor, by restoring flexible familist relationships. In the spring of 1929, while the first seven-story-high factory premises, stretching several kilometers along the railways, were being opened, it started the building of almost 2,000 houses, spread over several neighborhoods, mostly close to the core of the urban "spider." The expenses were unprecedented and amounted to half of total national social housing subsidies during 1929 and 1930. The new quarters were going to be inhabited by very large families (in the largest quarter, families had an average of more than eight children per family, most of them of wage-earning age), recruited from among the impoverished petite bourgeoisie of peripheral areas. These families were not only selected on the "daughters' criterion," though that was essential, but were also tested by "psycho-techniques" that laid the basis for the further development of applied psychology in the Netherlands. Fathers would get a job at Philips, too, as long as they could bring in at least three daughters at once (and more daughters later), since it was openly recognized that their wages would be "costly" and far exceed the men's actual contribution to production or profitability. The neighborhoods that were constituted in this way subsequently became the object of a well-developed company "social policy," ranging from social work to illness funds, pensions, house-supervisors, counseling, schooling, and leisure time associations. It made Philips into the classical example of company paternalism in the country, and a pioneer in the social management of industrialization. The Eindhoven experience of industrialization by public investment and social policy would subsequently play a considerable role in postwar Dutch reconstruction, as would its key designers.

This unique round of large-scale, state-sponsored urban and social investments between 1929 and 1931 enabled Philips to survive two consecutive mortal threats: first a local threat of hegemonic collapse, for which translocal linkages with the state became the solution; then a global threat, generated by the collapse of the stock markets and the consequent hypercompetition and international deflation, for which deepened and managerially restored local flexible familist arrangements became the weapon. The alliance with the state first allowed the company to regain control over labor, labor discipline, and productivity. In several waves, the lodgers, then the commuters, then other inadequate local workers got fired. In 1929–1930, accompanied by a surge of antiunion and antisocialist police repression, young mobile and "restless" workers were exchanged for the immigrant girls plus their overseeing fathers, who were just arriving in the new quarters (Kalb 1997: 213–225).

Revitalized flexible familism enabled Philips to counter the subsequent onslaught of hypercompetition and dumping by a concerted rationalization drive, predicated upon the newly won discipline (ibid.). In the process, the company could test out what local worker families had probably known all along: how uniquely flexible local employment arrangements were, and how easily they were geared to productivity enhancement. Starting in late 1931, Philips reduced its number of workers to its lowest possible point of fewer than 9,000, ostensibly to allow it to reduce stocks in the face of global overproduction. Immediately after their arrival, the new households in the Philips neighborhoods had on average more than six workers employed at the factories. This number was now reduced to about two: a father and one daughter. Sometimes even fathers were dismissed, if the mental predispositions of a family would seem to allow so. However, in combination with temporary reductions of housing rents, families were indeed kept from destitution, and protest was held at a minimum, while the actual personnel reduction was nevertheless drastic. Those who opposed the measures were offered a train ticket back to where they came from. The daughters kept on the payroll were the ones with the highest productivity scores. These disciplined, concentrated, and adroit girls were setting the norms from now on. Then, after some weeks, small groups of other family members were selected to be called back to the factories one after another and were individually trained to conform to the new strict standards. Flexible familism in this way not only allowed huge temporary cutbacks in employment, it also prevented protest and mass mobilization to break out. But on top of that, it facilitated a tremendous rise in labor productivity, an increase of not less than 300 percent between 1929 and 1933 (ibid.: 218). The result was a major paradox: By re-creating flexible familism from above and transforming the entire territorial morphology of Southeast Brabant and the city of Eindhoven, Philips succeeded in becoming a champion of export-led labor-intensive manufacturing in the middle of a world crisis precisely from a location in the last country in the Western world to leave the gold standard (1936).

Comparison and Prospective Practice

Flexible familism, ultimately, was based on a regional process of very gradual proletarianization of local households. Peasants, peasant workers, worker peasants and workers who moved into all sorts of wheeling and dealing, and, if they failed, back again into supplementary wage work, prevailed for a long time. Access to land and property remained important. Until the early twentieth century, this was largely a semiproletarian population not accurately captured by any statistics, nor by the notion of protoindustry. Familial networks were the key to survival, status, information, and property. Mutual support between spouses in a de jure patriarchal arrangement in which women were de facto sometimes surprisingly central (matrifocality) was essential. Children were supposed to be subservient to the family's overall reproductive needs, daughters much more directly so than sons, who were allowed to teach themselves the necessary social and technical skills of the "folk economy." As export-oriented light industry settled in the region, it did so first of all because of the locational advantage of immature labor markets, which meant low costs for a largely juvenile and female labor force, costs that did not cover the actual expense of producing and reproducing labor power, as epitomized by the Philips labor arrangement. The large entrepreneurs in the region acquired the hegemony they needed not primarily through the wage nexus, nor through any sort of "discourse" in the narrowly expressive sense, but through delegating authority to patriarchal familism and informally sharing profits with parents. Flexible familism was the intricate practice that sprang from these conjunctions.

Mature markets, as Gramsci has described for Fordism, generate capitalist hegemony at the point of production itself, through the wage nexus (Gramsci 1989: 277–320). Sure, we now know that Ford also developed complex personnel and social policies to regulate social life outside the factory. Ford's social package can be called "monetary moralism," where cash incentives are offered to those who are willing to supervise themselves and internalize Ford's ideal of the thrifty family man who is dedicated to industrial performance in order to support his 'healthy' consumer household (Kalb 1997: 226–233; Meyer, 1981). Mature (male) labor markets and monetary moralism belong together just as immature (young female) labor markets and flexible familism do; the former is paradigmatic for "the West," as a symbol even more than a place, while the latter emerges time and again in "Eastern" manufacturing spaces that try to export their way out of backwardness (Croll 2000; Ong 1987, 1999). The two forms have contrastive consequences for the emergence of critical identities and popular protest.

In the American Midwest, the classical topos of Fordism, the collapse of the New York Stock Exchange and consequent bankruptcies and deflation after 1929 caused a downward spiral of mutually reinforcing mass unemployment of male wage earners, impoverishment of households, defaults on mortgage payments, forced expulsion of families from dwellings, and so on. In short, the crisis of Fordism produced veritable uprooting. In response, the big cities of the Midwest developed a militant industrial unionism, and ultimately led to the New Deal and further electoral victories for a social democratic President Roosevelt (see, among others, Brody 1980). It thus even laid the electoral and programmatic basis for a new postwar world system. This new system was centered on the United Nations, the Universal Declaration of Human Rights, the International Bank for Reconstruction and Development, and an initially Keynesian International Monetary Fund to prevent another round of deflation. The dollar was offered as a world currency and the American consumer became the global consumer of last resort.

In comparison, the political spiral set in motion by the response to the same global conditions from a flexible familist industrial zone such as Eindhoven was deeply conservative and parochial. For a political historian such a comparison makes no sense as Eindhoven clearly had little independent political meaning, and wider national and European political circumstances played a role in any local outcome, too. But there was an inherent political dynamic to Philipsism that must be analyzed. That was a dynamic of strengthened gender and generational exploitation, of hyperrationalization and deepened export dependency, of patriarchal vocabularies of production and politics, of a social policy for stepped-up competitiveness. Ingredients of this supply-side conservative mix later featured in the postwar social compact in the Netherlands too, and even in muted form in the temporary success of the Third Way "Polder Model," after the fall of the Wall.

Less grandiose but not less real were the consequences for individual hope and aspirations. While the response to the crisis of the liberal Fordist model ultimately encouraged the legitimacy of, and a popular will for, high wages and abundant private consumption, the familist form would inspire strong desires for an escape from both patriarchal submission and from overcrowded complex households, as well as a redefinition, however cautious, of the family. Paradoxically, it was precisely the Philips firm itself which was going to bring this to its workers. As it expanded first nationally and then internationally, after the war, it created familist industrial communities around branch plants in new "immature" peripheries. It simultaneously transformed its base in Eindhoven into first a specialized industrial service center for small series productions and process development, and then ever more exclusively (after 1965 or so) into a headquarters and research function for a large multinational corporation. In Eindhoven, male blue- and increasingly white-collar work multiplied, while young female work strongly declined, but never disappeared, after the late 1950s. Wages gradually rose above individual reproduction costs. From the early 1960s onward, income rises finally allowed the transition to a family consumption economy for workers without formal diplomas. Please note the date: Yes, this late, in a core capitalist site.

But Maria Van de Velde and other working-class women in the early to late 1950s still encountered a myriad of obstacles on their way to extricating themselves from overbearing familial claims and to creating less demeaning and stressful, more independent and caring relationships. Parents continued to claim their earnings while the local housing market was factually bottlenecked by the huge cohorts of children from very large Philips families who were all longing to set up households of their own. It had been Philips's accumulation imperatives during the radio boom that had created the large demographic cohorts and the bottleneck in the first place. But, paradoxically, it was Philips again that was going to save them. The expanding firm saw itself ever more forced to offer housing to its personnel in an increasingly saturated labor market, again using state loans to do so. Housing shortages finally began to decline in the mid 1960s, at the very moment that the promise of a modest prosperity started to glow. As a consequence, the next generation of workers would tie itself again to the Philips firm. In close proximity to family and kin, near or actually in the factories and neighborhoods that had shaped their selves and their (lack of) youth and autonomy, young working-class couples of the 1960s, 1970s, and 1980s, having children of their own, would contemplate, renegotiate, and cautiously redefine, step by step, the meaning of childhood, family, gender, and work, surprised by and somewhat unsettled about the wealth, freedoms, and hedonism with which mature corporate capitalism was increasingly and openly legitimizing itself.

Conclusion

This essay has revolted against the pressure to be forced into the mold of one of the organizing bipolarities of social thought in the 1980s and 1990s, the figure of discourse versus class, in which class is the red herring and discourse the nice and communicative assistant. It must revolt because this figure, apparently enabling for a while in the 1980s, has turned into a vehicle of hegemony over academic fields. The program has become redundant.

This is not so because we need to retain the populist pulse of local resistance against injustice as associated with the *discourse of class,* as Eley and Nield contend—and Dirlik seems to agree with them. No doubt we must do that, too. But theoretically and strategically this is precisely the wrong way to go about it. Class must be rethought to regain a critical hold on the larger historical and spatial process of capitalism and its associated hegemonies and social divisions. It must be rethought to understand the contested terrain of place making, to capture the critical junctions, and to liberate bodily, material, and relational experience of individuals from the silencing by formal public discourse. And we need to rethink it, too, because we must root public discourse and action, as well as its reception and countervailing forces, much more firmly and dynamically in the actual contradictory patchworks of power and interest that manage the locales of work, family, and everyday life within the perpetually shifting spatial and temporal networks of the capitalist imperative.

Instead of recycling discourse against interest, or vice versa, this essay has tried to turn the program of class into a more flexible, contingent, and relational discovery procedure. The discovery was oriented toward what Eric Wolf has called the "key relationships" of social organization, that is, production and reproduction in a broad sense. These key relationships underpin what David Harvey has identified as the "structured coherence" of territorially engraved and spatially clustered modes of modern social life as they are made and unmade within a set of critical junctions that tie any locale into identifiable webs of space and time. The discovery procedure is connected to an ethnographic method of studying up and outward, as well as backward and forward, and seeks to identify the various struggles for place making and their shifting resource bases as people engage with the grand forces and human projects of modernity.

The example I have studied is an unlikely one. The absence of concerted class-based protest in this core region of manufacturing in the Netherlands has within the country itself almost always been explained by invoking discourse long before it became *en vogue* in the English-speaking academic world. Either paternalism or Catholicism, or a combination of both, has been used as an explanation. Both fail to scrutinize the cause, the modalities, and the actual grounds for reception of such public discourses offered from above. Such discourse-based explanations, moreover, have actively sponsored the continuing mystification of class, gender, and generational relations driving the industrialization process in these areas forward. They have left women in the dark. A refigured notion of class, wedded to a concern with critical junctions as worked out here, helps to discover how young women were socialized for "careful" exploitation within an alliance between employers and parents and how this fed into a specific, flexible familist form of urbanization and export-led industrial growth; how it prevented class-based action while it subjected women to painfully contradictory projects of becoming; and how such class relations and gender syndromes gradually shifted, though were never erased, in the course of time.

Notes

1. See Kalb (1997) for a more extensive discussion of class in history, sociology, and anthropology and for more lengthy examples and references. See also Tilly (2001) for a similarly relational approach as advocated here.
2. Eley and Nield's article (2000a) formed the start of a wider discussion in *International Labor and Working Class History*, with Frederick Cooper, Don Kalb, Stephen Kotkin, Joan Scott, and Judith Stein commenting and Eley and Nield (2000b) replying. My contribution here can be seen as one possible elaboration of my critique, which was, to my mind, largely supported in the contributions by Cooper and Stein.
3. Rewarding insights on anthropology and hegemony are to be drawn from Gavin Smith (2004), especially the difference between a cultural and relational reading of Gramsci and Raymond Williams.
4. A strawman because the new social history and the new urban sociology of "the seventies," and especially the political economy school in American anthropology, were well on their way of abrogating it. See Kalb (1997).
5. See Kalb (2000b) for an effort to work this out in relation to the globalization debate.
6. This story is based on Kalb (1997). Other key items on Philips, Eindhoven, and Southeast Brabant are: Bakker Schut (1933); Blanken (1992); Boonstra (1989, 1993); Van Drenth (1991); Heerding (1980, 1986); ILO (1932); Oorschot (1982); Otten (1987, 1991); Stoop (1992); Teulings (1976). On Dutch labor relations, see Windmuller and de Galan (1969). On the electrical industry and associated labor relations, see also Bright (1949) and Schatz (1983).
7. This fragment is extracted from Kalb (1997: 236–246).
8. Dr. Barentsen, a physician located in the area, described practices of gender repression in the early twentieth century in the largely protoindustrial countryside, reprinted as Barentsen ([1926] 1989).

References

Andersen, Michael. 1984. *Approaches to the History of the Western Family, 1500–1914.* London: Macmillan.

Appadurai, Arjun. 1996. *Modernity at Large.* Minneapolis: University of Minnesota Press.

———. 2000. "Grassroots Globalization and the Research Imagination." *Public Culture* 12, no. 1: 1–19.

Bakker Schut, F. 1933. *Industrie en Woningbouw.* Assen: Van Gorcum.

Barentsen, P. A. 1926. "Het gezinsleven in het oosten van Noord-Brabant." In *Mens en Maatschappij*, vol. 2. Reproduced in G. van den Brink et al., eds. 1989. *Werk, kerk en bed in Brabant.* 's Hertogenbosch: Stichting Brabantse Regionale Geschiedbeoefening.

Blanken, I. 1992. *De ontwikkeling van de N.V. Philips fabrieken tot electrotechnisch concern.* Leiden: Martinus Nijhof.

Blok, Anton. 1974. *The Mafia of a Sicilian Village, 1860–1960: A Study of Violent Peasant Entrepreneurs.* Oxford: Macmillan.

Boissevain, Jeremy. 1974. *Friends of Friends: Networks, Manipulators and Coalitions.* Oxford: Basil Blackwell.

Bonnell, Victoria, and Lynn Hunt, eds. 1999. *Beyond the Cultural Turn.* Berkeley: University of California Press.

Boonstra, O. 1989. "De dynamiek van het agrarisch-ambachtelijk huwelijkspatroon: Huwelijksfrequentie en huwelijksleeftijd in Eindhoven, 1800–1900." In *Werk, kerk en bed in Brabant*, ed. G. van den Brink et al. 's Hertogenbosch: Stichting Brabantse Regionale Geschiedschrijving.

———. 1993. *De Waardij van eene vroege opleiding: Een onderzoek naar de implicaties van alfabetisme op het leven van inwoners van Eindhoven en omliggende gemeenten, 1800–1920.* Wageningen: AAG Bijdragen.

Bright, A. A. 1949. *The Electrical Lamp Industry: Technological Change and Economic Development from 1800 to 1947.* New York: Macmillan.

Brody, David. 1980. *Workers in Industrial America: Essays on the Twentieth-Century Struggle.* New York: Basic Books.

Cooper, Fred. 2000. "Farewell to the Category-Producing Class?" *International Labor and Working Class History* 57: 60–68.

Croll, Elisabeth. 2000. *Endangered Daughters: Discrimination and Development in Asia.* London: Routledge.

Dirlik, Arif. 2001. "Globalism and the Politics of Place." In *Globalization and the Asia-Pacific: Contested Territories*, ed. Kris Olds, P. Dicken, P. F. Kelly, L. Wong, and H. W. Yeung. London: Routledge.

Drenth, Annemieke Van. 1991. *De zorg om het Philipsmeisje: Fabrieksmeisjes in de elektrotechnische industrie in Eindhoven, 1900–1960.* Zutphen: Walburg Pers.

Eley, Geoff, and Keith Nield. 2000a. "Farewell to the Working Class?" *International Labor and Working-Class History* 57: 1–30.

———. 2000b. "Reply: Class and the Politics of History." *International Labor and Working-Class History* 57: 76–87.

Gluckman, Max. 1958. *Analysis of a Social Situation in Modern Zululand.* Manchester: Manchester University Press.

Gramsci, Antonio. 1989. *Selections from the Prison Notebooks.* New York: International Publishers.

Gupta, Akhil, and James Ferguson, eds. 1997. *Culture, Power, Place: Explorations in Critical Anthropology.* Durham, NC: Duke University Press.

Hannerz, Ulf. 1991. *Cultural Complexity.* New York: Columbia University Press.

———. 1996. *Transnational Connections.* London: Routledge.

Harvey, David. 1989. *The Urban Experience.* Baltimore: Johns Hopkins University Press.

Heerding, A. 1980. *Geschiedenis van de N.V. Philips' Gloeilampen Fabrieken*. Vol. 1. Leiden: Martinus Nijhoff.

———. 1986. *Een onderneming van vele markten thuis: Geschiedenis van de Philips gloeilampen-fabrieken*. Vol. 2. Leiden: Martinus Nijhoff.

Hunt, Lynn, ed. 1989. *The New Cultural History*. Berkeley: University of California Press.

International Labor Organization. 1932. *Les Usines Philips*. Geneva: ILO.

Joyce, Patrick. 1991. *Visions of the People*. Cambridge: Cambridge University Press.

———. 1994. *Democratic Subjects: The Self and the Social in Nineteenth-Century England*. Cambridge: Cambridge University Press.

Kalb, Don. 1997. *Expanding Class: Power and Everyday Politics in Industrial Communities, The Netherlands, 1850–1950*. Durham, NC: Duke University Press.

———. 2000a. "Class (in Place) without Capitalism (in Space)?" *International Labor and Working-Class History* 57: 31–39.

———. 2000b. "Localizing Flows: Power, Paths, Institutions, and Networks." In *The Ends of Globalization: Bringing Society Back In*, ed. Don Kalb et al., 1–33. Lanham, MD: Rowman and Littlefield.

Katznelson, Ira. 1992. *Marxism and the City*. Oxford: Clarendon Press.

Kotkin, Stephen. 2000. "Class, the Working Class, and the Politburo." *International Labor and Working-Class History* 57: 48–52.

Meyer, Stephen. 1981. *The Five Dollar Day: Labor Management and Social Control in the Ford Motor Company, 1908–1921*. Albany: State University of New York Press.

Ong, Aihwa. 1987. *Spirits of Resistance and Capitalist Discipline: Factory Women in Malaysia*. New York: State University of New York Press.

———. 1999. "Clash of Civilizations or Asian Liberalism? An Anthropology of the State and Citizenship." In *Anthropological Theory Today*, ed. Henrietta L. Moore, 48–73. Cambridge: Polity Press.

Oorschot, Jan van. 1982. *Eindhoven, een samenleving in verandering*. 2 vols. Eindhoven: Gemeente Eindhoven.

Otten, Ad. 1987. *Volkshuisvesting in Eindhoven*. Zeist: Vonk.

———. 1991. *Philips woningbouw, 1900–1990*. Zaltbommel: Europese Bibliotheek.

Reddy, William. 1984. *The Rise of Market Culture: The Textile Trade and French Society, 1750–1900*. Cambridge: Cambridge University Press.

———. 1987. *Money and Liberty in Modern Europe: A Critique of Historical Understanding*. Cambridge: Cambridge University Press.

Schatz, Ronald. 1983. *The Electrical Workers: A History of Labor at General Electric and Westinghouse, 1923–1960*. Urbana: University of Illinois Press.

Scott, Joan W. 2000. "The 'Class' We Have Lost." *International Labor and Working-Class History* 57: 69–75.

Seccombe, Wally. 1995. *Weathering the Storm: Working Class Families from the Industrial Revolution to the Fertility Decline*. London: Verso.

Sider, Gerald. 1982. *Culture and Class in Anthropology and History: A Newfoundland Illustration*. Cambridge: Cambridge University Press.

———. 1993. *Lumbee Indian Histories: Race, Ethnicity, and Indian Identity in the Southern United States*. Cambridge: Cambridge University Press.

Sider, Gerald, and Gavin Smith, eds. 1997. *Between History and Histories: The Making of Silences and Commemorations*. Toronto: University of Toronto Press.

Smith, Gavin. 2002. "Effective Reality: Intellectuals and Politics in the Current Conjuncture." *Focaal—European Journal of Anthropology* 40: 165–180.

———. 2004. "Hegemony: Critical Interpretations in Anthropology and Beyond." *Focaal—European Journal of Anthropology* 43: 99–120.

Stein, Judith. 2000. "Where's the Beef?" *International Labor and Working-Class History* 57: 40–47.

Stoop, Sjef. 1992. *De sociale fabriek: Sociale politiek bij Philips Eindhoven, Bayer Leverkusen en Hoogovens Ijmuiden*. Leiden: Stenfert Kroese.

Teulings, Ad. 1976. *Philips: Geschiedenis en praktijk van een wereldconcern*. Amsterdam: Van Gennep.

Tilly, Charles. 2001. "Relational Origins of Inequality." *Anthropological Theory* 1, no. 3: 355–372.

Tilly, Louise, and Joan Scott. 1978. *Women, Work, and Family*. New York: Basic Books.

Weinstein, Barbara. 2000. "Where Do Ideas (about Class) Come From?" *International Labor and Working-Class History* 57: 53–59.

Windmuller, J., and C. de Galan. 1969. *Labor Relations in the Netherlands*. Ithaca, NY: Cornell University Press.

Wolf, Eric. 1964. *Anthropology*. Princeton, NJ: Princeton University Press.

———. 1969. *Peasant Wars of the Twentieth Century*. New York: Harper and Row.

———. 1982. *Europe and the People Without History*. Berkeley: University of California Press.

———. 1999. *Envisioning Power*. Berkeley: University of California Press.

———. 2001. *Pathways of Power: Building an Anthropology of the Modern World*. Berkeley: University of California Press.

Chapter Six

Prefiguring NAFTA
The Politics of Land Privatization in Neoliberal Mexico

Patricia Musante

... the world of humankind constitutes a manifold, a totality of interconnected processes, and inquiries that disassemble this totality into bits and then fail to reassemble it falsify reality. Concepts like "nation," "society," and "culture" name bits and threaten to turn names into things. Only by understanding these names as bundles of relationships, and by placing them back into the fields from which they were abstracted, can we hope to avoid misleading inferences and increase our share of understanding.

— Eric R. Wolf, *Europe and the People Without History*

Introduction

Eric Wolf's emphasis on interconnected, global processes in *Europe and the People Without History* (1982) provides a model for bringing the concerns of history, geography, and anthropology together to study the political economy of globalization, both past and present. To his list of "thingified" concepts I would add the *local* or the *community* which have been, and continue to be, reified within anthropological discourse and practice. The boundaries of the local or the community—however broadly they may be defined or imagined— are often taken as a given, and hence naturalized. This tendency continues even as anthropologists increasingly broaden their attention to include issues of globalization. We may recall here that the procedure in anthropology of

Notes for this chapter begin on page 148.

scale reduction, or "posing big questions to small settings," recently fell out of favor because it misrecognized the local as a microcosm of the nation, not because it incorrectly presumed a naturalness to the small setting. That is, although this misrecognition was less and less tenable as the boundaries of the nation itself became increasingly porous and permeable, anthropologists did not radically transform their basic understanding of the boundedness of localities. Rather, anthropologists still tend to attribute a preconstituted otherness to the local, which is then proposed as the last defense against the homogenizations supposedly inherent in the processes of globalization. Consequently, our understanding of the totality of interconnected, global processes and their political consequences, to which Wolf continually drew our attention, remains rather underdeveloped.

In this chapter, I am especially concerned with both geographical and cultural boundaries—how they are made, unmade, and remade—and the political alliances that they make possible or preclude. Emphasizing the constructedness of boundaries allows me to map out both political connections and spatial perspectives that transgress the local, as well as efforts by the state to reestablish the boundaries of the local and contain political struggle. I want to suggest that this approach, which draws equally upon the insights of Eric Wolf (1982) on global interconnections and Neil Smith (1984, 1992) on the production of space, moves us beyond the *ahistorical* approaches to the question of scale that have, thus far, limited the usefulness of anthropological understandings of the contemporary political conjuncture.

I pursue this line of critique on the question of scale in anthropological inquiry through a reconsideration of how local legacies of resistance figure into the complex negotiations over the terms and conditions of globalization. I will start by questioning the assumptions contained in both the dominant neoliberal development model charting the course toward more open global markets and the postmodernist critiques of globalization. Although posed in oppositional terms, both models tend to uncritically privilege local agency as strategically and analytically central to the issue of globalization. On the one hand, the neoliberal discourse and policies of development agencies and lending institutions start from the idea that both the state and the public sector have become outmoded forms of organization and power that hinder local initiative and decision making and thereby threaten the productivity and efficiency of capitalism.[1] On the other hand, postmodernist critics view the local as the premiere site of resistance to the forces of globalization, since its perceived autonomy provides a space for the creative production of identities and strategies in opposition to the cultural homogeneity associated with the accelerating flows of transnational capitalism (Escobar 1992; Featherstone 1996). I will argue for a more nuanced view that considers the renewed production and revitalization of the local in relation to both state power and global capital. From this perspective, the importance of local identities and political agency may be examined without resorting to a false dichotomy between the global and the local.

The focus of my consideration is a series of land invasions, part of a longer-term political campaign for the restitution of communal land that occurred during my field research in 1990–1991 in Tetelcingo, a village of Nahuatl- and Spanish-speaking peasants and mainly informal sector workers in Morelos, Mexico. They occurred on the eve of the momentous 1992 constitutional reform that newly sanctioned the privatization of *ejido* land that had been granted to organized agrarian communities as part of the consolidation of state power in the decades following the Mexican Revolution of 1910–1920.[2] The reform paved the way for the passage of the North American Free Trade Agreement (NAFTA) in 1994 which reduced political barriers to the free flow of capital on the continent. The Tetelcingeños' campaign for the restitution of communal land, then, offers a window into how the new intersections of transnational capital, the state, and particular localities are reworking existing social arrangements to create new forms of power and identity.

When I first arrived in the village, I was struck by what seemed to my eyes a rather strange site. A bunch of seemingly abandoned makeshift shacks peppered the dry, desolate, and otherwise vacant landscape on the eastern outskirts of the village. These tiny shacks, I soon learned, symbolized a political demand with deep historical roots by villagers for recognition of what they claimed to be their primordial rights to communal land that had been usurped by outsiders. Their claim was based on the elaboration and advancement of an interpretation of local historical experience as shaped by an encompassing system of ethnic domination. The recuperation of communal land was crucial to the continuing livelihood and survival of many of the villagers actively participating in the land campaign. Many either lacked enough land or adequate financial resources to secure a parcel that could meet their needs for living and working on the expanding urban periphery of Cuautla, just seven kilometers away.

Their adversary in the present land campaign was the Sindicato de Trabajadores de la Industria Azucarera de Casasano, the union of sugar industry workers, whose members worked in the nearby state-owned Casasano Sugar Mill. Union leaders claimed the land had been the private property of a nonresident landowner and they had purchased it legally. At stake in this dispute was the ability of a powerful group of outside investors, with strong ties to international capital, to acquire the Casasano Sugar Mill on the eve of the passage of NAFTA.[3] They were anxious to capture the profits that would likely flow from ownership of a sugar mill with the expected expansion of the processed food industry. As part of the complex negotiations surrounding this sale, the union demanded that the state and new owners honor longstanding government commitments to construct worker housing by matching the contributions that had been deducted over the years from the sugar workers' paychecks.

Globalism and the Historical Geography of Agrarian Conflict

In their property dispute with the union, villagers employed the legal procedure of restitution that recognized the claim of agrarian communities to prior ownership and subsequent dispossession of particular territories (Purnell 1999: 58–59). This procedure formed part of the set of agrarian reform laws contained in Article 27 of the 1917 Constitution. The inclusion of restitution in these agrarian reform laws owes much to the legacy of the revolutionary leader, Emiliano Zapata, and his peasant army who fought for the return of their villages' primordial lands that had been appropriated by sugar plantation owners under the protection of the Díaz regime. The death toll and property destruction wrought by Zapata's peasant army did not end until other regional leaders of the revolution agreed to their demand for justice: a return to the primordial boundaries and authority of the village.[4] However, the Zapatista vision of justice was fundamentally reframed in the process of concluding the armed struggle and institutionalizing the revolution in the 1920s and 1930s. Article 27 of the Constitution, which contains the agrarian reform laws, asserted national ownership of natural resources. Therefore, the nation, not the village, had the sole power and authority to grant rights to land (De la Peña 1981; Gilly 1998; Purnell 1999; Womack 1968). In the name of bureaucratic efficiency and national consolidation, war-ravaged villages were dissuaded from seeking the restitution of their primordial lands in favor of petitioning the state as agrarian communities for a land grant, or *dotación*.[5]

This paternalist settlement between the government and peasants not only facilitated the revolutionary elite's consolidation of power in the state, but also became the forcing ground of dominant ideas of the nation as the embodiment of the peasant revolution (Gilly 1998; Hamilton 1982; Joseph and Nugent 1994). Within this emergent nation-making discourse, local traditions and histories of struggle, such as Zapata's legacy of struggle for land, justice, and local autonomy in Morelos, were recuperated as "examples of the 'people's' humble contribution to the heritage of the nation" (Bommes and Wright 1982: 300). In this way, the idea of a common national heritage created an imaginary resolution to previously contradictory oppositions of peasant/state and local community/nation. But it was an extremely fragile resolution that could only be maintained through the formal institutionalization of the state/peasant compact, in which the state redistributed land and agrarian resources in return for political acquiescence (Gilly 1998; Hamilton 1982).

Indeed, the breakdown of the state/peasant alliance during the 1960s foreshadowed the resurgence in the 1970s of growing demands for the restitution of primordial village lands (Foley 1991; Saldívar 1982). This time, however, it was the state that advanced the idea of restitution as a legal option for peasant and Indian communities. The state's resurrection of restitution was an attempt to quell mounting agrarian unrest, expressed through participation in independent agrarian movements. These movements increasingly mounted well-organized land invasions onto private estates to force the state to live up to its end of the compact.

In 1974, hundreds of land-hungry villagers from Tetelcingo and its neighboring settlements active in independent agrarian movements staged a land invasion. Their goal was to press the government to resolve in their favor their fifteen-year-old petition to expand their insufficient *ejidal* grant onto the irrigated, cane-producing property of the owner, at that time, of the Casasano Sugar Mill. Tetelcingeños claimed that these lands had been intended as part of their original *ejidal* grant of irrigated land in 1936 but corrupt agrarian and municipal officials had transferred these lands to this new *hacendado*, the owner of the sugar mill. But unlike the successful land campaigns by displaced peasants and Yaqui Indians in northern Mexico, where the state expropriated large, expansionary agricultural and cattle estates, the agrarian committee that organized Tetelcingo's land invasion did not fare well in its negotiations with the government. Instead of expropriation, the state chose to prop up powerful, but nearly bankrupt, sugar-producing complexes like the Casasano Sugar Mill by financing reinvestment in the decapitalized plant (Jiménez Guzmán 1986, 1988; Singelman 1993). Indeed, the state pursued both military and legal channels to suppress this instance of peasant unrest. Within days of the occupation, the military forcefully expelled the land invaders. Following this show of force, government negotiators advised the agrarian committee to resubmit their petition for an expansion of their *ejidal* land using the newly revalidated legal procedure of restitution.

The official revalidation of the idea of restitution was a double-edged sword, however. While ostensibly containing mounting agrarian unrest within acceptable legal forms of expression, it also helped shore up and reconstitute popular traditions of struggle. The procedure of restitution seemingly validated local histories of struggle for land. But the very process of documenting these struggles opened up the discussion of local history to wider issues of political autonomy, ethnic dignity, and social justice, issues that historically had been intimately connected to peasant struggles for land and were the repressed legacy of Zapata. Zapata's reclaimed legacy resonated deeply with a new generation of displaced and insecure villagers whose attempts to earn an education and a livelihood increasingly spanned localities and regions, as well as cultural frontiers. Consequently, the key terms of Zapata's legacy, *Reform, Liberty, Justice, and Law*,[6] were rearticulated to the demands of this new social and economic landscape and helped energize a burgeoning, broad-based social movement.[7] A militant political meaning and agenda were inserted into the petition for restitution as this new generation of local peasant-workers joined in these wider struggles of students, teachers, and laborers for a livable, regular wage, job security, and urban services.

The growing militancy of the new social movements invigorated a struggle for municipal power. Like many Indian communities in Morelos's other municipalities, Tetelcingo initiated a campaign with its neighboring allied settlements to separate from the municipal seat of Cuautla (García Jiménez 1988). At stake was their ability to fragment the power domain of the regional elite tied to the long-ruling Partido Revolucionario Institucional (PRI) that had subordinated them politically, economically, and culturally. A key component of their radicalized agenda to form a new municipality was the redrawing of the political boundaries to correspond with those registered on the primordial maps that had been uncovered while documenting their claim for restitution.

The expanded political scope of the villagers' struggle for restitution was aided by their alliance with the progressive Catholic Church. This alliance provided their campaign with political support and protection. It also opened up new avenues of communication between the village and its allied settlements, as well as with other national and international groups and organizations involved in liberation and human rights struggles. Just as importantly, it imbued their campaign with a deepened moral significance and justification. The most critical support offered the campaign by the progressive Catholic leadership of Morelos, however, was the elevation of Tetelcingo to parish seat in the Church's hierarchy of places. This rise in status, part of the Church's own strategy to increase the representation of progressive priests in the bishop's council, significantly bolstered Tetelcingo's case for municipal independence, since it now assumed greater administrative and symbolic importance to Catholics in its neighboring settlements and in the region as a whole. The articulation of progressive Catholicism, municipal activism, and resurgent Indian identity proved politically potent. Accordingly, local Catholic ceremonies, now translated into Nahuatl by the young bilingual leaders in the village, empowered this campaign by infusing Christian symbolism of oppression and resistance into emergent understandings of their village's cultural history as told by the elders.[8]

During this period, Indianness came to symbolize a supralocal experience and political ties that were based on a shared history of exploitation and oppression, as well as a moral authority that predated the present state. As a potent marker of a differential morality and oppositional political stance, Indianness helped focus and energize widespread political resistance to increasing displacement and marginalization. As ethnic identifications came to articulate and empower their struggle against economic exploitation, political subordination, and cultural discrimination in the national political arena, factional expressions of local culture and politics, such as those previously found in the internecine feuding surrounding village fiestas honoring *barrio* saints, receded for a while into the background.[9]

The Remaking of Localism

Under enormous pressure from international lenders to stem Mexico's mounting debt crisis of 1982, the state embarked on a neoliberal course to boost economic productivity and control government spending (Cornelius 1985).

The social movements that connected communities independent of the ruling party posed a major political obstacle to this plan. As the economy worsened, these social movements increasingly aligned with opposition political parties to press their demands. Such an obstacle was posed by Tetelcingo's campaign for municipal autonomy whose leaders had just been elected to official political posts in the villages. The political threat posed by this campaign may be calibrated by the level of repression, intimidation, and mediation of local political and economic demands the state employed to resurrect the lines of conflict and contradiction that historically had separated Tetelcingo from its allied settlements economically, politically, and culturally.

This process resembled the localism described by Wolf (2001a, 2001b) and Carbonella (1996), in which a resurrection of localist cultural forms and the strengthening of community boundaries worked both to undermine wider political connections and limit the spatial perspectives of villagers. First, the state implemented the Municipal Strengthening Program, an economic development initiative that focused on delivering the crucial social and economic benefits demanded by the social movements over the past decade, but in ways and forms that aimed to reinforce the ideology of government benefaction and protection and, therefore, its political authority.[10]

Crucially, it sought to colonize the key organizational forms of the social movements. Proposals for local development projects were solicited from village and neighborhood-based committees that constituted the base of local support for these oppositional social movements. Moreover, these committees had to make their requests in grand public rituals of redistribution in the municipal seat presided over by the governor and his entourage.

Nevertheless, Tetelcingo continued to press their campaign for municipal independence by refusing to participate in this ritual in Cuautla. In an effort to win their participation, therefore, the government bestowed upon Tetelcingo a compromise political status, the first ever in the state, of *delegación municipal*. This administrative restructuring of the municipality implied greater power for Tetelcingo over its neighboring allied settlements while simultaneously maintaining its subordination to the municipal seat of Cuautla. Despite efforts to elicit the political collaboration of the elected local officials through patronage, the state's traditional method of bringing unruly local populations and their leaders in line, they forged ahead in the oppositional political movement for municipal autonomy. Therefore, the state moved to destroy the movement through military and paramilitary repression. In 1984, the movement's local leaders were arrested on trumped-up charges, fired from their jobs, and removed from local political office. Meanwhile, the local population as a whole was subjected to intense political intimidation through a six-month military occupation of Tetelcingo to enforce the state's new evening curfew and ban on political meetings. This military occupation enabled the state to install the previously long-ruling village faction loyal to the PRI in the newly vacant political offices.

Once the military had pacified the village, the state was better able to remake a localism in the image and service of a neoliberal project rapidly evolving on a national scale. A key element of this remaking was the rearticulation of identity to place. For example, community boundaries and localist sentiments were strengthened by sanctioning new, community-based monopolies of passenger van service. The municipality's archaic public transportation system, monopolized by one powerful family tied to the old guard of the PRI, was a major catalyst for the growth of the oppositional social movements in the municipality. The political opposition's widespread tactic of commandeering this family's buses to deliver crucial yet appallingly inadequate public transportation services to Cuautla's outlying villages and settlements had increased its appeal there, as well as inflamed their desire for municipal independence. To counter this, the state granted public transit permits in the name of the community to separate transportation committees that formed in each locality. This new arrangement increased both the availability and reliability of public transportation. Simultaneously, the taxes levied on these *transportistas* and redistributed by the newly imposed village officials helped fund local proposals for development projects during this period of state fiscal austerity. Crucially, however, it contributed to the resurgence of localism by tying the allocation of resources to continued party patronage because the permitting of community transportation monopolies and the funding of local development projects were contingent on political alignment with the PRI. *Transportistas* defended their monopolies against competition by guarding the borders of their communities against the political opposition, whom they now labeled as outsiders.

Further, the state strengthened localism by fostering an official commitment to the Indian as cultural heritage, a national treasure to be preserved for posterity, a commitment that cynically intended to counter the emergent identification of Indianness with a broader oppositional political stance. The state became the benefactor of ethnic customs, traditions, and languages through new government ethnological initiatives that reasserted the primacy of the locality in folklore, over and above processes of political strife and struggle that had been discovered to define those places in real time. Therefore, the state's elevation of Tetelcingo's political status vis-à-vis its allied settlements went hand in hand with its new role as promoter and benefactor of its local, ethnic culture. Tetelcingeños secured scarce government funds for the construction of a new Nahua ceremonial center in the village to honor and preserve their indigenous customs and rituals for future generations. In addition, an exhibit of the Nahua customs and traditions of Tetelcingo on display at the museum in Cuernavaca became a model of the rich cultural heritage of Morelos to be discovered by the increasing numbers of national and international tourists visiting the state. Finally, instruction in Nahuatl by several local teachers became available both through the Casa de la Cultura and the Universidad de Morelos in Cuernavaca. The "otherness" of the Indian in national culture persisted, however, and was symbolized by the fact that these courses were offered through the university's foreign language department.

State-supported localism, especially in the context of a developing neoliberal economy and morality, fostered heightened competition for scarce government resources between Tetelcingo and its neighboring settlements. As a result of its newly elevated political status, Tetelcingo received critical urban services, such as paved roads, a drainage system, and a medical clinic, while its neighboring settlements still struggled to acquire basic services like water and electricity. Crucially, this maneuver exacerbated long-standing political, economic, and cultural tensions between the settlements and helped fragment the political solidarity that had been slowly and carefully built up over the previous decade, a solidarity that had culminated in the campaign for municipal autonomy.

Restitution Remade

The political effect of the conflicts and contradictions of a remade localism became apparent in the shift of the political demand for restitution in the aftermath of the hotly contested 1988 presidential campaign between the neoliberal, Harvard-educated PRI candidate, Carlos Salinas de Gortiari, and the neo-populist candidate of the new Partido de la Revolución Democrática (PRD), Cuauhtémoc Cárdenas. The burning issue of the campaign had been the neoliberal intention to extend the privatizations of state-owned industries begun during the previous administration to include agrarian reform lands. Therefore, a neoliberal victory would mean the end of inherited ideals of the Mexican Revolution, such as the promise of land redistribution, no matter how tattered these ideals had become in actual practice (Gilly 1998).

The issue of restitution once again reared its head in the local campaign of this high-stakes election. With the help of the local ruling faction tied to the PRI now back in power in Tetelcingo, the sugar workers' union acquired a parcel of land adjacent to its neighboring settlement, Colonia Cuauhtémoc, on which to build worker housing. The government's promise to build worker housing was a critical piece in the volatile negotiations within the PRI to win the acquiescence of its labor sector to the sale of the state-owned Casasano Sugar Mill to a consortium of investors tied to Pepsico. But for most residents of Tetelcingo and Colonia Cuauhtémoc, where the prospect of a new, large residential development posed a serious threat to their already limited water supply, this promise to the union was perceived as the PRI's betrayal of their community. This perception was forcefully elaborated as part of Cárdenas's campaign against the pending neoliberal reforms and one-party rule. Once again, the issue of political autonomy was raised. Who had the right to define and allocate property rights within the community?[11]

The agrarian committee denounced the union's appropriation of this parcel using the primordial maps as proof of its illegitimacy. In the face of the serious challenge to the PRI posed by the PRD in Morelos, the governor issued a temporary injunction to halt work on the housing project.

The injunction was lifted once Salinas assumed control of the government in what was widely regarded as a highly fraudulent presidential election. Salinas selected a long-time national politician from the PRI as the new governor of Morelos. Apparently, he concluded that further development of the neoliberal agenda in Morelos would depend upon doling out this plum political post to a politician with strong connections and obligations to the labor sector of the PRI, which included the sugar workers' union. This was a politically astute move. Salinas clearly had one eye on the upcoming 1991 national legislative and municipal elections. The winners of that crucial election would either help or hinder the pending reform of Article 27 of the Constitution, which would open up agrarian reform lands to private investment. The PRI's political following in the region was at an all-time low, and only someone who could negotiate with the unions could be expected to shore up the PRI's political following at this crucial time.

With the promise of future land redistributions coming to an official close, the campaign for restitution of communal lands ceased being a significant component of a far-reaching demand for political autonomy, social justice, and ethnic dignity. Instead, it now focused on more narrowly achievable goals. By demanding the return of primordial lands, the villagers attempted to focus the argument on who had the right to benefit from privatization. They were not, however, questioning the inevitability of this process. This change reflected not only the shifting political terrain in the region, but also the growing divisions between Tetelcingo and its allied settlements resulting from the remade localism.

This fragmentation played out in the divergent strategies to recuperate communal land of Tetelcingo and Colonia Cuauhtémoc, reflecting, in large measure, the internal jealousies and shifting alliances of members of the agrarian committee. On the one hand, members of the agrarian committee from Colonia Cuauhtémoc maintained their focus on retrieving the parcel of land claimed by the sugar workers' union. They were allied with the PRD in the hope that its campaign against the old-party favoritism and heavy bureaucratic style of the PRI—with which the union was closely identified—would be victorious.[12] On the other hand, members of the agrarian committee from Tetelcingo concentrated on retrieving an adjacent parcel that had been acquired by a nonlocal businessman. With mixed political affiliations between the PRD and the PRI, they read the political winds differently. They understood that because of the new governor's ties to the labor sector of the PRI, continued struggle against the union's claim would likely fail. And, unlike Colonia Cuauhtémoc, Tetelcingeños had received many of the social, economic, and political benefits of the previous administration's Municipal Strengthening Program, and it was understood that they easily could be taken away.

These conflicts and contradictions at the local level strengthened the political hand of the neoliberal reformers. Just as construction on the housing project was about to commence in 1989, members of the agrarian committee from

Colonia Cuauhtémoc led a land invasion onto this parcel. The land invasion was relatively small and, therefore, politically weak. Mostly, it was comprised of fellow villagers from Colonia Cuauhtémoc due to the divisions between it and Tetelcingo. Although its leaders had framed their argument against the union in terms of local rights to the primordial lands claimed in their petition for restitution, they had begun to sell lots on the invaded parcel to people without roots in the community to increase their tactical power vis-à-vis the union. Paradoxically, this maneuver strengthened the political hand of the members of the agrarian committee from Tetelcingo, who were negotiating for the allocation of the adjacent parcel. They could now claim to truly represent the community as a whole in their denunciation of the leaders of the campaign against the union. Employing the discourse of localism, they questioned the right of these leaders to "sell" membership in the community and therefore access to its resources to outsiders. They asserted that these actions had delegitimized the village's moral claim, not only to this particular parcel, but to the more extensive primordial communal lands claimed in its petition for restitution. Preceding this denunciation was a behind-the-scenes negotiation between the members of the agrarian committee from Tetelcingo and many disgruntled participants from Colonia Cuauhtémoc. The latter disagreed with the tactics and strategy of the land campaign against the sugar workers' union and worried they would be left with nothing for their efforts if they continued fighting the union. Therefore, they defected into the political camp of the leadership from Tetelcingo with the understanding that they would be included in any settlement negotiated with the government. With their tactical power enhanced, the members of the agrarian committee from Tetelcingo organized a second, numerically superior land invasion onto this parcel in 1990.

Negotiations between the state and all parties in the dispute were settled just in time for the legislative and municipal elections. In return for delivering their votes to the ruling party candidates, the land invaders from Tetelcingo emerged victorious in their campaign. Those participants who defected from the campaign against the sugar workers' union were compensated by the union with more distant and less valuable alternative land. Finally, the participants who continued to press their campaign against the union were forcefully ejected by federal soldiers who arrived in a caravan of trucks and set fire to their shacks. They lost everything they had invested in this campaign.[13]

The ultimate winners to emerge from this campaign for restitution were the neoliberal reformers in Mexico City and their capitalist clientele who bought the Casasano Sugar Mill. As expected, the ruling party candidates won the legislative seats in the 1991 elections. Within a year, the state amended Article 27 of the Constitution, which enabled the privatization of national land. With the enactment of this reform, the individual certificates to lots on the parcel—bestowed upon the local victors in the land campaign by the new PRI municipal president in a public ritual held in the Nahua Ceremonial Center shortly after the elections—were converted into individual titles to private property.

Conclusion

The villagers' invasion onto land to which they claimed primordial rights pushes the issue of the construction of localist identities and their relation to political mobilization to the forefront of contemporary discussions of globalism. It would seem to fit into a postmodern understanding of social movements that tend to privilege the local as the premier site of resistance to globalism (Escobar and Alvarez 1992). But in reconstructing the history of their claim as a negotiated process, I have sought to underscore the continuing centrality of the state in Mexico in the thrust toward supposedly unbridled economic globalization. We have seen, for example, just how central the state remains in reconfiguring the local to the needs and requirements of neoliberal globalization. In both its institutional and discursive dimensions, the state has served, to paraphrase Edelman (1999: 187), as the central point of reference, focus of demands, and site of struggle of social movements despite assertions by postmodern theorists of the so-called new social movements that emancipatory politics takes place primarily in spaces outside or at the margins of the state. Following Gilly (1998: 275), I too believe that "[in] social practice, forms of resistance present themselves … as forms of conceiving and conditioning modernization from below and, once again, of negotiating the terms and not being excluded." And I would contend that what matters for our understanding of the construction of local identities and political strategies and their relation to globalism is not so much the forms of resistance—everyday or otherwise—in and of themselves, but the connections that are continuously made, unmade, and remade between these forms and state power.

Notes

Funding for this research was provided by grants from the Wenner-Gren Foundation for Anthropological Research, the National Science Foundation, and the Graduate School of the City University of New York, whose support I gratefully acknowledge. I thank Don Kalb and August Carbonella for their astute editorial suggestions, which greatly improved this essay.

1. The notion that the state has become obsolete is, of course, quite selective. Dominant development agencies, especially the IMF and the World Bank, are intimately connected with the U.S. goal of becoming *the state* of global capitalism, as Meszaros (2001) incisively points out in his study of the new imperialism.
2. *Ejido* land is national land to which peasants have use rights. This type of property regime was established by the agrarian reform laws that grew out of the revolution (see Whetton 1948).
3. For insightful discussions of the politics and economics of the privatization of Mexican sugar mills, see Chollett 1994 and Singelman 1993.

4. See Knight 1998; Wolf 1969; and Womack 1968. The essays in Joseph and Nugent 1994 provide especially useful discussions of popular participation in the period of revolutionary state formation.

5. *Dotación* did not require petitioners to show their prior ownership and illegitimate dispossession of the land. See De la Peña 1981; Nugent and Alonso 1994; Purnell 1999; and Vecinos de Tetelcingo 1981 for local accounts of the agrarian reform.

6. See Gilly's incisive discussion of the historical resilience of these terms in the context of the Zapatista rebellion in Chiapas in the 1990s (1998: 281–283).

7. García Jiménez (1988) provides a useful overview of this period's social movements in Morelos.

8. I developed these points further in Musante 2000.

9. Roseberry's introduction to *Anthropologies and Histories* (1989) begins with an analytically rich description of competing fiestas in Tepoztlan, which serves to illustrate the kind of internecine political feuding that I am referring to here.

10. See Estado de Morelos 1987 for an official description of this program, and García Jiménez 1988 for a critique.

11. Purnell (1999) provides an illuminating historical analysis of the issues of local political autonomy and control in the region of Michoacan with enactment of the nineteenth-century liberal land reform laws and the revolutionary agrarian reform laws of the twentieth century.

12. A discussion of the divisions between sectors within the sugar industry in Morelos and their effect on government actions to privatize the sugar mills in Morelos may be found in Singelman 1993.

13. Participants in the land invasion were required to put up an initial monetary sum to secure a lot plus money to meet the expenses incurred by organizers in the course of the campaign. They were also required to contribute time and endure great personal risk by participating in security details to guard the parcel against an invasion by other claimants.

References

Bommes, Michael, and Patrick Wright. 1982. "'Charms of Residence': The Public and the Past." In *Making Histories: Studies in History Writing and Politics*, ed. Richard Johnson, Gregor McLennan, Bill Schwarz, and David Sutton, 253–301. Minneapolis: University of Minnesota Press.

Carbonella, August. 1996. "Reconstructing Histories and Geographies: Some Dissident Remarks on Historical Anthropology's Unwaged Debate." *Focaal—tijdschrift voor antropologie* 26/27: 159–167.

Chollett, Donna L. 1994. "Economic Restructuring and Agroindustrial Complexes: The Case of the Mexican Sugar Industry." Paper presented at the 93rd Annual Meeting of the American Anthropological Association, 20 November–4 December 1994, Atlanta, Georgia.

Cornelius, Wayne A. 1985. "The Political Economy of Mexico under de la Madrid: Austerity, Routinized Crisis, and Nascent Recovery." *Mexican Studies/Estudios Mexicanos* 1, no. 1: 83–124.

De la Peña, Guillermo. 1981. *A Legacy of Promises: Agriculture, Politics, and Ritual in the Morelos Highlands of Mexico*. Austin: University of Texas Press.

Edelman, Marc. 1999. *Peasants against Globalization: Rural Social Movements in Costa Rica*. Stanford: Stanford University Press.

Escobar, Arturo. 1992. "Culture, Economics, and Politics in Latin American Social Movements Theory and Research." In *The Making of Social Movements in Latin America: Identity, Strategy, and Democracy*, ed. A. Escobar and S. Alvarez, 62–88. Boulder, Colo.: Westview Press.

Escobar, Arturo, and Sonia E. Alvarez. 1992. "Introduction: Theory and Protest in Latin America Today." In *The Making of Social Movements in Latin America: Identity, Strategy, and Democracy*, ed. Arturo Escobar and Sonia E. Alvarez, 1–15. Boulder, Colo.: Westview Press.

Estado de Morelos. 1987. *Municipios libres y fuertes*. Cuernavaca, Morelos: Gobierno del Estado.

Featherstone, Mike. 1996. "Localism, Globalism, and Cultural Identity." In *Global/Local: Cultural Production and the Transnational Imaginary*, ed. R. Wilson and W. Dissanayake, 46–77. Durham, NC: Duke University Press.

Foley, Michael W. 1991. "Agenda for Mobilization: The Agrarian Question and Popular Mobilization in Contemporary Mexico." *Latin American Research Review* 26, no. 2: 39–74.

García Jiménez, Plutarco. 1988. *Conflictos agrarios en Morelos, 1976–1986*. Cuernavaca, Morelos: Ediciones Equipo Pueblo.

Gilly, Adolfo. 1998. "Chiapas and the Rebellion of the Enchanted World." In *Rural Revolt in Mexico: U.S. Intervention and the Domain of Subaltern Politics*, ed. Daniel Nugent, 261–333. Durham, NC: Duke University Press

Hamilton, Nora. 1982. *The Limits of State Autonomy: Post-revolutionary Mexico*. Princeton, NJ: Princeton University Press.

Jiménez Guzmán, Lucero. 1986. *La industria canero-azucarera en Mexico (El estado de Morelos)*. Mexico City: Universidad Nacional Autonoma de Mexico, Centro Regional de Investigaciones Multidisciplinarias.

———. 1988. *La industria canero-azucarera en Mexico (El estado de Morelos), segunda parte*. Mexico City: Universidad Nacional Autonoma de Mexico, Centro Regional de Investigaciones Multidisciplinarias.

Joseph, Gilbert M., and Daniel Nugent. 1994. "Popular Culture and State Formation in Revolutionary Mexico." In *Everyday Forms of State Formation: Revolution and the Negotiation of Rule in Modern Mexico*, ed. Gilbert M. Joseph and Daniel Nugent, 3–23. Durham, NC: Duke University Press.

Knight, Alan. 1998. "The United States and the Mexican Peasantry, circa 1880–1940." In *Rural Revolt in Mexico: U.S. Intervention and the Domain of Subaltern Politics*, ed. Daniel Nugent, 25–63. Durham, NC: Duke University Press.

Meszaros, Istvan. 2001. *Socialism or Barbarism: From the American Century to the Crossroads*. New York: Monthly Review Press.

Musante, Patricia. 2000. "The Progressive Catholic Church and the Refashioning of Hegemony in Mexico: An Illustration from Tetelcingo." In *The Church at the Grassroots in Latin America*, ed. John Burdick and W. E. Hewitt, 33–52. Westport, Conn.: Praeger Publishers.

Nugent, Daniel, and Ana Maria Alonso. 1994. "Multiple Selective Traditions in Agrarian Reform and Agrarian Struggle: Popular Culture and State Formation in the *Ejido* of Namiquipa." In *Everyday Forms of State Formation: Revolution and the Negotiation of Rule in Modern Mexico*, ed. Gilbert M. Joseph, and Daniel Nugent, 209–246. Durham, NC: Duke University Press.

Purnell, Jennie. 1999. *Popular Movements and State Formation in Revolutionary Mexico: The Agraristas and Cristeros of Michoacan*. Durham, NC: Duke University Press.

Roseberry, William. 1989. *Anthropologies and Histories: Essays in Culture, History, and Political Economy*. New Brunswick, NJ: Rutgers University Press.

Saldívar, Américo. 1982. "Una década de crisis y luchas (1969–1978)." In *Mexico: un pueblo en la historia* (vol. 4), ed. Enrique Semo, 155–245. Mexico City: Editorial Nueva Imagen and Universidad Autonoma de Puebla.

Singelman, Peter. 1993. "The Sugar Industry in Post-revolutionary Mexico: State Intervention and Private Capital." *Latin American Research Review* 28, no. 1: 61–88.

Smith, Neil. 1984. *Uneven Development*. New York: Basil Blackwell.

———. 1992. "Contours of a Spatialized Politics: Homeless Vehicles and the Construction of Geographic Scale." *Social Text* 33: 55–81.

Vecinos de Tetelcingo. 1981. *Historia de Tetelcingo*. Cuernavaca, Morelos: Instituto Nacional de Antropología e Historia.

Whetton, Nathan L. 1948. *Rural Mexico*. Chicago: University of Chicago Press.

Wolf, Eric R. 1969. *Peasant Wars of the Twentieth Century*. New York: Harper and Row.

———. 1982. *Europe and the People Without History.* Berkeley: University of California Press.

———. 2001a. "Closed Corporate Peasant Communities in Mesoamerica and Central Java." In *Pathways of Power: Building an Anthropology of the Modern World.* Berkeley: University of California Press. (Orig. pub. 1957.)

———. 2001b. "The Vicissitudes of the Closed Corporate Peasant Community." In *Pathways of Power: Building an Anthropology of the Modern World.* Berkeley: University of California Press. (Orig. pub. 1986.)

Womack, John, Jr. 1968. *Zapata and the Mexican Revolution.* New York: Vintage Books.

Chapter Seven

Historical Anthropology through Local-Level Research

Marilyn Silverman and P. H. Gulliver

It is a common assumption today that two paradigms typify the growing nexus between history and anthropology. One paradigm, which typifies history, is "a movement away from social history … and towards a new cultural history" (Kalb, Marks, and Tak 1996: 7). In its concern with epochs, mentalities, and collective representations, it uses anthropology as a repository of concepts, methods, and empirical data that historians can raid. The other paradigm, which typifies historical anthropology, is the one through which anthropologists operate in order to do history, using a central method of local-level research[1] and exploring issues related to "autonomy, deviance, protest" and social change (ibid.). However, a problem with dividing the historiographic world in this way is that a basic division within historical anthropology itself is ignored: that of the distinction between "historical ethnography" and the "anthropology of history."[2]

Historical ethnography is a genre that analyzes a past era of a particular locality using archival sources and, when possible, local oral history. Very commonly, historical ethnographers try to link the past with the present, chronologically and processually, in order to explain the present by understanding the past. The concern here, then, is not only to record the past for its own sake but to show how things came to be the way they are now.[3] This is an orientation rarely shared with historians.

Historical ethnographies may also be produced for periods that are entirely in the past and for which only archival data can be used. Such work is, of course, a more straightforward invasion of the historian's field. It is also a

Notes for this chapter are located on page 165.

departure from conventional anthropological concerns with the present day. Because of this, such ethnographies are uncommon, although their numbers have increased in recent years.[4] Such studies may be synchronic or diachronic. The former are less common in anthropology than in history because the general anthropological concern with social dynamics and change and with individual decision making and strategizing make synchronic studies, of the past as well as of the present, unattractive.

Historical ethnographies assume a "recoverable past." They are analytical histories that are outsiders' constructions. Nevertheless, in using oral history, such accounts do not ignore "native points of view" or insiders' ideas of the past, even as they are anthropological constructions of that past. From this perspective, such historical ethnographies contrast with those anthropological studies that deliberately focus on the ways and cultural rationales by which a particular people envision, create, and re-create their own past and relate it to their perceived present. This we call the anthropology of history. It aims to record insiders' views and perceptions and to carry out analyses in the insiders' own sociocultural terms. Little attempt is made to produce an "objective" history. Instead, the concern is with what people know and remember about their past, how and why, how people make sense of the past and relate it to the present, and how people's perceptions and understandings of their past are a retrospective product of their present. Often, this form of historical anthropology is linked to a reflexive approach, with the anthropologist's experiences woven into the narrative to become an intrinsic part of the published ethnography.[5]

In this genre, the anthropologist is concerned with exploring a people's version of their own past, linking it to their present-day cultural conceptions and social arrangements. Thus, insofar as people explain the past to themselves as, consciously and unconsciously, they explain and justify their present, history is conceptualized in this genre as ideology and, therefore, it can be formed and reformed even as people believe it to be "true." It is the study of such transformation(s) that attracts the anthropologist of history. In this genre, too, history can be conceived of as "tradition," and its invention the object of study. Or the aim may be to analyze collective memory and the construction of identities (national, ethnic, local) through the use of historical symbols, meanings, narratives, and events. Thus, the genre will often discern several different histories in a given locale, related to gender, age, class, or other significant category. In this genre, then, the past as a contingent cultural construction is the object of anthropological study.

It may appear that the division within historical anthropology, as manifested in the ways in which history and historicity are integrated, follows an older and general divide between cultural and social anthropology. The former is concerned mainly with meanings and symbols and the latter mainly with social relations and processes. However, historical anthropologists have cut across these older divisions. Nevertheless, we suggest that essential elements of this divide are surfacing within historical anthropology. Such division concerns what should be privileged in analysis: the material or the symbolic, the action or the belief. The division, in turn, rests on the fact that no anthropological construction of the relation between what people do and what they believe has ever been universally accepted.

Points of Convergence: The Small Scale and the Context

The division within anthropology and the privileging of particular conceptual elements has never meant a total neglect of the other elements, nor has it ever produced a complete break. Rather, there has been a persistent concern for the reciprocal ties between action and belief, material relations and cultural meanings. This concern necessarily enters historical anthropology. So although particular anthropological studies of the past fall more or less into one or another of our two historical genres, aspects that inform the other are seldom neglected.

In part, this stems from the anthropological concern with holism—the notion that all aspects of social and cultural life are in some way interconnected. In part, too, it stems from empirical concerns that are common to both genres: exploitation and dominance, however phrased, are central. So, too, are the topics through which these are explored: class formation, colonialism, the state, protest, and resistance. Convergence also occurs because key concepts, although they may vary, derive from a shared history of changing paradigms within the discipline itself. Ultimately, commonalities emerge out of two other anthropological concerns: the notion of the local level or small scale, and the efforts made to contextualize this.

In the social sciences, various levels of human activity are perceived. These may be crudely designated as local, regional, national, and international. Disciplinary specializations on one or another of these levels produce different kinds of data, analyses, and understandings. It is anthropologists, however, who have long specialized in working at the small scale or local level; and those who do historical anthropology most commonly continue that tradition. In noting this, however, it is important to state that this does not mean that anthropologists assume that the smaller represents the wider society or culture—the "larger scale." Nor does it imply that the small-scale unit is seen as somehow typical of other small-scale units that share some of its features. In practice, the localities assumed by ethnographers vary in size, geographically and demographically, as determined partly by particular sociocultural contexts and partly by the interests of the researcher. A locality is not necessarily a so-called community; rather, it is an area within which it is convenient and reasonable to collect interconnected data, historical and/or contemporary. Thus, for example, a locality might be a single village, a cluster of villages, a small town, an urban ward, a stretch of country or of a town occupied by people with common interests and multiple interactions (e.g., farmers, fishermen, factory workers), or a politico-administrative area. In our own research in rural Ireland we took, as our principal locality, two adjacent electoral divisions, which covered a small town and much of its hinterland, for which statistical data had been collected by governmental agencies for a century and a half. However, for some purposes we included larger localities for which particular historical data were available or in order to take in a wider geographical range.

What then does local-level research mean? What is it that historical anthropologists can do, and are doing, in their continued concentration on the small scale? To begin with, every locality (however defined) within the same region, nation, or state has in some degree experienced different conditions—ecological, economic, demographic, political, cultural—and these have made for somewhat different histories as the reactions and choices of the inhabitants, with respect to local problems as well as to external opportunities and impositions, resonated through time and space.[6] Contrary to assumptions often made by those who study at more macrolevels, the experiences of people at different local levels, in varying places, are seldom identical. At the very least, the nature of historical homogeneity is a matter for enquiry. It is more useful, though, to accept that anthropological findings have long thrown great doubt on the existence of local uniformity even in the face of similar external pressures. This is, of course, because people seldom react uniformly to such stimuli. Only in exceptional historical circumstances are they mere pawns.

There is, then, great value in local-level research in the sense of examining how major, large-scale processes—the so-called important questions of historiography—have played out at the small-scale levels where people live and interact and where they experience both change and continuity, trying to make sense of what they encounter and deciding what to do. For example, major processes may be identified at the macro level: the emergence of capitalism or its consolidation, state formation, the decline of religious authority, the growth of xenophobic ethnicity, technological revolution. A more intensive and reliable understanding of such processes, though, can only be obtained by exploring these at the local level where cognition, belief and social interaction are actualized. The question then becomes how the so-called macroprocess actually worked amongst people as they lived their lives, engaged hopes and fears, experienced successes and failures, and dealt with intractable problems.

Complementing such insight into major transformative processes via locality-based research, and perhaps under its influence, other changes, perhaps less important from a macro viewpoint, may be highlighted and, when explored at the local level, may illuminate the larger scale. For example, the geographical range of marriage choices, the nature of neighborly cooperation, and the class origins of artisans or shopkeepers are the kinds of issues that escape attention at macro levels but directly underlie such large-scale processes as class formation and economic change. As well, conclusions and generalizations derived at a macro level can, and indeed must, be tested at small-scale levels. How far do they hold good? Do they need to be modified, held in abeyance, or even rejected? After all, it is at the local level that people communicate, express opinion and make decisions, cooperate, quarrel, and exploit. For example, demographic statistics may show a trend to, say, earlier marriage or fewer children; but it is at the local level that people choose and act (consciously or not) and express their ideas and motivations. Demographic statistics, in other words, are only generalizations of the results of choices made by people in their own localities. As another example, the origin, nature, and reproduction of the bourgeoisie may be conceptualized at macrolevels, but it is at the level of actual life that capital, both financial and cultural, is appropriated and accumulated and both power and privilege exercised.

Local-level research, in other words, allows and promotes better understanding of both particular and general processes. This is because there are variations in action and reaction, perception and ideas, at different local levels and because locality-based research allows an exploration of the contingent factors. Anthropologists, therefore, find confusing the ways that historians and others working at nonlocal levels seek locally derived, apt illustrations of the conditions and processes they are studying. Thus, they may take an illustration from one locality for one point while an illustration of another may come from a different locality in the same region or, even, from the far side of the country. A third feature may be illustrated from another locality. This analytical sleight of hand disregards the probability that pertinent conditions likely vary significantly in each of the localities and that the illustrations may very well have been affected by those differences. Quite apart from the fact that such casual illustrations cannot prove anything—although too often they are taken to clinch an argument—they may in reality be misleading because of small-scale variability.[7] The historical anthropologist, on the other hand, usually feels obliged (often with some frustration) by the disciplinary notion of holism and its research methodology to examine and report on a set of social-cultural features as they have been actualized simultaneously and interconnected within the same milieu, among the same people. Locality-based research, in other words, encourages contextualization; and contextualization gives a validity to anthropological understanding.

A final aspect of local-level research that must be emphasized is that regional or national histories—and the data and analyses by which they have been constructed—are in large part composed of facts, events, ideas, and processes that occurred in a myriad of local places. There should be, therefore, a dialectical relation between a set of local histories and a macrohistory. To understand the dynamics of that dialectic, historical anthropologists provide an essential perspective that, unfortunately, is too often neglected by historians and macrotheorists.

In all these ways, "scale reduction and scope expansion go hand in hand" (Kalb, Marks, and Tak 1996: 7) in historical anthropology, and although such anthropology may be divided by empirical foci, centralizing concepts, and, ultimately, genre, the fact of local-level concentration is key. Indeed, it is the ways in which and reasons why this occurs that differentiates historical anthropology from the historians' use of anthropology.[8]

What also distinguishes historical anthropology is its concern with context. It is a truism in sociocultural anthropology today to say that the small scale (local places, meanings, and social relations) is enmeshed in "wider arenas" or contexts and that this must form part of any study. However, how the wider context is conceptualized leads to the variations in methods, concepts, and theories that now permeate historical anthropology, regardless of genre. Three common contextual strategies can be highlighted: that local realities are enmeshed in a global (capitalist) system; that they are integral parts of ideological, cultural, and/or material systems of power, domination, and/or hegemonic processes; and that they are spatially incorporated in larger geographical units.[9]

These three ways of conceptualizing context are not, of course, mutually exclusive. However, an emphasis on one does tend to orient and affect historical understandings. This is because the varying ways of constructing context reflect, in part, the long standing anthropological way of dividing societies and cultures into economic, political, ideational, and social systems. Thus, it is fair to say that context defined as a world capitalist system typified an economistic approach that, in the 1980s, privileged the analyses of social relations as these were manifested in production and which, in the 1990s, privileged the analysis of those social relations, as well as the ideology, that are enmeshed in exchange and commoditization. Similarly, context defined as domination, power, or hegemony reflects the more recent concern with ideational systems and, importantly, the resurfacing of the political domain after a period of neglect because of the primacy given to economic concerns.

Context constructed as a sociospatial dimension in anthropology, however, has tended to cross-cut social relations, economy, polity, and ideology. This is because it had a different origin and history within the discipline. It reflects the move from studying bounded units (e.g., bands, tribes, villages, etc.) in the earlier years of anthropology to a current recognition of the contingency of local sociocultural life. In this sense, space as context serves to structure our historical understandings in a fashion that complements the other two contextual strategies.

All this is not to suggest that the construction of context is always a deliberate act. Very often, the nature of the context emerges seamlessly out of conceptual choices and the research problem. Moreover, although the specification of context has a methodological dimension in that it tends to emerge out of the kinds of data encountered in the field, context is more often seen by anthropologists as an outgrowth of the theoretical premises that underlie the study. Thus, the construction of context complements, in a theoretical way, the choice of small-scale locale, which is seen, in contrast, as a heuristic or methodological, and not a theoretical, device.

What all this suggests is that historical anthropology, however defined, reflects the flavor, trends, and biases of the discipline at large. To that extent, we suggest that historical anthropology is not a field or subdiscipline. It is simply one way of doing anthropology. It is not, at least not so far, specifically linked to any particular paradigm or theoretical orientation.

Local-Level Research: Two Empirical Explorations

To illustrate the nature and usefulness of local-level research in historical anthropology, and as examples of historical ethnography, we present briefly two cases drawn from our ongoing researches in Ireland.[10] Both cases demonstrate the advantages of collecting and analyzing data from a small-scale locality.

Case 1: Retailers and Retailing

In our endeavor to gather historical and contemporary information on all categories of people in Thomastown, county Kilkenny, we sought data on retailing and shopkeepers as far back as could be traced. We began with a list of all retailers active in the 1980s and worked back, via archival and oral sources, through the sequences of proprietors of each shop, noting also owners of shops that had closed at earlier times. From this work it proved possible to construct a continuous record back to about 1840 although disparate information was available on some earlier retailers. Since 1840 the number of retailers in Thomastown at any time ranged between thirty-seven and fifty, with a total of some four hundred in all. Systematically, we sought data on the origins and tenure of these retailers, their kinship connections, and those of their spouses; on their children's careers and marriages; on the kinds of goods and services supplied and the changes in these and in shop premises through time; on the activities of retailers outside of their shop businesses; and on retailers' strategies, values, and attitudes as these changed over the years.

To accomplish this task, we used a variety of sources: the knowledge and memories of Thomastown people; family histories and genealogies; parochial registers of baptisms and marriages; such business ledgers and shop records as we could discover; valuation records made for local taxation purposes; all items in the county newspapers that referred in any way to retailers; Poor Law Union and Rural District Council minute books and records; legal records from the national Deeds Registry, Land Registry, and National Archives; local school registers; and minute books of local associations.[11]

In accumulating this information, it was crucial that it formed part of an intensive and wider anthropological enquiry in the chosen locality. We collected data for the nineteenth and twentieth centuries on other categories of people, other kinds of economic activities, and all kinds of social and political affairs. As a result, a good deal of invaluable information about retailers was obtained indirectly—as a by-product, as it were—from enquiries about nonretailers and nonretailing matters in and beyond the locality. A few brief examples will illustrate this. Bequests and references to retailers in other people's wills only became known to us because we looked at *all* wills probated for *all* people who had lived in the locality. Information on retailers was gained from other people's genealogies and family histories, from accounts of political events and charitable organizations, from other people's cases in the local courts, and so on. Clearly, without this additional information our data would have been significantly poorer and, therefore, our insights into the lives of retailers less satisfactory.

For a small locality such as Thomastown parish (population in 1846, 7,410; 1981, 2,650), it proved possible to obtain an almost comprehensive record of all retailers who were in business during a period of about 150 years, together with a great deal of information on their activities, strategies, ideas, and social relations. To accomplish this for a much larger number of retailers—say, for a larger town or a whole region—would scarcely be possible with that degree of intensity. This is because a larger number of retailers presupposes a larger number of contemporaneous nonretailers and their relationships and activities. This means that information would be required on *all* those other people, *all* political events, *all* court cases, and much more in the sure expectation of discovering important data on the retailers. Moreover, a larger number of retailers would require resort to sampling procedures with problems of sample selection in an unknown population.[12] Potential biases could arise as some retailers were more prominent publicly, or more successful, thus leaving behind better records and more persistent memory, while others led a quieter life and left meager record. In addition, sampling would exclude an unknown number of different kinds of individuals and businesses: for instance, larger and smaller businesses, inherited and purchased shops, varieties of specialization, and lengths of tenure. And to produce a stratified sample using these criteria would, in turn, have required the comprehensive research to have been done beforehand. In short, a larger-scale study could never be as comprehensive as a holistic one in a smaller locality. It would, necessarily, be a rather different kind of study, less intensive, valid enough for some purposes, of course, but yielding different kinds of results.

What, then, is to be gained for understanding the history of retailing from an intensive anthropological study? First, a high degree of accuracy and comprehensiveness are possible. The researcher can trace virtually all careers, social linkages, and activities of many kinds for the complete range of retailers. Inter alia, this is valuable in detecting repetitive and changing patterns of tenure, or retail practices or marital strategies, throughout the period and for different kinds of businesses. It also furnishes a profusion of in-depth case studies for analytical and presentational purposes.

Second, such accumulation of data prevents an artificial homogenization of the category of retailer, allowing clearer recognition of differentiation amongst the various retail specialties and combinations of them, or amongst the different sizes of businesses. It raises apparently simple, but effectively complex, questions as to what was a "shop" and who was a "retailer." For example, what, if anything, was common to, on the one hand, the butcher whose shop became a smaller part of a most profitable business that included livestock rearing and trading and the wholesaling of meats and, on the other hand, a small grocer, open at all hours, with a few feet of counter and a limited range of goods, or the man who sold insurance policies from his own house? In our research project, these kinds of questions raised issues concerning the theoretical validity and analytical inclusiveness of such key concepts as "lower middle class" and a Marxist "petite bourgeoisie."

Third, comprehensive local-level data allow one to address generalizations that have been assumed in macro studies. For example, we were led to review and to revise the common assumption that small businesses are inherently family enterprises in which wives and children are essential participants. Another assumption that has been taken for granted by historians and sociologists is that, in Ireland, retailers have largely been recruited from farmers' families, have married into such families, and have maintained strong relationships and cultural commonalities with farmers. For Thomastown retailers, this stereotype proved to have only limited validity. Another general assumption in Irish historiography has been that retailers have been prominent, as leaders and executives, in political organizations and protest movements. This has not been the case in Thomastown. In the light of local-level historical data, such macrogeneralizations can be questioned, demonstrating the need and the way to modify and elaborate them and indicating the processual significance of associated socioeconomic conditions.[13]

Case 2: The Great Famine, 1845–1849

A seminal moment in Irish history was the so-called Great Famine produced by the repeated failure of the potato crops. Its story has long been told through a well-developed Irish historiographic tradition that was formulated in the later nineteenth century as part of an indigenous land reform and nationalist movement. It is a story that all Irish people "know"—regardless of class, age, or locality. What they know, briefly, is the following.

In an overpopulated country of poor tenant farmers and rapacious absentee landlords, people lived on potatoes and sold all their other produce to pay rents. A series of potato failures after 1845 caused massive starvation and fever, which the British state, with its laissez-faire policy, failed to alleviate. Minimal government efforts included, first, some public works projects in the early years to provide employment so that people could buy cheap food; then soup kitchens; and, finally, a total reliance on the harsh and hated poor law and workhouse. Given the unconcern of landlords alongside the state's ideology, financial austerity, and racism, the Irish starved.

Until today, this story is "common sense" in Ireland, having been disseminated through school texts, political rallies, and churches for more than a century. Revisionist historiographic work in the last few decades has moderated the story somewhat.[14] Statistical analyses of counties have shown that famine was unevenly distributed and that the west of the country was worst affected. Demographic analyses also have shown that the poor (laborers and small land holders) were, by far, the worst afflicted. Nevertheless, contemporary historiographic work still takes its research agenda from the nationalist version. It is therefore concerned mainly with two issues: the way in which the structure of the pre-Famine economy contributed to the Famine and the trajectory of the Famine itself (mortality rates, British policy, etc.). In this macro approach, the experiences of small localities are ignored, except for apt illustration, in favor of statistical modeling and national, or sometimes regional, patternings. Qualitative data, when used, are taken largely from the west of the country where famine was most dramatically experienced.

In our own archival and field research in Thomastown, we explicitly sought data on the Famine in the locality and region. However, county newspapers, government reports, parliamentary sources, and local stories yielded only meager information. Did this mean that we could say nothing about this major historical event? Was local-level research so narrow in its focus that such a great event could not be addressed? Could we not do "real" history because of our concern with the local level? Was the only way to do history the way of the orthodox historian—with events and memories from a diverse multitude of places amalgamated into synthetic, homogenized versions?

We collected what we could at the time. It was only recently, though, that we tried to write an article on the Famine. We scoured our files for our few references. We also began to look more consciously at what was missing, such as reports of potato yields, of deaths, and of extensive admissions to the workhouse. We also looked at what had been happening in the locality in the decades prior to the Famine—not only in its economy, but in its political and ideological life, and in the everyday relations between landlords, tenant farmers, and laborers. What emerged was a story that was different from the nationalist or revisionist one, and this was because different topics and issues necessarily formed its framework.

In this story, very briefly, we argue that a "culture of dearth"[15] had underwritten relations between the gentry and the poor in the decades prior to the Famine. At times of severe and exceptional distress, the "deserving poor" were temporarily relieved, amidst public fanfare, by the moral and material interventions of locally resident landlords and notables. Such public crisis relief worked, for example, in the post-Napoleonic depressions of 1816 and 1820, high unemployment in 1830, and virtual famine in 1840. Not surprisingly, the first potato failure in 1845 elicited no response. Local gentry saw it as a minor problem that would be dealt with as usual if conditions worsened.

During the same pre-Famine decades, our data also showed that, despite a laissez-faire ideology in economic matters, the English state had been dramatically expanding its control over two key areas: the means of violence and of administration. By exploring these, we found that the Famine story could be reframed through a particular local perspective.

Pre-Famine Ireland was reputed for its violence (agrarian outrages, homicide, arson, threats, banditry). Yet in Thomastown and its region, the violence was always sporadic in time and space. Nevertheless, a growing sense of crisis was created as Insurrection Acts (1814, 1822), a new police force (1822), an expanded military (1820s), and growing media concern throughout the 1820s convinced the locally resident gentry that all Ireland was aflame and that increased state coercion was essential. The resulting collusion of the gentry with the state in turn convinced state agents that ever greater coercion was both necessary and welcomed. In response, violence did escalate, culminating in the "Tithe War" in southern county Kilkenny in 1830. By 1835, however, the state had quashed it; and except for minor outbreaks, violence never came back to southern Kilkenny.

Meanwhile, the colonial state was expanding its administrative interventions: its agents and rules were visible everywhere. New courts imposed the law; regulations on weights and measures came to control an expanding retail trade; public works (roads, bridges, canals) established new transport routes; Thomastown's town government was abolished and its functions given to gentry who now sat on boards established by the new Poor Law; laws regulating imports affected the local milling industry; state-organized Loan Funds undercut local usurers; and state valuators were in the locality in 1845 collecting data for a national tax system. In other words, the pre-Famine period in southern county Kilkenny was one in which an expanding state administration underwrote a growing coercion. The state was pervasive, and many local people approved.

With the potato crop failures after 1845, the locally based culture of dearth quickly collapsed under the weight of bureaucratic regulation that accompanied state intervention in famine relief. In the early years, the gentry were ordered by the state to provide proposals for public works, to form relief committees, and to set local taxes. They did so. For southern county Kilkenny, there were virtually no reports of independent gentry relief measures that would have typified a subsistence crisis prior to 1845. Instead, in expectation and action, the gentry quickly gave way to the state, as was not uncommon; and the state, in managing famine relief with gentry collusion, furthered the expansionary process that had begun decades before.[16]

The process was aided, and state relief was more effective in southern Kilkenny, in part because the Famine was not as severe as in western areas of the country. We say this in the face of the absence as well as the presence of data. For example, the local newspapers at the time reported on famine elsewhere in Ireland, and Europe, rather than in county Kilkenny itself. County newspapers also gave few details on the local state of potato crops, distress, or death. The absence of data, in other words, suggested that famine conditions were not excessively harsh. The occasional positive piece enhanced that conclusion. For example, one report noted that only one hundred Thomastown people, with its population of more than seven thousand in 1841, had entered the workhouse during the height of the Famine. Another report cited a farmer who told of other foodstuffs his family ate instead of potatoes. Most important, though, were reports on the building of a railway from Kilkenny to Waterford, through Thomastown, between 1846 and 1850. More than £300,000 in public and private capital was expended and hundreds of workers were continuously employed. Working people in the locality, in other words, had been able to afford alternate foods.

One hundred forty years later, in Thomastown in the 1980s, there were virtually no Famine stories, even from old people whose grandparents had lived through it. They remembered only that a particular road had been built and a soup kitchen had operated. In contrast, everyone we asked could tell us a detailed story of the Famine as they had learned it in school. However, in reviewing our data, we came across a 1937 letter to a local newspaper written by a Thomastown laborer. He complained of working conditions on a government building site and compared them to what "old people often refer to [as] that unhappy period of our history known as 'the time of public works.'" In this, for us, was finally crystallized and encapsulated both the folk and factual views of the Great Famine in Thomastown and southern county Kilkenny, which we had been struggling to understand for more than a decade. It was indeed a time of public works—of soup kitchens, roads, and railways. It was a time of extensive penetration of public and private capital and of state consolidation. It was a time when the local culture of dearth failed to hold up under the pressures of state formation.[17]

Conclusion: Through the Perspective of Local Research

Through a research project with a particular, local perspective and an in-depth focus, we found new information that led us to question previous general assumptions and to make fresh suggestions about retailers and shopkeeping. We also discovered a framework and a Famine story that in some important respects differed from general "common sense" and historiographic verities. Thus, local-level research allowed us to access conditions, events, actions, relationships, and meanings at ground level, to raise new questions, and to use the opportunity to search for answers. Thus, insofar as local conditions differ from the generalizing assumptions of macro description and analysis, this calls for explanation and some enquiry into the reasons and consequences. Conversely, it indicates the need for more than a casual or passing reference to local variations because these often will suggest modifications to the generalizations.

All this is possible because of the anthropologist's intensive knowledge of the interrelated facets of local social life such that particular matters of interest can be seen within a local context—as well as in more macro contexts of region and nation—and, therefore, the effects from and upon contingent factors. Moreover, it is possible for the anthropologist to go beyond the data that have survived and to appreciate the significance of what is missing—in the Famine case, for instance, both the kinds of local newspaper reports that were published and the kinds of information that, deliberately or not, were ignored.

Local-level description and analysis need not—indeed, must not—be merely self-contained and of interest only to those already concerned with the particular locality. Nor is the anthropological task to supply local cases that may be used to exemplify macro generalizations. Rather, the results of local-level research—both the "facts" and the analytical conclusions—must be shown in their relation to macro processes such as state formation and penetration, colonialism, class relations, economic innovations, demographic trends, and so on, so as to contribute to identifying and understanding them. In so doing, new ways of seeing and assessing old historical phenomena may emerge and new foci of attention may be generated—all with the potential of reformulating both research agenda and theoretical patternings.

To take a single example: our own particular study led us to focus on the progressive penetration of the colonial state into local affairs. This was a process that had begun well before the Famine years but intensified during them. This appears to contrast with the common emphasis on the failure of the state to deal adequately with the horrendous conditions of starvation and fevers in Ireland and on the laissez-faire doctrine of the British government of the time, which made it reluctant to interfere with market conditions and the rights and power of landlords. There is, however, no reason to conclude that this is an unacceptable inconsistency. The colonial state may well have not done what was needed in the circumstances—although the idea that it could and should have done more indicates a notable assumption about the capability and responsibility of the state to intervene (by people at that time or in later decades). However, what the state did provide—at least in our locality—was strictly under its own burgeoning bureaucratic control. It therefore superseded the previous culture of dearth dominated by landlords and notables. To what extent this was a local phenomenon is as yet unclear, although we strongly suspect that it was not so restricted. It was, in a particular time and context, a part of the development of the colonial state in Ireland. It was also a new Famine story, a different way of seeing (both empirically and theoretically), and a potential basis for an expanded research agenda in future. This kind of result, in our view, is the contribution of contextualized, locality-based research and of historical anthropology.

Notes

1. This strategy was referred to as "scale reduction" in Silverman and Gulliver 1996, where parts of the present argument appeared.
2. This distinction was first proposed in Silverman and Gulliver 1992.
3. Examples include Silverman 1980, Behar 1986, Sider 1986, B. O'Neill 1987, Parman 1990, Adams 1994, and Gulliver and Silverman 1995.
4. Early examples include Dening 1980, Netting 1981, Wolf 1982, Silverblatt 1987, Hastrup 1990, and Sabean 1990.
5. Some examples are Sharp and Hanks 1978, Sahlins 1985, Parmentier 1987, Hoskins 1987, Tonkin and Chapman 1989, and Ohnuki-Tierney 1990.
6. A good example of such local variations was given for Alpine Italy in Cole and Wolf 1974.
7. Examples by Irish historians are Donnelly 1975, Hoppen 1984, and K. O'Neill 1984. See also Tilly 1984.
8. This is discussed at length in Silverman and Gulliver 1992 and Rogers 1992.
9. See, for example, Vincent 1982, Roseberry 1983, Smith 1985, Comaroff 1985, and Trouillot 1988.
10. Field and archival research in a small town and its hinterland—Thomastown, county Kilkenny—began in 1980 and continues. To date we have each logged more than forty-eight months in the field. See Silverman and Gulliver 1986, Gulliver and Silverman 1995, and Silverman 2001.
11. A more complete account is given in Gulliver 1989.
12. Our own investigations strongly suggest that lists of retailers in commercial directories—so often used for larger-scale studies—are not altogether reliable. Some retailers, often the smaller ones or those situated beyond the commercial center, and some specialties were not included.
13. Detailed discussion of these questions is in Gulliver and Silverman 1995.
14. Historical revisionism in Ireland is commonly taken to have begun with Edwards and Williams 1957. Brief discussions were given by Foster 1986 and Fanning 1988. See also Mokyr 1983 and Ó Gráda 1989.
15. We take this term from Vincent 1992.
16. In 1848, the Kilkenny Poor Law Board, comprising mainly landlords and gentry, was summarily dissolved, and state-appointed paid officials took over.
17. A more detailed study of the Famine years in the Thomastown area is in Silverman and Gulliver 1997.

References

Adams, Jane. 1994. *The Transformation of Rural Life: Southern Illinois, 1890–1990*. Chapel Hill: University of North Carolina Press.

Behar, Ruth. 1986. *Santa Maria del Monte: The Presence of the Past in a Spanish Village*. Princeton, NJ: Princeton University Press.

Cole, John, and Eric Wolf. 1974. *The Hidden Frontier: Ecology and Ethnicity in an Alpine Valley*. New York: Academic Press.

Comaroff, Jean. 1985. *Body of Power, Spirit of Resistance: The Culture and History of a South African People*. Chicago: University of Chicago Press.

Dening, Greg. 1980. *Islands and Beaches: Discourse on a Silent Land—Marquesas, 1774–1880*. Chicago: Dorsey Press.

Donnelly, James. 1975. *The Land and People of Nineteenth-Century Cork*. London: Routledge.

Edwards, R. D., and T. D. Williams, eds. 1957. *The Great Famine: Studies in Irish History*. Dublin: Gill and Macmillan.

Fanning, Ronan. 1988. "The Meaning of Revisionism." *Irish Review* 4: 15–19.

Foster, Roy. 1986. "We Are All Revisionists Now." *Irish Review* 1: 1–5.

Gulliver, P. H. 1989. "Doing Anthropological Research in Rural Ireland: Methods and Sources for Linking the Past and the Present." In *Ireland from Below*, ed. Chris Curtin and Thomas Wilson, 320–338. Galway: Galway University Press.

Gulliver, P. H., and Marilyn Silverman. 1995. *Merchants and Shopkeepers: A Historical Anthropology of an Irish Market Town, 1200–1991*. Toronto: University of Toronto Press.

Hastrup, Kirsten. 1990. *Nature and Policy in Iceland, 1400–1800: An Anthropological Analysis of History and Mentality*. Oxford: Clarendon Press.

Hoppen, K. T. 1984. *Elections, Politics and Society in Ireland, 1832–85*. Oxford: Clarendon Press.

Hoskins, Janet. 1987. "The Headhunter as Hero: Local Traditions and Their Reinterpretation in National History." *American Ethnologist* 14, no. 4: 605–622.

Kalb, Don, Hans Marks, and Herman Tak. 1996. "Historical Anthropology and Anthropological History: Two Distinct Programs." *Focaal—European Journal of Anthropology* 26/27: 5–18.

Mokyr, Joel. 1983. *Why Ireland Starved*. London: Allen and Unwin.

Netting, Robert. 1981. *Balancing on an Alp: Ecological Change and Continuity in a Swiss Mountain Community*. New York: Cambridge University Press.

Ó Gráda, Cormac. 1989. *Ireland before and after the Famine: Explorations in Economic History, 1800–1925*. Manchester: Manchester University Press.

Ohnuki-Tierney, Emiko, ed. 1990. *Culture Through Time: Anthropological Approaches*. Stanford: Stanford University Press.

O'Neill, Brian. 1987. *Social Inequality in a Portuguese Hamlet: Land, Late Marriage, and Bastardy, 1870–1978*. Cambridge: Cambridge University Press.

O'Neill, Kevin. 1984. *Family and Farm in Pre-Famine Ireland: The Parish of Killashandra*. Madison: University of Wisconsin Press.

Parman, Susan. 1990. *Scottish Crofters: A Historical Ethnography of a Celtic Village*. Fort Worth, TX: Holt, Rinehart and Winston.

Parmentier, Richard. 1987. *The Sacred Remains: Myth, History, and Polity in Belau*. Chicago: University of Chicago Press.

Rogers, Nicholas. 1992. "The Anthropological Turn in Social History." In *Approaching the Past: Historical Anthropology through Irish Case Studies*, ed. Marilyn Silverman and P. H. Gulliver, 325–370. New York: Columbia University Press.

Roseberry, William. 1983. *Coffee and Capitalism in the Venezuelan Andes*. Austin: University of Texas Press.

Sabean, David. 1990. *Property, Production, and Family in Neckarhausen, 1700–1870*. Cambridge: Cambridge University Press.

Sahlins, Marshall. 1985. *Islands of History*. Chicago: University of Chicago Press.

Sharp, Lauriston, and L. M. Hanks. 1978. *Bang Chan: Social History of a Rural Community in Thailand*. Ithaca, NY: Cornell University Press.

Sider, Gerald. 1986. *Culture and Class in Anthropology and History: A Newfoundland Illustration*. Berkeley: University of California Press.

Silverblatt, Irene. 1987. *Moon, Sun, and Witches: Gender Ideologies and Class in Inca and Colonial Peru*. Princeton, NJ: Princeton University Press.

Silverman, Marilyn. 1980. *Rich People and Rice: Factional Politics in Rural Guyana, 1902–70*. Leiden: E.J. Brill.

———. 2001. *An Irish Working Class: Explorations in Political Economy and Hegemony, 1800–1950*. Toronto: University of Toronto Press.

Silverman, Marilyn, and P. H. Gulliver. 1986. *In the Valley of the Nore: A Social History of Thomastown, County Kilkenny, 1840–1983*. Dublin: Geography Publications.

———. 1992. "Historical Anthropology and the Ethnographic Tradition." In *Approaching the Past: Historical Anthropology through Irish Case Studies*, ed. Marilyn Silverman and P. H. Gulliver, 3–72. New York: Columbia University Press.

———. 1996. "Inside Historical Anthropology: Scale Reduction and Context." *Focaal—European Journal of Anthropology* 26/27: 149–158.

———. 1997. "Historical Verities and Verifiable History: Locality Based Ethnography and the Great Famine in Southeastern Ireland." *Europa* 3, no. 2: 141–170.

Smith, Carol. 1985. "Local History in Global Context: Social and Economic Transitions in Western Guatamala." *Comparative Studies in Society and History* 26, no. 2: 193–228.

Tilly, Charles. 1984. *Big Structures, Large Processes, Huge Comparisons*. New York: Russell Sage Foundation.

Tonkin, Elisabeth, Maryon McDonald, and Malcolm Chapman, eds. 1989. *History and Ethnicity*. London: Routledge.

Trouillot, Michel-Rolph. 1988. *Peasants and Capital: Dominica in the World Economy*. Baltimore: Johns Hopkins University Press.

Vincent, Joan. 1982. *Teso in Transformation: The Political Economy of Peasant and Class in Eastern Africa*. Berkeley: University of California Press.

———. 1992. "A Political Orchestration of the Irish Famine, County Fermanagh, May 1847." In *Approaching the Past: Historical Anthropology through Irish Case Studies*, ed. Marilyn Silverman and P. H. Gulliver, 75–98. New York: Columbia University Press.

Wolf, Eric. 1982. *Europe and the People Without History*. Berkeley: University of California Press.

Chapter Eight

ANTHROPOLOGY AND HISTORY
Opening Points for a New Synthesis

Gerald Sider

1. The conjunction of history and anthropology (and similarly, the peculiar specialist discipline of "ethnohistory") remains undeveloped. Much has been written about history and anthropology; indeed, the topic became a fad that is now fortunately coming to an end. Most of the writings on this conjunction have not proved useful analytical bases for understanding or developing strategies against the intensifying expansion of exploitation and domination. Yet the potential of this conjunction may still be significant, but the interweaving of the two disciplines—or better, projects—probably needs to be rebuilt from scratch. And the conjunction, as the title of this volume recognizes, is indeed antagonistic: putting the two kinds of perspectives together, in less superficial ways than usual, ought to lead to very basic criticisms of, and changes in, each.

2. The term "history" has, in English, a triple meaning. "History" refers to what has happened and is happening in the real world (the narcissistic claims of the postmodernists to the contrary notwithstanding); history also refers, simultaneously, to the descriptions and explanations we construct about what has happened and is happening; and history also refers to what is, or is about to become, gone, lost, finished: the past definite perspective in action or what we might jokingly call "the conditional past definite in forward motion," as in the phrases "that's history" or "if the boss does that to me again I'm history." Taking these multiple meanings all together, history most of all references the hopes and claims for a different future, and the struggles and the outcomes that our hopes and actions partly create—all of which develop in conjunction

---

References for this chapter are located on page 176.

with our changing sense of the past, and all of which are encapsulated in the intensely compressed phrase "making history." "Anthropology," by contrast, does not refer to any processes in the real world, or to anything in the real world that we want to, or must, make, or remake, nor does it (yet) reference any processes of making claims upon, or against, the emerging future.

The conjunction of history and anthropology, as it has been formulated, thus begins from a hidden, but fundamental, imbalance. "Anthropology" does not reference even the potential existence of any processes in the real world that we are necessarily implicated in, transformed by, and most of all, forced to confront in our ordinary daily lives. "History," despite its superficially apparent removal from the concerns of current daily life—as in the phrase "that's history"—has an implicit immediacy and a confrontational directness that anthropology can never have. History addresses the unavoidable problems that both continuity and change confront us with, not just socially but also simultaneously and equivalently intensely personally, as those our lives are interwoven with do or do not grow up, go away, get old; as "the relations we must enter into in order to produce the conditions of our existence" change, or harden, or evaporate, revealing themselves to be not only "eras of production" but the constantly changing waters of any one life's seasons.

There could thus be no anthropological equivalent to Thompson's *The Making of the English Working Class*, forcing people to judge their situation as it has developed from and against their history: the closest anthropology came to this was in some of the works by Margaret Mead, which led people to think comparatively, and ahistorically, about sex and child rearing, or in the earlier work of Boas and Kroeber, which sought to separate "race," language, and culture both from each other and, less directly, from actual social-historical processes. Anthropology is the only major social science discipline in which there was, for the first half of the twentieth century, no significant Marxist component, and this is neither accidental nor epiphenomenal. Despite all the nonsense that has been written about anthropology as constituting "the mirror for man," and despite the obsequious attempts of anthropologists throughout the early mid-twentieth century to serve the interests of their colonial office, anthropology has remained, at the level of its basic concepts, the most analytically static and politically passive of all the major social sciences. Further, we have only to start to think about the ways in which historians have grabbed hold of such vacuous anthropological concepts as "thick description," and the uses historians have made of such concepts, to realize that the long-standing fundamental political passivity of anthropology is not only revealed by, but has been contagious to, the conjunction with history.

3. To transform the analytical stasis of anthropology we must first explore it further. If we claim that the central fact of the world about us is its continual change, then we must also cope with the fact that there is nothing in the fundamental concepts of anthropology that forces us to address process or transformation. Hence, anthropologists have been led into a series of fundamental

analytical blunders that have characterized almost the entire twentieth-century development of the discipline:

- the use of the "ethnographic present" tense as a framework to depict fantasy reconstructions of the past;
- the concept of "acculturation" (and its successor concepts, such as "globalization," "transnationalism"), which misread the entire logic of differentiation by failing to grasp that power not only destroys but simultaneously, and fundamentally, also creates difference;
- using the paired concepts of "tradition" and "custom" without realizing that these labels reference necessarily fluid forms of creating, reproducing and transforming local inequalities; the local social relations of domination and value extraction that situate the local, contradictorily, both in partial alliance with and in partial opposition to larger systems of domination and exploitation;
- the current outgrowths of a so-called reflexive anthropology (which flourished only briefly in the 1970s but left a long trail of intellectual havoc) leading to the midst of the "postmodern" forms of textual analysis and hermeneutics, which not only eliminate history but trivialize the ongoing transformations of the real world;
- the "weapons of the weak" perspectives (Scott 1985), through which the exploited and oppressed are removed from historical processes by not considering their relations—of anger, as well as of supportive coinvolvement—to one another: relations that lie at the core of their capacity to force change (just as the struggles within the working class or amongst an oppressed ethnic group are often not simply an obstacle to, but a key part of, confrontations with domination and exploitation).

The list could continue; it suffices to underscore the point that the conjunction of history and anthropology is not just unproductive but, in the current state of anthropology, unworkable. All anthropology can at present do is to borrow some conceptually indigestible methodologies from history—indigestible because they do not effect the basic analytical frameworks of anthropology. Further, anthropology is not in a strong position to critique history—particularly British Marxist social history and the British cultural studies perspectives, which to my mind are both the best of the current approaches to understanding history and also deeply in need of theoretical—and thus, simultaneously, political—critique.

This critique is particularly needed on two grounds for which a redeveloped anthropology ought to be of use: the presumptive rationality that British Marxist history has imposed on social relations, particularly in analyses of class formation, which does not fit well with reconceptualized anthropological understandings of culture (or even the complex senses of folk culture that emerged from well-done ethnography), and the politically dangerous failure of this historical perspective to address the description and, more importantly, the analysis of changing tensions and struggles amongst the ordinary people of the working class, and amongst oppressed and exploited minority groups. "Class" thus remains a historically vague abstraction from the changing relations of production—vague because the struggles that must be engaged seem delineated by these relations. The major conceptual gain of social history over anthropology is thus reduced to the realization that the social relations of production are indeed a crucial component of any full social analysis; "borrowings" from anthropology seem most often used to evade this, rather than to further develop Marxist perspectives. It is noteworthy that the major leftist historians of culture in the British Marxist tradition, such as Stuart Hall and Raymond Williams, did not use anthropology in any significant way, nor did E. P. Thompson, despite his more serious interest in it, nor do most of the politically engaged, activist feminist social historians.

4. Indeed, all varieties of social history have largely used anthropology in the worst possible ways, either to reinforce what they would have done anyhow—for example, "thick description"—or to avoid addressing process: invoking anthropological studies of "meaning" that ignore the ways meanings are ordinarily the foci of struggle; studies of local classificatory systems (ethnobotany, color classification, disease, etc.) that depict how some people presumably try (unsuccessfully in reality, but successfully in the analytical models) to order their universe. These studies also usually ignore those people in a social system who are hardly likely to invoke, explicitly or indirectly, those kinds of presumptive orderings. Perhaps the most problematic of all methodologies that history has routinely "borrowed" from anthropology are those from the study of "kinship systems," which in anthropology achieve a level of idealism and distance from actual social relations matched only by bourgeois economics. Anthropology lacks a set of concepts and methods—and above all, a real-world problematic—that would press other disciplines to use it in more constructive ways.

This is not a universal condemnation. There are people who have relatively successfully brought anthropology and history together (Cooper 1993; Mallon 1983; Moore and Vaugh 1994; Roseberry 1991; Smith 1989; Vincent 1982; Wolf 2001). But this work remains, for the most part, fragmented and individualized: no general perspective or methodology has developed from these works (or from any other combination of politically progressive and historically sophisticated anthropologists), and their works have led to no basic reformulation of anthropological or historical concepts. Historical anthropology has not been a challenge to either history or anthropology. The point now is to start to make it so.

5. To do this we can begin by rethinking an established and rightly marginal form of anthropology called "ethnohistory." There is a small journal in the United States by that name, which is notable for the way that it illustrates how

over the years the notion of what constitutes ethnohistory continually changes. It started as the history of people who are "ethnics" of a sort—Native Americans, in particular—the kinds of people North American anthropologists usually then studied. Its central project became redefined as doing histories of peoples who did not seem to have the usual historical records (primarily the same "ethnics" as before), which necessitated relying on other kinds of evidence, such as oral history. While oral history is usually as important as other kinds of evidence, the claim that it must substitute for those other kinds is often made by people who have only a hazy notion of how to find and access documentary evidence—a topic for which the vast majority of anthropology programs give no organized training whatsoever.

"Ethnohistory" has also been used to refer to the history of peoples who are, in Lévi-Strauss's terms, historically "cold"—lacking the inner fires that fuel change from within their own social system. The interesting point here is how the legislative powers of nation-states have characteristically forced indigenous communities to adopt this very peculiar perspective on themselves, rooting the claims for their future that they are allowed to make on the pretense that they have had no effective history, or even historical knowledge of their own. As native land claims cases in Canada, for example, came to be rooted in the continued existence of "hunting territories," native peoples have been forced to financially subsidize the resurrection of their colonial fur-trapping practices. In the case of the Mistassini Cree and their struggles against the land grabs of Quebec Hydro's monstrous dam projects, they have tapped into the comparatively scant payments they receive for the alienation of their land to subsidize fur trappers, in part to be able to better sustain their "aboriginal claim" to their land in the Canadian courts. Similarly, aboriginal territorial claims in Australia are allowed to be presented if they meet two major criteria: (1) patrilineal descent from the aboriginal inhabitants of a territory—a criterion derived from invoking Radcliffe-Brown's poorly done analysis of native kinship systems, which artificially emphasized patrilineality, and combining this with a desire to exclude the maximum possible numbers of descent-based claims, for it excludes all those offspring of mixed parentage where the father, rather than the mother, is "white," and (2) a "religious coloring" to the aboriginal claim, for which the courts usually require reference to a special role for the territory in "the dreamtime." The "dreamtime," however, is largely a Euro-Australian fantasy about aboriginal culture, but one that the native peoples must now participate in sustaining (Wolf 2001). In such characteristic contexts, what has been called ethnohistory turns out largely to be both the study and the mystificatory denial of our cultural impositions upon relatively powerless peoples. We are studying people who must use, in part, our fantasies to resist our brutal realities.

There are a number of other approaches to ethnohistory, all with substantial problems, of which I should mention only one, as I have used it in ways that I now regard as insufficiently dynamic. This is using "ethnohistory" to reference a people's own sense(s) of history, and how this becomes intertwined with their attempts to reshape the connections between past, present, and future. The mistake that I made was to not sufficiently appreciate the extent to which "history," used in this context, names a domain of *inescapable* struggles, not only between a people and those that oppress and exploit them, but simultaneously among a people (or a class, or within an ethnic ghetto, etc.). Just as Marx, in his analysis of capital, provided the conceptual framework for understanding class formation and the necessary emergence of the kinds of class struggles that transform capital, so a redone ethnohistory (or historical anthropology) should seek to provide the analytical basis for understanding why and how other forms of differentiation than class *must* emerge, and how a far broader and complexly interwoven range of struggles becomes both necessary and transformative.

To develop this broader perspective two kinds of changes in anthropology are necessary. First, we must learn to see that the basic anthropological concepts—for example, "culture," "kinship," and "social organization" (primarily in the sense of the social relations of daily life and work)—delineate terrains of struggle over the ways local inequalities are formed, made materially consequential, and reproduced. Second, we must develop new conceptual tools for describing and analyzing the characteristic ways in which localized systems of inequality take shape simultaneously separate from, in alliance with, and in opposition to larger systems of domination and exploitation. Taken together, these changes will be the basis for a historical anthropology of multiple forms of differentiation.

One aspect of such broad processes of differentiation is particularly relevant here: people becoming antagonistically separated from their own histories. A few preliminary remarks on this may be helpful.

6. John Berger once wrote that if everything had a name there would be no need for stories. Here are three brief stories about people *having* history, as a prelude both to thinking about people making history, and about the way we go about (what is politely called) "doing" or "knowing" history.

In the mid-1970s, in a Newfoundland fishing outport, I was in the fishing shed of a middle-aged fisherman, a man I liked and respected very much, just talking. Leaning in the corner of his shed was a very large wooden mallet, much battered. I asked him what it was for, and he said: "It's to pound the ice off my boat when I goes fishing in the winter: see?" And with the word "see" he held his hand out in front of me, his knuckles red and swollen with arthritis and permanently bent. His hand was his illustration of the mallet: his history was carved upon his body in ways that both joined him irrevocably to his past and confronted him, antagonistically, in his very own body, with this past.

Such struggles occur, frequently hidden, *within* the clamor of more open confrontations: for example, all the protest and controversy over building the Vietnam Memorial in Washington, D.C., eventually focused on an attempt to divert the call to sanity and reality from the memorial wall by erecting, directly in front of the wall, a "realistic" statue of three soldiers in battle uniform. In the midst of all the protest and the very public controversy about remembrance, commemoration, and patriotism that the advocates and opponents of the wall generated, we must deal with the so far utterly uncontroversial, unfortunately completely unprovocative, and almost entirely unrecognized fact that more American Vietnam veterans killed themselves after the war ended than died during the war. Struggles with history are inescapable no matter how they are masked, and they are characteristically both intensely, and hardly ever simply, personal: these postwar deaths were very likely to be, in part, confrontations with our inability to see or hear that they were happening and are still continuing to happen.

The anthropologist Linda Green (1996) has worked in Guatemala with Mayan Indian women whose husbands have been killed by government troops, often gruesomely and with their families and fellow villagers watching and listening. Many of these widows' sons were drafted into the army, and the government practice is to assign substantial numbers of young, rural Mayan men to the elite battalions that do such work (in other regions of the country). For a variety of reasons, from protection to family, some of the women who have had their husbands butchered, often while they were forced to watch, have photographs of their sons, in the uniform of the units that do this, on the walls of their homes.

The same "history" that the left wants peasants and workers to "make," and that peasants and workers have struggled with and for at such appalling cost, remains irreducibly tangled into knots and spasms of ambivalence and ambiguity, along with the passions of both hope and terror—tangled and multiplex beyond our wildest imagination. Most significantly, we have yet to begin to try to understand how struggles are constructed as much within as against the chaos that power routinely engenders.

7. To begin to do so entails, particularly for historians, a thorough-going rejection of Weberian approaches to "historical social science," including especially the Weberian notions that power and culture, and the conjunction of power and culture (e.g., the whole concept of "stand"—a status grouping—and the notions of political legitimation), are forms of social order, or of social ordering, rather than names for, on the one hand, domains of chaos imposed upon daily life and, on the other, the necessary, unavoidable (and, often, order-creating) struggles that continually emerge within and against this chaos. We might well invoke the concept of "stand" because it seems to help us discuss the middle class—*die Mittelstand*—but does it help us to understand the situation of, say, the Turks in Germany, or the blacks in the United States, to refer to them as a "stand"? Does the concept of "legitimation" help us to understand the current upsurge in government-sponsored assaults on the well-being of the poor?

So we should begin to construct our historical anthropology by substantially reformulating basic concepts: to start with anthropology, the concepts of culture, of kinship, and of social organization. To the contrary of the ways they are ordinarily used, "culture" names an often violent struggle over what "values" will and will not be shared, and by whom; "kinship" constitutes one of the primary domains for the formation and transformation of local inequalities (a point that is rather widely known, but its implications for a theoretical and political understanding of kinship systems remain almost completely undeveloped); a social system or a community (and also a mode of production) is probably never rooted in *a* social organization but in the conjunctions and disjunctions of multiple, and at least partly incompatible, forms and processes of the social organization of daily life and work.

The core of historical anthropology, in sum, should become the analysis of processes of differentiation within, as well as between, social systems, communities, classes, modes of production, and so on, and the formation of new kinds of social systems, and new cultures, in and against these processes of—and struggles about—differentiation. But we must focus on processes of "differentiation" with the realization that the term itself is deceptive, implicitly suggesting an orderliness that denies the actual situations of the poor and the oppressed. Could one say either to or about the increasingly displaced Mayan widows that we need to examine how they are being differentiated? What we could do, in such situations, is to try to understand the enormous range of struggles such women engage—struggles that are many times fought in utter public silence— and through the order-creating and chaotic consequences of such struggles, come to see how differentiation develops.

It is on the basis of a direct engagement with processes of differentiation that emerge from the multiple ways in which power, and the struggles against power, simultaneously generate both chaos and a necessarily transient orderliness that anthropology, or more precisely, a newly historical anthropology, becomes both theoretically and politically crucial. Class, we have come to realize, emerges simultaneously from at least two domains: the relations of production (i.e., the social relations through which surpluses are formed, appropriated, and used) and the struggles that people in different positions within the relations of production *must* fight (Thompson 1978). If class struggle occurred simply between classes, or could be reduced to issues directly connectable to those emerging from the relations of production, there would be no particular need to develop a Marxist historical anthropology: our current praxis would be adequate to the tasks at hand. Historical anthropology is born from the understanding that materially consequential, unavoidable struggles occur within, as well as between classes—for reasons that are directly connected to understanding that we cannot separately conceptualise hegemony and class consciousness. These struggles within classes are not fully reducible to the sources and consequences of differential access to the means of production: they also emerge across the terrain of culture, kinship, gender, ethnicity, the social relations of daily life—across, in sum, all the modes of differentiation.

More to the point: it is on the basis of critiques of our present praxis—critiques that should lead us to fundamentally reformulate our concept of "struggle"—that a historical anthropology could contribute to understanding how new kinds of social relations develop both from and as the basis of such newly successful struggles against oppression as that now being waged by the people of Chiapas. Understanding how and why struggle develops among, as well as between, classes should help us to understand how new kinds of relations develop among and between the oppressed, and how, from these new relations, new possibilities emerge.

References

Cooper, Frederick, Allen Isaacman, Florencia Mallon, William Roseberry, and Steve Stern, eds. 1993. *Confronting Historical Paradigms: Peasants, Labor, and the Capitalist World System in Africa and Latin America*. Madison: University of Wisconsin Press.

Green, Linda. 1996. *Fear as a Way of Life: Mayan Widows in Rural Guatemala*. New York: Columbia University Press.

Mallon, Florencia E. 1983. *The Defense of Community in Peru's Central Highland: Peasant Struggle and Capitalist Transition, 1860–1940*. Princeton, NJ: Princeton University Press.

Moore, Henrietta L., and Megan Vaughn. 1994. *Cutting Down Trees: Gender, Nutrition, and Agricultural Change in the Northern Province of Zambia, 1890–1990*. Portsmouth, NH: Heinemann; London: J. Currey.

Roseberry, William, and Jay O'Brien, eds. 1991. *Golden Ages, Dark Ages: Imagining the Past in Anthropology and History*. Berkeley: University of California Press.

Scott, James C. 1985. *Weapons of the Weak: Everyday Forms of Peasant Resistance*. New Haven: Yale University Press.

Smith, Gavin A. 1989. *Livelihood and Resistance: Peasants and the Politics of Land in Peru*. Berkeley: University of California Press.

Thompson, Edward P. 1978. "Eighteenth-Century English Society: Class Struggle without Class?" *Social History* 3: 133–165.

Vincent, Joan. 1982. *Teso in Transformation: The Political Economy of Peasant and Class in Eastern Africa*. Berkeley: University of California Press.

Wolf, Eric. 2001. *Pathways of Power: Building an Anthropology of the Modern World*. Berkeley: University of California Press.

CONTRIBUTORS

August Carbonella is Assistant Professor of Anthropology, Memorial University of Newfoundland, St. Johns, and Visiting Research Scholar in Anthropology at the Graduate School, City University of New York. His 1998 PhD dissertation examined the shifting temporal and spatial matrices of working-class political agency in an industrial region in the United States between 1920 and 1990. He is currently researching and writing on the anti-imperialist and internationalist politics of radicalized soldiers and veterans of the United States' invasion of Vietnam.

Christian Giordano is Professor of Social Anthropology at the University of Fribourg (Switzerland) and Doctor honoris causa of the University of Timisoara (Romania). His main interests are political anthropology, economic anthropology, and historical anthropology. His recent publications include *Die Betrogenen der Geschichte. Überlagerungsmentalität und Überlagerungsrationalität in mediterranen Gesellschaften* (1992; coeditor); *Europäische Ethnologie— Ethnologie Europas* (1999; coeditor); *Bulgaria: Social and Cultural Landscapes* (2000; editor); *Borderline: Die Sozialwissenschaften zwischen Grenzziehung und Grenzüberschreitung* (2001); "Europe: Sociocultural Aspects" (2001); *Constructing Risk, Threat, Catastrophe: Anthropological Perspectives* (2002; coeditor); "Interdependente Vielfalt: Die historischen Regionen Europas" (2003).

P. H. Gulliver is Distinguished Research Professor Emeritus, York University, Toronto, Canada. He was previously Professor of African Anthropology, University of London. He has undertaken research in various parts of eastern Africa and in Ireland. His interests include dispute management processes, local-level politics, network theory, processes of social change, and historical anthropology. Among his publications are *Neighbours and Networks* (1971) and *Disputes and Negotiations* (1979). He has also co-authored, with Marilyn Silverman, *In the Valley of the Nore* (1986) and *Merchants and Shopkeepers: An Historical Anthropology of an Irish Market Town, 1200–1986* (1995).

Don Handelman is Sarah Allen Shaine Professor of Anthropology, the Hebrew University of Jerusalem, and a member of the Israel Academy of Sciences and Humanities. Among his recent publications are *Models and Mirrors: Towards an Anthropology of Public Events* (1998); *God Inside Out: Siva's Game of Dice* (1997; coauthored with David Shulman); *Siva in the Forest of Pines: An Essay on Sorcery and Self-Knowledge* (2004; co-authored with David Shulman); *Nationalism and the Israeli State: Bureaucratic Logic in Public Events* (2004), and *Playful Power and Ludic Spaces: Studies in Games of Life* (*Focaal—European Journal of Anthropology* 37, special section, 2001, edited with Galina Lindquist).

Don Kalb is Associate Professor of Sociology and Social Anthropology at Central European University, Budapest, and researcher at the Anthropology Department of Utrecht University, the Netherlands. He was a senior fellow at the Institute for Human Sciences (IWM) Vienna, and directed IWM's SOCO (Social Consequences of Economic Transformation in East Central Europe) program between 1998 and 2000. His publications include *Expanding Class: Power and Everyday Politics in Industrial Communities, The Netherlands, 1850–1950* (1997); *The Ends of Globalization: Bringing Society Back In* (2000; coeditor); and *Globalization and Development: Themes and Concepts in Current Research* (2004; coediter). His recent research focuses on problems of economic restructuring, culture, class, and citizenship in Eastern Europe. He is the (founding) editor of *Focaal—European Journal of Anthropology*.

Patricia Musante is a doctoral candidate in the Department of Anthropology at the Graduate Center of the City University of New York. She is completing her dissertation on the politics of land in neoliberal Mexico. Her research interests include the construction of social memory, globalization, ethnicity and state formation, comparative social movements, and urbanization.

Hermann Rebel received his PhD in History from the University of California at Berkeley in 1976. He has taught in the History Departments of York University in Toronto and the University of Iowa in Iowa City, and is currently at the University of Arizona in Tucson. Publications include *Peasant Classes* (1983) and numerous articles, including "Peasantries under the Austrian Empire" in *Peasantries of Europe* (1998), and "Dark Events and Lynching Scenes in the Collective Memory" in *Agrarian Studies* (2001).

Gerald Sider is Professor of Anthropology with a joint appointment at the College of Staten Island and the Graduate Center, City University of New York. He also holds an appointment as Adjunct Professor of Anthropology at

Memorial University of Newfoundland, and has been a member of the anthropology and history working group at the Max Planck Institut für Geschichte, Göttingen, since 1978. He is currently engaged in several projects addressing the historical transformations of suffering, violence, chaos, and silence, including differential mortality in African famines, Labrador Inuit and Innu youth suicide, and the recent severe economic decline and differentiation both in rural Newfoundland and in North Carolina. His publications include *Between History and Histories: The Production of Silences and Commemorations* (1997; coedited with Gavin Smith), *Between History and Tomorrow: Making and Breaking Everyday Life in Rural Newfoundland* (2003), and *Living Indian Histories: Lumbee and Tuscarora People in North Carolina* (2003).

Marilyn Silverman is Professor of Anthropology, York University, Toronto, Canada. She has carried out field research in Guyana, Ecuador, and, most recently, Ireland. Her areas of interest are local-level political economy, historical anthropology, labor studies, and agrarian processes. Her ethnographies include *An Irish Working Class: Explorations in Political Economy and Hegemony, 1800–1950* (2001); *Merchants and Shopkeepers* (1995; with P. H. Gulliver); and *Rich People and Rice: Factional Politics in Rural* (1980). She has edited several volumes, including *Approaching the Past: Historical Anthropology through Irish Case Studies* (1992; with P. H. Gulliver) and *A House Divided? Anthropological Studies of Factionalism* (1978; with R. F. Salisbury).

Herman Tak is Assistant Professor of Social Sciences at Utrecht University, University College Utrecht, and Roosevelt Academy Middelburg, the Netherlands. He has published *South Italian Festivals: A Local History of Ritual and Change* (2000) and *Feste in Italia meridionale* (2000). He is an editor of *Focaal—European Journal of Anthropology*.

INDEX

Lightning Source UK Ltd.
Milton Keynes UK
UKOW06f2340070716

277931UK00025B/1218/P